Contents

Acknowledgements

This book was written during a personally and professionally busy and exciting time. Being involved in a wide range of projects, I am both amazed and thrilled that I was able to find the time to write *Communities, identities and crime*, particularly as identity issues seem so relevant to contemporary social and cultural dynamics. Firstly, I should like to thank Alia Imtoual at Flinders University, who played a key role in enabling me to be a visiting scholar at the University of Adelaide during Spring 2006, where, as well as enjoying the great and unforgettable Australian outdoors, I was able to write the first half of this book.

I should also like to thank members of the Institute of Applied Social Sciences at the University of Birmingham: Ann Davies, my mentor who has guided me since my arrival at Birmingham University, David Prior, Sedouh LeGrand, who helped do the research for this book, and Salah el-Hassan, together with the teaching team: John Doling, Tina Hearn, Nathan Hughes, Bob Matthews, Stephen McKay, Robert Page, Lizz Ross and Karen Rowlingson.

I should also like to thank various individuals at the Centre for Crime and Justice Studies: Will McMahon, Rebecca Roberts and Enver Solomon, for their support. My thanks also go to Bob Lambert at Exeter University, Steve Savage at Portsmouth University, Peter Gilbert at Staffordshire University and Sandra Walklate at Liverpool University for their support of, and input into, some creative research/writing endeavours.

My thanks, as always, go to my family and friends, who enrich my life, their colourful stories and experiences helping to keep me grounded. In particular, my love and special thanks to Neil Whitehead for his tolerance and support, my thanks to Natassja Smiljanic whose spiritual journeying has resonated hugely with me, my thanks to Marek Spalek for tennis, humour and camaraderie, my thanks to my parents, Wincenty and Wiktoria Spalek, whose journeys have been truly inspiring, and thanks as well to Andy Fiol, H, Mick, Andrzej, Jan and Pauline.

COMMUNITIES, IDENTITIES AND CRIME

Basia Spalek

First published in Great Britain in 2008 by

The Policy Press
University of Bristol
Fourth Floor
Beacon House
Queen's Road
Bristol BS8 1QU
UK

Tel +44 (0)117 331 4054
Fax +44 (0)117 331 4093
e-mail tpp-info@bristol.ac.uk
www.policypress.org.uk

British Library Cataloguing in Publication Data
A catalogue record for this book is available from the British Library.

Library of Congress Cataloging-in-Publication Data
A catalog record for this book has been requested.

ISBN 978 1 86134 804 3 paperback
ISBN 978 1 86134 805 0 hardcover

Cover design by Qube Design Associates, Bristol.
Front cover: image kindly supplied by www.panos.co.uk
Printed and bound in Great Britain by Hobbs the Printers, Southampton.

Introduction

This book is very much a product of contemporary theorising and discussion about the social and cultural processes taking place in liberal democratic societies. Many writers have attempted to capture the social, economic and cultural dynamics of contemporary western society, using words like risk, anxiety and uncertainty to describe a time of huge transformation from an earlier post-war 'Golden Age' of increasing affluence and full employment in Europe and North America. It is argued that social identities have become increasingly problematic and contestable in contemporary western society because traditional social affiliations, based on family or social class, have been increasingly eroded; moreover, rising individualisation, alongside the fragmentation of communities, has led to the self becoming a task that is under continuous construction. At the same time, contemporary democratic societies are marked by social differences in terms of ethnicity, religion, sexuality, age and so forth, and these differences can bring to crisis core tenets of liberal democratic states relating to notions of citizenship and individual rights, which themselves are under stress from factors such as globalisation and migration.

This book involves placing a critical lens upon the notions of identity and community, exploring the issues that these raise for a criminal justice context. Civil disturbances involving conflict between different 'racial', ethnic and/or religious groupings, such as those occurring in Birmingham, England, in 2005, which featured Black, and Pakistani and Bangladeshi, youth, illustrate the problems of disorder and violence that can arise from the formation and expression of resistance identities, which are generated by actors who perceive themselves to be in devalued positions. Moreover, a number of high-profile cases – including, for example, the racist murders of Stephen Lawrence in 1993 and Zahid Mubarek in 2000, and the homophobia-motivated murder of Jody Dobrowski in 2005 – illustrate further the significance of social identities when considering crime, victimisation and criminal justice. Indeed, the burgeoning 'equality and diversity industry' that is now endemic to the criminal justice system, and the focus given to community participation, engagement and dialogue, bear further testimony to the centrality of identity and community issues.

This book is also a reaction to a number of crises facing contemporary criminology. The seemingly close relationship between state apparatuses that inflict pain on vast numbers of people who are deemed criminal, and academic and research institutions that carry out state-sponsored work has led a number of observers to question the (moral) validity of criminology. At the same time, factors such as the pressure to raise research money and to publish journal articles in quick succession have helped to create a situation whereby there is a general lack of critical reflection in relation to the ways in which research is carried out on crime and victimisation, with there being little reflection about how criminological knowledge production might marginalise the perspectives and voices of minorities, contributing to a suppression of social and epistemological difference. This book therefore consists of an attempt to broaden out criminological work, through a focus upon identities and communities. This book illustrates that, in taking a critical stance towards the notions of identity and community, this necessitates an exploration of sameness/difference, how researchers and policy makers can take account of the Other, those social groupings that are comprised of the delegitimised, marginalised and excluded, and raises questions about what counts as social justice, including whose perspectives are considered in criminal justice policy-making arenas. This introductory chapter will briefly set out a summary of the chapters that feature in this book, but firstly, a critique of contemporary criminology will be made as this provides the background context to *Communities, identities and crime*.

Criminology in crisis?

Questioning the (moral) validity of criminology

Critical perspectives are increasingly questioning the validity of criminology as a discipline or as a set of discursive practices. Researchers appear to be increasingly questioning the meaning of having a subject discipline such as criminology, where crime itself is a social construct and therefore has no ontological validity. Moreover, criminological work might be viewed as being complicit with state processes of criminalisation, which themselves involve the suffering of a large number of people, in particular those who are poor and marginalised:

> Since its inception criminology has enjoyed an intimate relationship with the powerful, a relationship determined largely by its failure to subject to critique the category of crime which has been handed down by the state and around which the criminal justice system has been organised. (Hillyard et al, 2004: 18)

It seems that critical criminologists are increasingly questioning the morality of working within a subject discipline that narrowly only considers those social harms that are most easily labelled as crime by the state. Therefore it has been suggested that being engaged in criminological research can produce harms as this can involve supporting state agendas that consist of increasing criminalisation and control and ever-expanding criminal justice systems (Hillyard et al, 2004). The close links between criminology and the state were commented on over 30 years ago, when Taylor et al (1975) observed that the science of criminology was one of the most state-dominated branches of social science (in Carrington and Hogg, 2002). More recently, Scraton (2002) has highlighted how generous Home Office funding in the UK has led to burgeoning academic work consisting of evaluation studies in relation to crime prevention strategies, government surveys and audits. Critical perspectives lament the decline of theorising, due in part to pressures placed upon academics to generate research money and the short-term thinking underpinning many research agendas.

Gelsthorpe (2006), in a plenary speech at the British Society of Criminology conference in Glasgow, raised the question 'What is criminology for?'. For Gelsthorpe, because criminology is a moral enterprise, there is a need for disciplinary reflexivity. That there is some questioning of the criminological enterprise is perhaps not surprising, given that reflexivity is a characteristic of late modern society, involving individuals, collective groups and/or institutions intentionally and rationally reflecting upon the part that they play in the perpetuation of identified social problems (Lash, 1994; McGhee, 2005). The extent to which criminology has, or ever can have, a normative project is therefore questionable, where normativity might be defined as 'a system of thought and belief which is concerned in some way to improve society' (Dodd, 1999: 2). Therefore, the question of abandoning criminology altogether has been raised because of its inadequate focus upon law, crime and criminal justice, this focus essentially helping to reproduce a skewed criminal justice system based on class (Hillyard et al, 2004).

Some critical researchers are arguing that a focus on social harm rather than crime might be more beneficial, where a social harm perspective might be viewed as one that moves beyond the narrow confines of criminology to look at harms that people experience, whether those harms are defined as crime or not (Hillyard et al, 2004: 1). In focusing upon social harm rather than crime, researchers are asking broader questions about how, in an unequal society where criminal justice cannot be guaranteed, social justice might be achieved. Social justice might be viewed as people enjoying full citizenship, in terms of the civil, political and social (Marshall, 1950, in Cook, 2006). However, full citizenship may be unachievable for individuals belonging to minority groups due to wider social structures of inequality (Cook, 2006). It might further be argued that in taking a social harm perspective this necessitates an acknowledgement and inclusion of social identities, and minority groups in particular, as these will hold perspectives and experiences that help shed light on discriminatory norms and structures that traditionally have largely been marginalised through a focus upon, and a utilisation of, the narrow lens of criminal justice. Therefore, the voices of those individuals who occupy outsider status will need to be increasingly included in research. This can also help to challenge the narrow confines of criminological knowledge production, as will be discussed below.

Homogenisation of social difference; feminist, critical, postmodern perspectives as comprising the Other

A further dimension to the crisis confronting criminology is in relation to its being a discipline of modernity, underpinned by Enlightenment philosophy, where modernity itself has been criticised for creating racial (and other) hierarchies that have helped to institutionalise oppression and discrimination, through the production of Others. 'Otherisation' involves the perpetuation of dominant norms and the suppression of difference, so that those identities that lie outside dominant regimes of power are constituted as the Other – the devalued – and their voices and perspectives are largely suppressed. It might be argued that criminology has also been complicit in the suppression of social difference, not only through largely focusing on those harms defined as criminal by regimes of power, and therefore ignoring or marginalising the viewpoints of individuals who lie outside these regimes (but who at the same time have to endure the oppression and control generated from within these regimes), but also through insufficiently exploring social difference and insufficiently engaging with the voices of those who occupy the margins, thereby leading to the homogenisation of knowledge production.

According to Seidman, 'there is a political unconscious to the human sciences. This refers to ways disciplinary conventions operate, often without the explicit intentions of social scientists, to suppress, if not erase, epistemological and social difference' (1997:22). Criminology emerged from modernity, constituting a rational and scientific attempt to study crime (Morrison, 1995; Garland, 2002). Thus, for Garland (2002), the origins of criminology lie in a Lombrosian and a governmental project, both of which used scientific frameworks of understanding and analysis. Enlightenment philosophy underpins modernity through the belief that science holds the key to social progress. According to Seidman (1997), Enlightenment thought consists of a utopian ideal of society comprised of abstract citizens who are equal before the law. Although Enlightenment thought has produced social good, it has nonetheless legitimised 'the destruction of particular social identities and multiple local communities and traditions that have given coherence and purpose to the lives of many peoples' (Seidman, 1997: 6). Although feminist, critical race, postmodern and other perspectives have questioned the legitimacy of Enlightenment philosophy, modernity constitutes the dominant framework within criminology, thereby consigning feminist, critical and postmodern perspectives to the category of the Other, the delegitimised. As Gelsthorpe (2006) highlights, there is an increasingly scientised conception of criminology, influenced by the Research Assessment Exercise (RAE), the Economic and Social Research Council (ESRC) pushing quantitative skills in the training of social scientists, as well as by Home Office research that seems to prioritise statistical 'What Works' analyses over work that would seek to engage offenders by asking what intervention programmes are most meaningful to them.

So research approaches that, for example, stress the fluidity of identities, the value of focusing upon emotions, the importance of drawing upon individuals' own accounts of their experiences and involving communities in the research process, and so on, immediately stand in opposition to modernist agendas, being viewed as somehow less valid and objective, and more partisan in nature, and therefore 'suspect', particularly if an inclusion of voices, community perspectives and the like can at times stand at odds with logical, rational reasoning so valued within frameworks of modernity. For Jefferson, human behaviour is the product of cognition, reason and, importantly, emotion, making 'the peculiarly passionless subject of criminology hard to comprehend' (2002: 152). For Gelsthorpe (2006), psychoanalytic thinking can potentially make a significant contribution not only to criminological research, but also in relation to developing a more informed understanding of criminal justice policy.

Exploring the construction of social identities and working with communities inevitably includes handling the nature and complexity of subjectivity, and so presents the opportunity to develop a psychosocial criminology, using Jefferson's (2002) terminology. Therefore, *Communities, identities and crime* might be viewed as an inherently political project, attempting to widen the boundaries of the subject discipline of criminology to include marginalised, Otherised perspectives. Although the term 'crime' is used throughout the book, the author acknowledges that crime is a social construct, and that it is problematic to use this terminology as harms that are committed by individuals in powerless positions are often labelled as criminal acts, yet harms generated by the state, corporations and individuals in positions of power are rarely labelled as criminal. Whether this book is ultimately part of a longer-term project of abandoning criminology altogether as a result of its generally limited focus upon criminal events and processes is a question that only future work and developments will answer. For the author, *Communities, identities and crime* is part of a political stand that seeks to find meaning and understanding of, and ways of exploring, experiences of social harms through engaging in a holistic struggle in relation to knowledge production that refuses to reproduce the narrow confines of much criminological research. As such, the notions of identity and community are used here as a way of challenging the somewhat narrow borders to criminological knowledge production.

Perhaps identities in relation to gender, 'race'/ethnicity, religion/spirituality, sexual orientation, disabilities and age are focused upon in this book rather than class, because the author views these former categories as holding more potential to broaden the narrow confines, and to challenge the homogenisation of knowledge production evident within criminology. This is not to argue that class is irrelevant to analyses of crime and victimisation, as poverty is very much an important issue; rather, other collective identities are focused upon in this book for a political purpose: to help challenge what has been conceptualised here as a crisis of homogenisation within criminology. Furthermore, although there seems currently to be a backlash against identity politics, with some perspectives increasingly questioning the focus upon 'race'/ethnicity, in particular, as well as perspectives that seek to focus upon human rights that might encompass all identities, the author's position is that a focus upon identities is still desirable, particularly when dominant regimes in relation to patriarchy, whiteness, secularism, heteronormativity, able-bodiedness and youth continue to comprise the broader structural contexts to people's lives. Thus, a critical focus upon gender, 'race'/ethnicity, religion/spirituality, sexual orientation, disability and ageing might start to make visible discriminatory norms that help reproduce discrimination and oppression, as it seems that a modernist agenda has largely failed to give sufficient voice and form to these broader norms.

Now that the background context to *Communities, ientities and crime* has been presented, a brief summary of the chapters will be outlined below.

Summary of chapters

Chapter One explores the relevance of identity formations for criminology and their significance in a criminal justice context. Conceptualising today's society as late modernity, it is argued that identities might be viewed as being constituted through both modern and postmodern processes: the expression of collective identities and interests, alongside the fragmentation, individualisation, and fluidity of identities. It is argued that within a criminal justice context, offender and victim identities are relevant, as are identities in relation to gender, 'race'/ethnicity, religion/spirituality, sexual orientation, disability and ageing.

In Chapter Two the book examines equality legislation, policy and practice in the UK, particularly in a criminal justice context. It is argued that in many instances there continue to be differences in the level of protection afforded to different social groupings with respect to gender, 'race'/ethnicity, religion, sexual orientation, disability and age; however, contemporary policy developments suggest that hierarchies of equality provisions are being levelled out so that there is growing harmonisation of protections afforded to different groupings. Furthermore, at the same time that policies are being targeted at a wide range of group collectivities, there is a growing sense of the artificially constructed nature of these collectivities. Therefore, there is also a search for more nuanced methods and approaches in relation to promoting equality and documenting diversity, which might acknowledge specificities of experience. These developments suggest that alongside the modernist agenda underpinning equality and diversity strategies, postmodern processes are also at play, involving the fragmentation of socially constructed identities.

Chapter Three focuses upon exploring some key methodological questions, including ethical ones, when researching communities and when focusing upon identities as a way of understanding the social world. It is argued that researchers, whilst documenting specificity of experience, and acknowledging differences between people, should not lose sight of power relations that generate and reproduce inequalities and injustices. Thus, discourses that claim no knowledge beyond that which is local and situated cannot challenge forms of social organisation that are unjust, and localisms do not produce discourses that are absent of power, as power is inherent to all knowledge claims, no matter how nomadic they may be. Chapter Four looks at the notion of community, this featuring significantly in criminal justice policy and practice. It highlights how an emphasis upon community participation in criminal justice reflects broader developments in governance, whereby responsibility and accountability for crime is increasingly concentrated at local levels, whilst at the same time centralised control in terms of resources and target-setting is maintained (Prior et al, 2006). Furthermore, this comprises a form of institutional reflection (Lash, 1994) that involves criminal justice institutions opening themselves up to the communities that they serve, with the lay public engaging with, as well as critiquing, rival forms of expertise. Individuals, and the communities to which they belong, are therefore being encouraged to identify and define the problems that they face and to put forward solutions to those problems, as well as to work with, and alongside, agencies of the criminal justice system. The chapter also highlights the contentious nature of community, this being open to many different interpretations, particularly within the context of late modernity.

The next chapter examines gender in relation to crime, victimisation and criminal justice. It is argued that apparently neutral, objective scientific research, when applied to women, has been found to be underpinned by sexist assumptions. As a result, feminist researchers have challenged gender-biased distortions by using the voices of female offenders and by concentrating upon their experiences to provide a more accurate picture of women offenders. At the same time, feminist work has questioned some of the male-orientated assumptions underpinning traditional victimological work, which has led to women's behaviour being judged and implicated in the crimes that have been committed against them. Chapter Five further highlights how researchers, policy makers and practitioners increasingly acknowledge diversity amongst women. Population movements due to war, globalisation and economic deprivation can have a substantial impact upon practitioners' work as women arriving from different countries with different cultural traditions may have different needs and sets of experiences that need to be taken into account.

Chapter Six looks at 'race'/ethnicity in relation to crime and criminal justice. The issue of the difficulties involved when collecting data about 'race' is raised, highlighting that this is a social construct that is influenced by historical, social and political contexts that attach particular labels to particular groups of individuals at particular points in time. Other issues that are looked at include institutional racism, racist victimisation and knowledge claims arising from Black, Asian and minority ethnic communities, and how these need to be legitimised when a scientific paradigm holds sway within policy-making circles. Moreover, this chapter highlights how the application, and predominance, of a (social) scientific approach to 'race' is problematic when viewed from a perspective that actively engages with, and acknowledges, the harms caused under the guise of Enlightenment philosophy, since modernity has been linked to the creation of racial hierarchies that have helped to construct, and to dehumanise, racial Others. Chapter Seven explores faith identities in relation to crime, victimisation and criminal justice, suggesting that religious identities are increasingly featuring in criminological discourse, as well as in criminal justice policy and practice. It is argued that a focus upon faith identities can lead to the adoption of innovative research techniques and theoretical frameworks of enquiry. However, this work carries with it the potential of being delegitimised due to the predominance of secularism within contemporary western society, whereby an artificially constructed binary opposition of secular/sacred serves to place work that includes a focus on the sacred into the category of the deviant Other.

The following chapter, Chapter Eight, focuses upon the experiences of lesbian, gay, bisexual and transgender (LGBT) communities in relation to crime, criminal justice and victimisation, as these people have traditionally been marginalised by policy makers and researchers. It is argued that when considering LGBT minority experiences it is important to consider the oppositional binary Heterosexual/Homosexual that is said to underpin western society, casting same-sex desire into the category of the Other, the delegitimised. Thus, within a criminal justice context, LGBT communities have criticised agencies of the criminal justice system for assuming that all peoples are heterosexual, and for acting in discriminatory ways towards those who are not. This chapter also looks at knowledge claims arising from LGBT communities and the challenges that these identities pose for criminological knowledge production. Chapter Nine looks at two further minority groupings that have traditionally been marginalised by criminologists: older people and people with disabilities. It is argued that in criminology there seems to have been a tendency to focus upon young people, particularly as offenders, although some research in relation to the fear of crime and victimisation has included a consideration of older people. People with disabilities who experience crime, on the other hand, have been labelled 'invisible victims' because crimes committed against these individuals are often hidden and not reported to agencies of the criminal justice system. This chapter presents key research and policy issues in relation to older people and people with disabilities, both as offenders and as victims of crime. At the same time, this chapter also explores some of the issues that the inclusion of identities in relation to ageing and disability pose for criminological knowledge construction. It is argued that research with older people and people with disabilities places focus upon the body, the body as ageing or the body as 'impaired'. Chapter Ten is a conclusion, drawing upon the key themes that have been developed throughout the main chapters. Having outlined the chapters that feature in *Communities, identities and crime*, it is time to turn to the main body of the book, to Chapter One.

References

Carrington, K. and Hogg, R. (2002) 'Critical criminolgies: An introduction', in K. Carrington and R. Hogg (eds) *Critical criminology: Issues, debates, challenges*, Cullompton: Willan, pp 1–14.

Cook, D. (2006) *Criminal and social justice*, London: Sage.

Dodd, N. (1999) *Social theory and modernity*, Cambridge: Polity Press.

Garland, D. (2002) 'Of crimes and criminals: The development of criminology in Britain', in M. Maguire, R. Morgan and R. Reiner (eds) *The Oxford handbook of criminology* (3rd edn), Oxford: Oxford University Press, pp 7–50.

Gelsthorpe, L. (2006) 'What is criminology for? Looking within and beyond', plenary speech presented at the British Society of Criminology conference, University of Strathclyde, Glasgow, unpublished presentation.

Hillyard, P., Pantazis, C., Tombs, S. and Gordon, D. (2004) *Beyond criminology: Taking harm seriously*, London: Pluto Press.

Jefferson, T. (2002) 'For a psychosocial criminology', in K. Carrington and R. Hogg (eds) *Critical criminology: Issues, debates, challenges*, Cullompton: Willan, pp 145–67.

Lash, S. (1994) 'Reflexivity and its doubles: Structure, aesthetics, community', in U. Beck, A. Giddens and S. Lash (eds) *Reflexive modernization: Politics, tradition and aesthetics in the modern social order*, Cambridge: Polity Press, pp 110–73.

Marshall, T.H. (1950) *Citizenship and social class*, Cambridge: Cambridge University Press.

McGhee, D. (2005) *Intolerant Britain? Hate, citizenship and difference*, Maidenhead: Open University Press.

Morrison, W. (1995) *Theoretical criminology: From modernity to post-modernism*, London: Cavendish.

Prior, D., Farrow, K., Spalek, B. and Barnes, M. (2006) 'Can anti-social behaviour interventions help to contribute to civil renewal?', in T. Brennan, P. John and G. Stoker (eds) *Re-energizing citizenship: Strategies for civil renewal*, Hampshire: Palgrave Macmillan, pp 91–111.

Scraton, P. (2002) 'Defining power and challenging knowledge: Critical analysis as resistance in the UK', in K. Carrington and R. Hogg (eds) *Critical criminology: Issues, debates, challenges*, Cullompton: Willan, pp 15–40.

Seidman, S. (1997) *Difference troubles: Queering social theory and sexual politics*, Cambridge: Cambridge University Press.

Taylor, I., Walton, P. and Young, J. (eds) (1975) *Critical criminology*, London: Routledge.

ONE

Social identities in late modernity: offender and victim identity constructions

Introduction

The subject of the construction of social identity in contemporary western societies is a growing area of research interest. Conceptualising today's society as late modernity, fluid modernity or postmodernity (amongst other signifiers), researchers argue that social identities have become increasingly problematic and contestable as a result of the demise of the so-called 'Golden Age' of post-war Europe and North America of full employment and rising affluence, together with the emergence of uncertainty, risk and insecurity with a concomitant questioning of, and focus upon, identity as a source of meaning (Beck, 1992; Lyon, 1999; Young, 1999; Bauman, 2000).

Unsurprisingly, therefore, numerous books and articles have increasingly focused upon and explored questions of identity (see, for example, Calhoun, 1994; Craib, 1998; Lyon, 1999; Gilroy, 2002; Woodward, 2002; Castells, 2004; Taylor and Spencer, 2004). Whilst traditionally, class, gender and racial/ethnic identities have generated substantial social scientific research interest, other groups are now receiving greater focus, specifically those relating to sexual orientation, religion, disability and age. At the same time, work by Giddens (1991), Beck (1992), Lash (1994a) and Bauman (2000, 2004) includes a focus upon the construction of self in late modernity since it is argued that increasing individualisation means that human identity is a task under continual construction, with actors having responsibility for this, mediated by abstract expert systems of knowledge. Within this approach, a critique and deconstruction of collective identities can be located, so that although group collectivities continue to be relevant in social, political and policy arenas, specificity of experience is increasingly being acknowledged and pursued by policy makers, state agencies and researchers.

Identity formations are of crucial significance when attempting to examine some of the important contemporary developments within the criminal justice and community safety sectors. For example, recently, bias-motivated offending has entered the criminological terrain, with the introduction of hate crime legislation in the US, the UK, Australia, as well as in other western democratic societies. Within this approach to crime, agencies of the criminal justice system are required to take into consideration victims' and offenders' identities and victims' perceptions when considering the motivation for an offence, so that crimes motivated by racial, religious or homophobic hatred (as well as other forms of prejudice) are dealt with more severely.

Civil disturbances involving conflict between different racial, ethnic and/or religious groupings, such as those occurring in Birmingham, England, in 2005, which featured Black, Pakistani and Bangladeshi youths, and in Sydney in 2005, involving White and Lebanese Australian youths, illustrate the problems of disorder and violence that can arise from the formation and expression of resistance identities, which are generated by actors who perceive themselves to be in devalued positions, thereby building 'trenches of resistance' on the basis of difference (Castells, 2004: 8). Efforts are increasingly being made by agencies of the criminal justice system, government officials, community leaders and community groups to mitigate the harms associated with racial and religious backlashes, amid the pursuit of policies and initiatives aimed at encouraging community engagement, community participation and community representation within criminal justice and community safety contexts. These developments both constitute and portray institutional reflection (Beck, 1992; Lash, 1994a), whereby agencies of the criminal justice system are reflecting more and more upon the part that they themselves may play in instigating and perpetuating the formation and expression of resistance identities, and work towards alleviating forms of discrimination and prejudice.

The development and implementation of policies aimed at promoting equality and at reducing discrimination and prejudice is a feature of all agencies of the criminal justice system in western societies today. Race relations legislation has led to the monitoring of minority ethnic groups' experiences of the criminal justice system, in the UK (as evidenced, for example, by Section 95 of the 1991 Criminal Justice Act), in Australia and in the US. More recently, in the UK, the accusation of 'institutional racism' in the Metropolitan Police Service (Macpherson, 1999) has stimulated fresh examination of racial/ethnic bias in policing policies, practices and procedures. At the same time, over the last decade, national, European and international policy developments in respect of direct and indirect discrimination, the provision of public services and employment law suggest that equality provisions are now being targeted at a broad range of group collectivities, including those based on religion, sexual orientation, disability and age. These developments reflect the emergence of new social movements consisting of politicised identities based on race, ethnicity, faith, gender, sexual orientation, disability and age, whose activities include demands for a recognition, or greater recognition, of their identities within the public sector.

Clearly, the issue of identity has important implications for criminal justice and community safety policy and practice. However, the notion of identity is itself elusive and open to substantial debate, and so this chapter aims to examine the nature, formation, maintenance and multiplicity of identity formations in late modernity, and to explore their implications for criminal and community justice. It is argued that contemporary manifestations of identity can best be understood through the social dynamics characteristic of late modernity. Late modernity does not signify a radical separation from modernity, but rather, consists of the interaction of two contradictory yet inter-related mechanisms: the 'imperative of order' (Lash, 1994a, critiques this) arising out of, and located within, the framework of modernity, whereby group collectivities are formed around politicised identities in relation to 'race'/ethnicity, faith, gender, sexuality, disability and age, these being underpinned by a belief in emancipation from oppression. At the same time, standing in contradiction to – but also interacting with – this imperative is rising individualisation, the growing fragmentation and liquidity of identity attachments, and increasing institutional and self-reflection. These processes are integral to understanding the construction and maintenance of social identities. First, however, it is necessary to focus upon and explain modernity and its characteristic features.

Modernity

Modernity has been linked to the historical period of time of the Enlightenment, after the Middle Ages (Tait, 2004), when reason emerged as the dominant paradigm through which to view the emancipation of humans from the pre-modern static order, the 'ancien régime' (Lash, 1994a: 112). Enlightenment values include the pursuit of scientific methods of enquiry; a belief in the concept of progress, that social problems can be identified and overcome; and a belief in truth and discovery (Smart, 1992). Free from pre-modern traditional feudal societies, and thrust into the world of industrial society that contained inequalities and oppressions, individuals originally grouped together to form collectivities based around class, gender and race, as evidenced by the emergence of labour and socialist movements and the women's and race equality movements, which, although often linked with the radicalised era of the 1960s, actually have a much longer, 200-year, history (Calhoun, 1994).[1]

It can be argued that in modernity, group collectivities, although formed rather than inherited, contain individual members who share a wider group consciousness, maintained by the coalescence of past, present and future members, and thereby, to use Bauman's (2000) terminology, possess a sense of solidity. But it would be a mistake to view the collectivisation of identities in a solely positive way, since group identities are formed and reinvigorated through the 'threat and practice of exclusion' (Bauman: 2004: 21), and so the potential for violence is ever present (Castells, 2004).

Late modernity

Late modernity is a phrase used by social scientists to try and capture the social and economic transformations that have occurred in western society during the last 40 years, beginning in the late 1960s. Traditional social affiliations, based on family or social class, have been eroded, as evidenced by, for example, the reduction in union and party political membership, rising divorce rates and the decline of the nuclear family (Beck, 1992; Furedi, 1997; Bauman, 2004). These developments have taken place amid the rapid demise of the manufacturing and industrial sectors, leading to a reduction in the primary labour market and in tenured secure employment, and to an increasingly insecure work environment requiring a mobile labour force, thereby dislocating people from their local communities (Furedi, 1997; Young, 1999). For Young, the 1960s heralded a movement from modernity to late modernity, 'from a world whose accent was on assimilation and incorporation to one which separates and excludes' (1999: 1). Thus, whereas a 'Golden Age' post-war Europe and North America might be characterised by rising affluence, full employment and the increased inclusion of social movements based on class, gender and race, late modernity might be characterised as a world that separates and excludes, a world of uncertainty and risk (Young, 1999).

According to Bauman (2000), in late modernity communities are becoming increasingly short-lived and fragile, so that any sense of belonging that individuals experience is likely to be transitory and fleeting, and any attachments formed to a community are likely to be easily discarded (Bauman, 2004):

> Communities are formed that are fragile and short-lived, scattered and wandering emotions, shifting erratically from one target to another and drifting in the forever inconclusive search for a secure haven: communities of shared worries, anxieties or hatreds – but in each case 'peg' communities, a momentary gathering around a nail on which many solitary individuals hang their solitary individual fears. (Bauman, 2000: 37)

A similar position can be found in the work of many other sociologists, who write about the loss of a sense of historical continuity and the decline of traditional community life with the concomitant emergence of more individualised ways of being (Lasch, 1980; Giddens, 1991; Lash, 1994b; Young, 1999). For example, in his book entitled *The culture of narcissism*, Lasch (1980: 5) argues that late modernity contains a 'spiritual crisis' in that people are quickly losing a sense of belonging to a succession of generations, and are starting to live for themselves rather than for wider community or family orientated goals. According to Beck (1992: 7), 'collective and group-specific sources of meaning', which he links to modern, industrial society, are breaking up and suffering from exhaustion and disenchantment. Both Lyotard (1984) and Baudrillard (1993) have portrayed late modernity as a world in which the grand narratives of progress and truth have been increasingly replaced by the construction of many different truths produced in many different locations. Therefore, the growing individualisation in conditions of late modernity creates pluralism, ambiguity and disagreement (Young, 1999). According to Giddens (1991), self-identities are actively constructed, consisting of a constant questioning and reconstruction of self, amidst a plethora of choices. However, those choices are themselves constrained by social and economic factors, so that people with the smallest amount of resources tend to have the fewest options available to them.

Whilst much has been written about the condition of contemporary western society as a movement away from modernity, it is important to stress that whilst collective sources of meaning seem to be breaking up, and according to Beck (1992) individuals are being released into a post-industrial late modern society where populations are increasingly being governed according to statistical analyses of risk (Simon, 1988; Ewald, 1991; O'Malley, 1992), nonetheless collectivised forms of identity and meaning continue to be relevant. As a result, social commentators will often refer to late modernity rather than postmodernity when discussing contemporary western society, to illustrate that contemporary social conditions do not signal the rise of a totally new era, but rather, amidst increasing fragmentation and individualisation, the characteristic features of modernity continue to be relevant. Indeed, according to Giddens (1990, 1991), it is premature to speak of the end of modernity, and Tait (2004) argues that most of the central features of modernity are still firmly in place.

Social identities in late modern society

The discussions in the above paragraphs suggest that when writing about the nature of social identities in contemporary western society, it is important to consider the interplay, tensions and contradictions between modernity's 'imperative of order' (Lash, 1994a), including the expression of collective identities and interests, and the fragmentation, individualisation, and fluidity of identities associated with conditions of late modernity. Both processes are at play and serve to produce, perpetuate, deconstruct and influence the nature of identity formations within particular contexts. Indeed, similar social and economic transformations can bring about both the unification and fragmentation of identity. For example, according to Castells (2004), over the last 25 years, as people's control over their environments has reduced, expressions of collective identity have surged forth. At the same time, Craib (1998) argues that a loss of control has also led to increasing fragmentation and individualisation, involving a constant questioning and reconstruction of the self.

Identities are socially constructed, being influenced by micro and macro factors in relation to historical, geographical, cultural, institutional, biological and psychological processes, as well as many other kinds of building material (Castells, 2004). Both processes can occur at a micro level, at the level of the individual, so that the construction of self may, in certain contexts, involve the construction of unitary categories, like Woman or Black, since these may be constituted from, and underpinned by, socio-structural and institutional processes that serve to perpetuate commonalities of experience according to gender, race, class and so forth (Brah, 2003). At the same time, particular social contexts and cultural processes may promote fragmentation of any constructed unitary aspects of self, thereby encouraging pluralism and multiplicity of subject positions. The integration and fragmentation of identities take place simultaneously, so that the ways in which unitary categories of identity are used, constructed and experienced by individuals are themselves mediated by other aspects of individuals' identities, and the nature and experience of identity pluralities is influenced by pressures towards the unification or collectivisation of identity. Similarly, at institutional and systemic levels, the interplay and tensions between the construction of 'catch-all' generalised categories of identity and the development of more nuanced approaches that take into account specific identities can be seen. The classificatory systems used by government agencies to mark social relations may use broad-based identity constructions that, although marking out difference, may also group together many different peoples (Woodward, 2002). At the same time, since institutional reflexivity in late modernity involves a client-centred approach to service delivery (Lash, 1994a), the multitudinous nature of identity is increasingly being focused upon and acknowledged, so that when responding to individuals, agencies are more often taking into account individuals' multiple subject positions and their multiple needs.

Importantly, in late modernity the decline of the influence of institutional settings – such as the Church, labour unions and political parties – on identity formations (Castells, 2004), alongside the fragmentation of communities and the rising significance of global networks and flows, has led to an increasingly amnesic society less able to maintain memories and experiences bound by tradition and history. As a result, interaction between the propensity to form group and collective identities and the propensity to fragment and individualise can lead to progressively more volatile and unpredictable social identities. Thus, in the context of late modernity, where identity attachments have become more fluid (Bauman, 2004) and the influence of traditional and civil institutions has declined, the flexibility and unpredictability of identities at the individual, group and collective level has heightened. For example, Castells (2004) argues that historical African American identity is being fragmented and individualised, without being integrated into a multiracial open society. Alongside the gradual loss of Black identity[2] in the US, new manifestations of collective identities have emerged based on religion[3] and gender.[4] At the same time, Black identities have become more localised and fragmented where defensive communities and/or gangs have formed, built out of ethnic materials rather than race (Castells, 2004).

In the UK, research suggests that some young Asian men may be constructing a 'strong' Islamic identity for themselves as a way of resisting the 'weakness' that they perceived to be associated with the category Asian (Archer, 2003). Similarly, Saeed et al (1999) argue that the concept of 'ummah' means that a global Islamic community supersedes national or ethnic identities. Therefore, young people may be claiming an Islamic identity for themselves because this places them within a global community so that they no longer feel so marginalised. But collectivisation around Islam is also accompanied by fragmentation and individualisation, so that individuals' (particularly young people's) beliefs become more 'personal, detached and heterogeneous' (Davie, 2002: 8). Indeed, it has been claimed that increasing numbers of young Muslims in Britain are using the Qur'an and hadiths directly as a resource rather than accepting the traditional views passed on to them from their parents (Joly, 1995).[5] Therefore, whilst the expression of Islamic identities in late modernity may, at some points, emerge from or feed into collective notions of Islam or the ummah, at other points it may consist of highly individualised and personal beliefs, practices and experiences of (un)belonging.

Social identities in relation to criminal justice and community safety

Turning specifically to a criminal justice and community safety context, the subject of identities is relevant in many ways. At a rudimentary level, two categories around which the criminal justice system operates are in relation to 'offender' and 'victim', and where these categories are internalised by an individual they become part of their self-identity. When discussing the construction of offender and victim identities, it is important to give some focus to the notion of power. As Castells (2004: 7) observes, 'the social construction of identity always takes place in a context marked by power relationships'. It is perhaps beneficial here to draw upon the work of Michel Foucault, which implicitly recognises power through the notion of governance, entailing 'the conduct of conduct: that is to say, a form of activity aiming to shape, guide or affect the conduct of some person or persons' (Gordon, 1991: 2). Recently, much work has focused upon documenting the emergence of an 'actuarial regime' in late modernity, which refers to the governance of populations through statistical analyses of risk (Simon, 1988; Ewald, 1991; O'Malley, 1992). It has been argued that whereas in previous eras criminal justice agencies sought to rehabilitate offenders, through the professions of welfare, regulatory power is now in operation, which is more concerned with managing populations through statistical analyses of risk rather than attempting to reform offenders (Simon, 1988; Ewald, 1991; O'Malley, 1992). Importantly, the movement towards actuarial forms of governance within criminal justice suggests the fragmentation of offenders' identities (Simon, 1988). Although agencies of the criminal justice system continue to collect information about individuals, this is transformed into classificatory systems that have little to do with an offender's traditional social affiliations in terms of their class, gender, 'race' and so forth, but which generate 'new offender subjects', for example the high-risk offender, or the career criminal (Kemshall: 2003: 28).

It is important to stress, however, that the rise of actuarial justice does not necessarily mean that the modernist agenda is no longer relevant within criminal justice, nor that it has been replaced. Disciplinary power continues to work through the criminal justice system, so that subjects are constructed through discourses emerging from the human sciences that make human behaviour visible and subject to intervention (Rouse, 1994). Kemshall (2003) argues, for instance, that agents working within criminal justice continue to use their 'professional judgement' rather than formal risk assessment tools when working with offenders, so that there is grassroots resistance to actuarial forms of governance. Essentially, whilst disciplinary and regulatory power have different levels of significance according to which historical period is analysed, both occur simultaneously (Burchell et al, 1991). As such, identities including offender gender/'race'/ethnicity continue to constitute sites of intervention, control and controversy within criminal justice jurisdictions.

Similarly, regarding the 'victim' category, Sykes (1992) and Furedi (1997) argue that the rising significance of victim issues in late modernity reflects increasing individualisation, with people claiming victim status for themselves as part of a wider 'culture of complaint', driven by selfish claims for financial compensation. Within government policy arenas, victims are viewed as being consumers of a criminal justice system, who have certain basic requirements such as the need for financial compensation or for information about the progress of their cases, thereby serving to individualise victims' reactions so that they are encouraged to think about themselves as individuals with needs that are linked to the criminal justice process rather than as individuals who belong to wider groups or other social collectivities (Spalek, 2006a). At the same time, however, it is important to stress that a significant feature of victim claims-making activities, which can be left out of analyses that attempt to situate victim issues within accounts of late modernity, is the involvement of action and support groups. Victim action groups may belong to broader social movements such as the feminist, race relations or the human rights movements, whose members share common politicised identities and whose work may seek to change wider societal injustices (Elias, 1993; Spalek, 2006a). In this way, the prevalence of victim issues in late modernity reflects not only individualisation but also collectivisation and shared experiences of victimisation.

Struggles take place over the definitions of offender and victim categories, and they may be labels that are imposed upon people. At the same time, however, offender or victim categories may be actively sought out by individuals themselves, with power relations being at play. Importantly, occurrences that take place within criminal justice may influence identity formations in other, broader, contexts, and may have implications for community safety issues. Similarly, events that take place beyond the criminal justice arena may affect the social construction of identities within criminal justice. The following sections therefore focus upon offender and victim identities in more detail.

Offender identities

Labelling theorists have argued that no behaviour is inherently deviant or criminal, but only comes to be considered so when this label is attached to the act by others. According to Becker (1963), dominant social groups who own the means of mass communication and control the reins of political power have the greatest capacity to impose labels upon people. This is true not only in terms of class positions but also with respect to other groupings in relation to 'race', gender and so forth (Sumner, 1994). For some categories of crime, or for certain types of agent, it may be more difficult to impose the category 'offender' than for others. For instance, legal infractions by businesses are not always considered to be suitable for criminalisation, and so corporations carrying out illegal activities may not be charged with, or found guilty of, any offences (Nelken, 1994; Croall, 2001). White-collar offenders may be eloquent individuals with a fair amount of legal knowledge, which means that they perhaps more easily avoid the label 'offender' being imposed upon them (Braithwaite, 1984; Bosworth-Davies, 1987; Punch, 1996). Where agencies of the criminal justice system disproportionately target the types of deviance associated with poor, working-class, marginalised communities, then individuals from within these communities will be increasingly identified as 'offenders'. Where the label 'offender' is imposed upon a person, it may lead to them internalising this label so that it becomes part of their identity and understanding of selfhood and, according to labelling theory, this may mean that they are more likely to engage in deviant activity in the future (White and Haines, 2001). Moreover, certain labels may contain more affective, 'sticky' characteristics, provoking particularly strong and negative reactions from within wider society (Ahmed, 2004). The offender label may stigmatise individuals so that their rehabilitation and acceptance back into society is particularly difficult, thereby increasing the likelihood of them reoffending.

But the category offender is only one aspect of identity formations with respect to criminal justice. As social identities are multitudinous, offender categories can only be understood in relation to other parts of individuals' self-identities, different aspects of which will emerge, become more significant or be accentuated by particular contexts within the criminal justice and community safety sectors. At different points in the criminal justice system, at different time periods, different identities will become more dominant, influencing the extent and type of state intervention and control, and an individual offender's experiences of the police, courts and prisons. At the same time, the systems of classification used by agencies and practitioners of the criminal justice system will themselves influence the construction and maintenance of offender identities, which may be linked to the kinds of illegal activities that individuals have committed as well as their subject positions in terms of their class, ethnicity, gender, faith, sexual orientation, age and so forth.

Offender identities and prison

Much has been written about the nature of offender identities in prisons as a result of Sykes' (1958) and Goffman's (1961) groundbreaking work regarding the effects of 'total institutions' upon those who have been institutionalised. It might be argued that as well as disrupting the social roles that prisoners may previously have held outside prison, penal institutions are sites of power inequalities, and identity serves as an important factor in the negotiation of relationships of domination.

Within prison, a 'hierarchy of identities' can operate, one aspect of which includes the crimes that prisoners have committed and their reputations as 'hard men'. Prisoner autobiographies directly refer to this hierarchy; John McVicar (1982) writes that a prisoner who informs on his attacker to the authorities is condemned as a 'grass', and that this label will place him lower down in the hierarchy than convicted sex offenders. As well as the crimes that prisoners have committed, their identities in relation to their ethnicity, faith or other subjectivities may influence their experiences of imprisonment and the negotiation of power. For example, Bosworth and Carrabine's (2001) research suggests that strategies of resistance that prisoners draw upon when incarcerated reflect their 'race', gender and sexuality. Furthermore, the over-representation of certain ethnic groupings in prison may lead to forms of solidarity within those groupings as a way of managing the effects of imprisonment (Bosworth and Carrabine, 2001). Similarly, according to Beckford et al (2005), some Asian Muslim prisoners in British jails follow the contours of regional and tribal loyalties in Pakistan. At the same time, however, this work has also uncovered extensive evidence of mutual support and cooperation among the majority of Muslim inmates and therefore a wider connectivity between prisoners on the basis of their faith. A pilot study of Muslim converts in prison by Spalek and El-Hassan (2007) suggests that converting to Islam may be an inmate's way of negotiating their personal safety, since this may be part of the construction of a masculinist identity that places the inmate higher up a hierarchy. According to Goodwin (2002), who studied Christian converts in British prisons, conversion to Christianity is a process through which individuals actively seek to adopt a new world-view and reformulate their sense of self. Therefore, religion can replace existing ways of interpreting the world, and can be used by inmates in order to create new forms of self-identity.

The ways in which identities are played out within the penal system are a product of – and reflect – many individual, situational, institutional, historical and social factors, some of which may relate directly to the penal context itself but which may also be linked to broader processes occurring within wider society. At certain points in time particular aspects of individuals' identities may become more pronounced for the individual concerned as well as for the prison authorities. In a post–11 September 2001 context, when many terror attacks have been committed around the world by Islamist extremists, some of which have been carried out by Muslim converts, those individuals who convert to Islam while incarcerated have generated considerable concern among prison officials, leading to an increased scrutiny of these inmates; this scrutiny may itself influence the content and expression of Muslim identities within prison. Racist incidents in prison or in wider society may influence the expression and formation of racial and/or ethnic identities within penal institutions. Localised events occurring within a particular jail constituting racial harassment, abusive language and/or assault, involving inmates and/or members of staff (Burnett and Farrell, 1994), may serve to radicalise identities within that particular institution or within the wider penal archipelago, leading to the production of resistance identities based on 'race' and/or ethnicity. The absence of particular identities from the classificatory systems that are used by prison services may also influence the ways in which particular identities are constructed and played out. For example, in France since the second half of the 1990s it is illegal to ask someone to declare their religious faith, and so there are no official data concerning the religious or ethnic identity of French people in prison (Beckford et al, 2005).[6] Beckford et al (2005) argue that, in contrast to England and Wales (where religious identity is categorised by the prison authorities), French prisons give rise to highly individualised expressions of Islam, and opportunities for collective prayer are scarce in French jails (Beckford et al, 2005).

Summary

The discussions above provide only a few examples of the ways in which identity is socially constructed and enacted within prisons. Certainly, more research is needed here. In particular, the linkages between the collectivisation of identities and the emergence and maintenance of group formations, and the fragmentation and individualisation of identities, must be further explored, taking into account both local and global influences.

There are also many other sites at which identities are at play throughout the criminal justice system and within a community safety context. For example, within some Muslim communities, perceptions of policing may include the notion that the communities are being criminalised, that police officers are operating 'religious profiling' when deciding whom to stop and search, and that young Muslims are being unfairly targeted (Spalek, 2005). It is also well documented that Black communities have been stereotyped as deviant by state agencies and have experienced over-regulation, over-policing and state control (see, for example, Bowling and Phillips, 2002; Chigwada-Bailey, 1997). Therefore, it seems that individuals' identities very much shape the experiences that they have of crime and criminal justice, and so the question of social identity is likely to feature implicitly in the policies and practices of all agencies of the criminal justice system. This issue will be returned to in later chapters of this book.

Victim identities

Victim identities are also socially constructed, and in constant negotiation and flux, being influenced by cultural, social, situational and criminal justice processes. In late modern societies, the notion of an 'ideal' victim, who is 'innocent', having played no part in their victimisation, is perpetuated and mass marketed, and stands as the prototypical identity against which all other victims are judged (Spalek, 2006a). The ease with which the victim status is afforded to individuals is influenced by their subject positions and their social roles. For instance, older people, children and women often receive a more sympathetic response to their victimisation than working-class males (Elias, 1993). Individuals whose jobs expose them to potentially high risks of victimisation, for example police officers, fire fighters or medical practitioners, may be denied a victim identity by wider society. Offenders are also often denied victim status, due to the mutual exclusivity of the offender and victim categories as perpetuated in social and political arenas, even though the categories of offender and victim often overlap (Farrall and Maltby, 2003). This can clearly be seen in court cases involving individuals charged with committing a particular crime, who portray themselves as being a victim in order to explain and to try to present mitigating circumstances for their behaviour. For example, women who have killed their husbands or partners may argue that underlying reasons for their behaviour relate to them being physically or mentally abused, the so-called 'battered women's syndrome' (Burnley et al, 1998).

In some cases, individuals will be labelled 'victims' in the wider social arena even though they do not necessarily view themselves in that way. Indeed, people may actively oppose a label that they feel has been imposed upon them. If the stereotype of victim as 'passive' and 'helpless' is perpetuated in dominant representations of victimhood during a time when individual strength is valued in society, then individuals may not situate themselves in terms of victimhood, despite the harms experienced, because of their distaste for the label 'victim' and the kinds of stereotypes that it elicits (Spalek, 2006a). Other aspects of individuals' identities, such as their gender, 'race' or class, are likely to influence whether or not they embrace victimhood as an aspect of their self-identity. Men may particularly resist calling themselves victims, due to the threat that notions of passivity and helplessness may have for their masculinity, when the dominant representations of manliness valued in western society appear to include men as 'being able to look after themselves and their families', as men who are 'strong' and 'resilient' (Newburn and Stanko, 1994).

It may be the case that because the criminal justice system constitutes an apparatus of government, and government technologies serve to subjectify people so that they behave in ways consistent with government objectives and priorities

(Garland, 1997), processes that occur within criminal justice encourage individuals to adopt particular kinds of victim identity. Discourses of 'consumerism' and 'active citizenship' that underpin approaches to victimisation, particularly in the UK context, serve to individualise victims' reactions so that people view themselves as individuals with particular needs as well as responsibilities, thereby threatening the expression of collective and/or group identities in relation to victimisation (Spalek, 2006a). Indeed, practitioners operating within the criminal justice and community safety sectors may themselves directly or indirectly influence the formation of certain kinds of victim identity, as they may encourage individual victims to behave in a way consistent with survival, so that people are penalised if they are perceived as remaining as 'passive victims' for too long (Williams, 1999).

The social identities of victims will also influence the very process and experience of victimisation. For instance, a study by Neville et al in 2004 suggests that race and cultural factors contribute to post-rape recovery. Neville et al (2004) argue that a 'race'–gender stereotype of Black women as being sexually loose, as identified by Black feminist academics, may be internalised by some Black female victims of rape and this may reduce their self-esteem and increase their self-blame after rape so that it is more difficult for them to 'recover' from this experience. Victims whose faith is an important aspect of their identities may not recognise that their experiences constitute victimisation because pain and suffering may be seen as an integral part of life (Spalek, 2006a).

The issue of whether an experience of victimisation may serve to re-awaken dormant identities, bringing forth aspects of a person's identity that were once less significant and perhaps deeply buried but which take on increased relevance in the aftermath of the crime, is an area that deserves greater exploration. It may be the case, for example, that a victim undergoes a process of radicalisation in the aftermath of crime, where radicalisation might be understood as adopting a more politicised stance, advocating thorough reform of systems that reproduce oppression (Spalek, 2006b). This may be particularly likely to be the case in relation to hate crimes, as these offences are motivated by a prejudice towards particular identities or belief systems. An attack motivated by racial hatred, for example, may lead to 'race' and/or ethnicity becoming a more predominant part of the self-identity of the victim, influencing their perceptions, frameworks of understanding regarding their experiences in relation to the social world, and their behaviour. It may lead to the victim adopting a more politicised stance in relation to the aspect of their identity that has been re-awakened, which may have positive or negative outcomes. For example, a victim of hate crime may join a group that they feel represents the part of their identity that has been attacked, which campaigns peacefully for social change. A victim may also join a generic peace movement, whereby individuals' identities are subsumed within the wider goal and ideology of promoting peace. At the same time, however, a victim of hate crime may join an extremist group that advocates the use of violence in order to defend identities that they deem to be under attack. Victims may also form 'resistance identities' that involve the formation of defensive communes, constructing collective forms of resistance to oppression (Castells, 2004). An example here might be Webster's (1995) work in relation to young Asian men defending particular parts of territory in Keighley, West Yorkshire, as a way of responding to racial hostility and violence. Similarly, Moazzam Begg, who spent three years in detention in Afghanistan and Guantanamo Bay in Cuba, as a teenager joined a gang called the Lynx, which was dedicated to self-defence and fighting racism in Birmingham, where right-wing extremist groups like the National Front and the Anti-Paki League were active (Hattenstone, 2006). Certainly, more research is needed in order to explore and capture the many different pathways that victims take when responding to the crimes that have been committed against them.

It is also important to stress that hate crimes may have an impact upon the wider communities that direct victims belong to (Hall, 2003). Communities may be imagined as well as real, so that the effects of a particular incident of hate crime may have far-reaching consequences through potentially re-awakening or radicalising a myriad of identities. In late modernity this is likely to take on a global dimension as a result of technological advancements, so that occurrences that take place in one part of the world may affect other locales elsewhere on the globe (Giddens, 1990; Chesneaux, 1992). Particular concern has been generated towards the radicalisation of Muslim identities following the terror attacks on the World Trade Center in September 2001 and then the subsequent attacks in Bali, Madrid and London. In the aftermath of each terror attack, Muslim communities have reported higher levels of victimisation as a result of their being targeted by members of the public and by far-right groups. Thus, Muslim women and men have been physically and verbally abused and attacked, and mosques have been vandalised (Spalek, 2002). It may be the case that this violence and abuse, and the fear generated by it, has shaped individuals' self-identities, leading to a significant number of individuals from minority ethnic groups who were nominally Muslim to claim Islamic identities for themselves more vigorously.[7] The impact of anti-terror legislation that has been introduced by western governments has further compounded this, leading perhaps to dormant Islamic identities being re-awakened.

An experience of hate crime may also lead to the victim hiding or denying parts of their identities that they deem to put them at risk. A decision not to veil so as to hide one's Islamic identity, a decision not to show signs of affection in public if part of a homosexual relationship, or a decision not to speak in public places for fear of arousing hostility due to one's foreign accent or language, are all ways of trying to reduce the risk, and manage the fear, of crime. Of course, some identities are easier to hide than others, and those with physical attributes like gender or 'race'/ethnicity are particularly difficult to conceal. Another strategy in managing personal safety is for those who experience oppression to claim for themselves spaces in which they are able to freely construct, reproduce and show their identities. This process has been referred to as 'queering' space in gay and lesbian literature (Felsenthal, 2004). Another way of avoiding victimisation might be to stress particular aspects of one's external social identity even though there is little or no internal acceptance of this identity. An example that can be provided here is in relation to a White Muslim man whose religious identity is more important and significant to him than either his 'race' or his masculinity. However, when witnessing Islamophobic abuse being carried out by another White man against an Arab woman on the basis of an Islamic identity that the attacker perceives the woman to have, the White Muslim male may stress commonalities of identity in terms of 'race' and 'gender' with the abuser in order to secure his own safety and also perhaps to reason with the White abuser so as to try and protect the woman who is under attack.[8] At the same time, an offender's perceptions of the identity of a victim may not correspond to the victim's own perception of themselves. In the aftermath of 11 September 2001 not only were Muslim communities attacked but also Sikh and Christian Arab minorities due to their perceived resemblance to Muslims and/or members of al-Qaeda (Spalek, 2002). Research suggests that factors that are likely to feature in offenders' perceptions when carrying out hate crime on the basis of 'race', faith and sexual orientation include the victim's dress, their skin colour and their location.

Experiencing victimisation on the basis of one's identity also means that this is likely to be a recurring and, in severe cases, a constant, feature of one's everyday life. Individuals' daily lives as framed by actual, or perceived threat of, violence and abuse have been well documented in relation to gender, racial/ethnic, gay, lesbian, bisexual and transsexual identities and disability (Stanko, 1990; Chahal and Julienne, 1999; Tatchell, 2002; Bowling and Phillips, 2002; Disability Rights Commission, 2005). The notion of 'travelling identities' may be particularly relevant here (see Gilbert, 2005).[9] Continual harassment and abuse can lead to the gradual emergence of new aspects of self, which can coexist with more familiar constructions of self, influencing everyday behaviour and experiences. In contrast to the 'victim as survivor' identity that is mass marketed within western society, whereby victims are portrayed as individuals who have become 'stronger', 'better' people as a result of their experiences (Spalek, 2006a), the process of victimisation can bring forth new aspects of self that victims dislike and which may cause them much pain and distress. In severe circumstances, where the victimisation is ongoing, this may lead to the victim making themselves as invisible as possible to try and reduce the potential for violence and abuse (Chahal and Julienne, 1999).

Victims' identities can also influence the ways in which agencies of the criminal justice system respond to their victimisation. In the aftermath of the inadequate and misguided police response to the murder of Black teenager Stephen Lawrence, a report by Lord Macpherson labelled the police as institutionally racist, thereby suggesting that Black victims might experience inappropriate, poor and/or discriminatory treatment from the police. Individuals with disabilities who are the victims of crime may find that their complaints are not taken seriously by agencies responsible for prosecuting and investigating cases. Indeed, this may have an impact upon the broader population of disabled people, since individuals may be afraid to leave institutional care settings to live in wider society if they are aware of acquaintances who have been victimised in the community, and who may not have had their complaints taken seriously (Williams, 1999). Gay, lesbian, bisexual and transgender communities tend not to report crimes that they experience to the police because of their fear of police harassment or as a result of their belief that the police will not be sympathetic to their plight (Tatchell, 2002). Older people who are the victims of abuse may also be too frightened or embarrassed to go to the authorities. A report by the House of Commons Select Committee in 2004 highlights the lack of training of professionals in recognising, reporting and treating elder abuse (Health Committee, 2004). These are just a few examples of the ways in which victims' identities affect their experiences of crime, criminal justice and community safety. The issues raised by these examples will be elaborated upon more fully in the chapters that follow.

Social identities, institutional reflexivity and reflection

When writing about social identities in relation to the criminal justice and community safety contexts, it is important to draw upon the notion of 'reflexive modernity' as outlined by Lash (1994a) and developed by Beck (1992) and Giddens (1991). According to Lash (1994b: 200), Beck's (1992) notion of reflexivity consists of the ways in which the side effects, the dangers or 'bads' arising out of modernity are dealt with in order to minimise insecurities associated with the social changes here. Thus, it might be argued that the criminal justice system constitutes an example of the ways in which government institutions and agencies have evolved in order to respond to the social problems of crime and disorder (Lash, 1994a). More importantly in the context of this chapter, reflection is a constituent part of reflexivity in late modernity, whereby individuals, collective groups and/or institutions intentionally and rationally reflect upon the part that they play in the perpetuation of identified social problems as well as reflecting upon ways in which they can intervene and act so as to minimise harms (Lash, 1994a; McGhee, 2005). Given that in late modernity, identity is increasingly a source of meaning through which experience is mediated (Lyon, 1999), reflexivity within the criminal justice system also involves the acknowledgement, monitoring and production of – as well as engagement with, and minimisation of harms in relation to – social identities.

Reflection may take many different forms. It may involve the pursuit of a 'representative democracy' (Lash, 1994a), whereby criminal justice institutions open themselves up to the communities that they serve, with the lay public engaging with, as well as critiquing, rival forms of expertise. The phrases 'community participation', 'community engagement' and 'community scrutiny of performance' are often found in government and criminal justice policy documents, with the prosecutorial and criminal justice authorities such as the prison service, police service, probation service and Crown Prosecution Service (CPS) actively pursuing aims that strive to achieve these goals across a wide range of contexts. For example, in the UK, when drawing up policies on the prosecution of religiously and racially aggravated crime, as well as crimes motivated by hostility towards lesbian, gay, bisexual and transgender communities and individuals with disabilities, the CPS consulted many different community groups (CPS, 2004). Illustrating the importance with which community engagement is viewed, good practice guidance on this has been produced by the CPS, and the development of a strategic and sustainable approach to community engagement features in the CPS Business Strategy 2005–08.

Police engagement with local communities can take place on many different levels. Every police service in England and Wales has a police authority that must ensure that community consultation takes place regarding the ways in which a particular area is policed, also with respect to the policing priorities that a particular police service adopts. Police authorities can also work with local police services on community engagement, and many important initiatives have been developed, aimed at building the trust of local communities, and seeking to increase community involvement in policing (Myhill et al, 2003). For instance, a key organisation working with the Metropolitan Police Service (MPS) is the Muslim Safety Forum. The forum is an important mechanism through which Muslims' concerns about police tactics and approaches are regularly raised (Spalek, 2005).

Institutional reflection may also involve community engagement with training packages that are developed for members of staff working for the various criminal justice agencies. For example, following the publication of *Diversity matters*, issued by the HM Inspectorate of Constabulary in 2003, police training is likely to reflect increasingly the local communities that separate police forces serve, and to include members of local communities in the training programmes targeted at police officers. The CPS is also encouraging community participation in the learning requirements, the design or the evaluation of CPS staff training programmes. For instance, representatives from community and faith groups contributed to a national training programme on racially/religiously aggravated crime. Community scrutiny of the effectiveness of new CPS training procedures is also taking increased significance, for example by gaining feedback about the impact of newly introduced training programmes from local communities (Spalek, 2005).

Institutional reflection might also involve agencies of the criminal justice system reflecting upon the ways in which different identities are represented in their workforces. The British government, for example, is seeking to achieve a 'truly representative police service' and a national target of 7% for minority ethnic officers by 2009 has been set (Home Office, 2002). According to Lash (1994a), as employees become more educated and, in late modern conditions, more individualistic and less bound by tradition and convention, then they are more likely to question their working practices and the orthodoxies underpinning these.

It is perhaps unsurprising, therefore, that employees of the criminal justice system are grouping together on the basis of 'race'/ethnicity, gender, sexual orientation, age and disability to question and challenge what they view as oppressive employment practices and conditions. The National Black Police Association in the UK and the National Association of Black Law Enforcement Officers in the US, the Association of Black Probation Officers, the British Association of Women Police, the Gay Police Association, the Association of Muslim Police in the MPS and the Disabled Police Officers' Association of Northern Ireland (which represents serving as well as retired police officers) constitute just a few examples, but they illustrate how employees can demand organisational change and so institutions may be forced to reflect upon their policies and practices by the claims-making activities of their own members of staff. Indeed, employees' identities may powerfully challenge the identities that agencies of the criminal justice system themselves have created, adopted or perpetuated. Whitfield (2004) argues, for example, that the first Black police officer, Norwell Roberts, challenged the MPS's White identity that maintained that 1960s' British society was not yet prepared to accept Black police officers. The case of Norwell Roberts clearly illustrated that the real issue within the MPS was the reluctance of the White Commissioner and other White senior members of the police force to appoint Black police officers.

External factors may also lead to increasing institutional reflection. For example, the years following the publication of the 1999 Macpherson Report, which found evidence of institutional racism in the MPS (Macpherson, 1999), stimulated much self-examination by the MPS in relation to policies and practices affecting minority ethnic communities. Similarly, after the murder of Zahid Mubarek by a racist inmate in 2000 at HMP Feltham, alongside other highly publicised incidents at HMP Brixton and HMP Full Sutton, the Commission for Racial Equality (CRE) conducted a formal investigation into HM Prison Service and the director general announced that the service is institutionally racist. This led to HM Prison Service committing itself to work with the CRE to build race relations into all aspects of its work, whereby a five-year joint Prison Service/CRE Action Plan, entitled 'Implementing race equality in prisons: A shared agenda for change', was launched in December 2003 (HM Prison Service, 2004), covering areas such as employment, staff development and training, and performance improvement.

Another aspect to institutional reflection may involve the development and use of targets and specific indicators to help formulate strategies and plans of action for agents of the criminal justice system to follow. These may be formulated at government, national or local levels. For example, the British government has introduced a series of public sector agreements aimed at agencies of the criminal justice system. These contain specific targets that agencies are expected to meet, for example in relation to raising the public's, as well as Black and minority ethnic communities', confidence in criminal justice, and also ensuring that victims and witnesses are treated with respect and understanding (HM Government, 2004).

Police services are particularly active in using tension indicators in order to help assess whether certain types of activities that they carry out might lead to civil disturbances from particular groups within society. The US Department of Justice, for instance, advocates the use of tension indicators to help assess the likely reaction to particular types of police intervention at particular moments in time. The following types of indicators can be used: a rise in racist attacks, a rise in racist graffiti, a rise in racist activity on the internet, and a rise in the activities of the far right. This kind of information can be gathered by police observation in liaison with other agencies as well as local communities (Tupman and O'Reilly, 2004). Tupman and O'Reilly (2004) suggest that a similar approach can be utilised in relation to counter-terrorism policing activities, so that police intervention can be assessed and future policy drawn up in relation to indicators that help to measure the likelihood of terrorism-related backlashes, using measures such as a rise in anti-westerner or anti-foreigner attacks or graffiti, or a rise in the activities of militias. However, it is important to stress that any attempts by local police services or other agencies of the criminal justice system to manage violent backlashes produced by resistance or politicised identities may be undermined by wider, global events that serve to help produce and maintain these. Thus, in the context of counter-terrorism policing and the attempt to reduce the pool of resistance identities from which extremists may draw for the commission of terrorist attacks, events that take place in the global arena such as the war in Iraq and its aftermath, and the treatment of detainees at Guantanamo Bay in Cuba, may reduce any efforts made by local agencies themselves.

Conclusion

This chapter illustrates some of the ways in which the notion of social identity is important in the criminal justice and community safety sectors. In discussing the social construction of offender and victim identities, the chapter has shown that these are multitudinous, and are linked to other aspects of individuals' identities in terms of their gender, 'race'/ethnicity, faith, and so on, subject positions, being constrained and influenced by a wide range of factors, including social, political and institutional issues. Importantly, this chapter illustrates how power lies at the core of identity formations, since identity is both a product of an individual's internal constructions of self as well as their social location and how they are categorised by others.

Research is increasingly focusing upon the construction of offender identities in prison since identities may play an important role in the negotiation of power in this context. Researchers have examined, for example, the influence of 'race'/ethnicity, gender, sexuality and faith in the construction of inmates' identities and in the negotiation of their personal safety. Studies suggest that both the unification and fragmentation of identities are taking place within prisons, since inmates may group together on the basis of wider social collectivities, for example, on the basis of a particular faith, but also at the same time may group together in more specific ways, in terms of specific ethnicities. Inmates may also respond to their incarceration in an individualised way by reconstructing their sense of self, involving taking on new identities. The classification systems used by the prison authorities may themselves influence the formation and expression of certain identities, and the pursuit of actuarial forms of governance may serve to fragment offenders' identities and to create new subjects that have little to do with traditional social affiliations. Certainly, more research is needed examining the issue of the construction of identity within a penal setting.

Research exploring the construction of victim identities suggests that these are multitudinous in nature, and can be influenced by policies promoting particular responses to victimisation that underpin the criminal justice and community safety sectors. Thus, it might be argued that notions of an 'active citizen' and 'consumer' as included in government strategies serve to influence victims' reactions so that they think of themselves as individuals rather than as belonging to wider group and social collectivities. Nonetheless, victims' reactions to the crimes that have been committed against them may include engaging in collective responses. These responses may take the form of the development of resistance identities that stress separation from wider society; at the same time, however, victims may develop and join wider social movements that try to engage in dialogue with mainstream society in order to effect change. The issue of hate crimes is particularly relevant here, as hate crimes are targeted at people because of the particular identities and belief systems that they are perceived to have by the offender. But, while victims' responses to hate crime may include a politicisation of aspects of their identities, responses may also include denying parts of their self so as to try to reduce the risk of being re-victimised. In severe circumstances, it may lead to the invisibilisation of certain identities.

A core theme underpinning this chapter is that in order to understand the social construction of identities in contemporary western society, it is important to take into consideration the 'imperative of order' as associated with modernity, and fluidity and fragmentation of meaning and experience as associated with conditions of late modernity. Both mechanisms occur simultaneously and influence the formation of social identities, so that at the same time that collective and group identities are constructed and expressed, and beliefs in progress and group emancipation from oppression may surface in particular contexts, identities are simultaneously fragmented and individualised. The next chapter considers equality and diversity issues in relation to the public sector, whereby it will be illustrated that developments that are taking place here suggest that policies are being implemented to promote equality between different group collectivities based on 'race'/ethnicity, faith, gender, sexual orientation, disability and age. At the same time, however, there is rising awareness that the distinct voices and experiences of certain specific groups of individuals are obscured within such broad-based approaches, and so, increasingly, more nuanced approaches to equality and diversity are being adopted, whereby the needs of specific communities and individuals are progressively being taken into account. Thus, the theme of the interplay between modern and late modern processes in relation to the construction of identity is further pursued.

Notes

[1] Calhoun (1994: 23) argues that the women's movement has roots at least 200 years old, and that communes were as important in the early 1800s as in the 1960s.

[2] Indeed, Stuart Hall (2003) writes about the end of the essential 'Black subject' in Black cultural politics.

[3] As evidenced by the growing influence of Farrakhan's Nation of Islam as well as Black churches (Castells, 2004).

[4] As evidenced by the 1995 Million Men March in Washington DC built around Black male pride (Castells, 2004).

[5] This suggests that in the context of late modernity the Durkheimian notion of religion as a form of collective memory or collective consciousness, based upon a community of past, present and future members, as well as tradition (Davie, 2002) may not be so relevant.

[6] In France there is a set of secular, republican values and institutions known as 'laïcité', whereby State and Church are clearly separated (Beckford et al, 2005).

[7] Indeed, the author has heard anecdotal evidence that suggests that after the publication of Salman Rushdie's *The Satanic Verses* in 1989, some Muslim women began to wear the hijab.

[8] This example is based on a real-life story as related to me by a Muslim student.

[9] The notion of a travelling identity refers to the fluidity of self constructions and suggests that painful experiences can lead to the emergence of new aspects of selfhood (Gilbert, 2005).

Chapter questions

What is the material from which social identities are built?

What are 'resistance identities' and what is their relevance to a criminal justice context?

To what extent does the question of fluid and transitory social life, as identified in accounts of late modernity, apply to all contexts? That is, does this apply to rural areas?

Case study
Moazzem Begg

He was born 37 years ago in Birmingham to secular Muslim parents. His mother died when he was six, and his father sent him to the Jewish King David School in Birmingham, because he thought it inculcated good values. For the next six years Begg wore a yarmulke (skullcap), learned Hebrew, recited Jewish prayers and mixed almost exclusively with Jewish friends. He smiles as he talks about how secure and contented he felt, even though he realised there were differences – he did not go to synagogue on Saturday, and he went to Qur'an lessons.

No wonder he was confused. He wasn't sure whether he was Pakistani or Indian (his family had crossed to Pakistan at partition); his father showed him photos of his grandfather and great-grandfather as heroic warriors with terrifying eyes and told him they were Mongols; he was born and bred in Britain and was given a thorough Jewish education.

Then came secondary school and another identity crisis. The National Front and Anti-Paki League were doing big business in Birmingham, his brother was hospitalised after being beaten in a racist attack and, rather than feeling that he had a toe in every cultural camp, Begg began to feel like a persecuted outsider. He joined a gang called the Lynx, dedicated to self-defence and fighting racism. Begg shows me pictures of gang members, most of them wiry with precocious moustaches, dead ringers for Thin Lizzy's Phil Lynott. Begg is at the corner of the picture, smiley and tiny. That was another problem – his size. There is another boy towards the opposite corner, bigger, cooler, charismatic. That's Sigi, a German Asian, a hard-nut, a negotiator, and Begg's best friend. Like many in the gang, he got into drugs and petty crime, and by his early 20s he was dead, having suffocated on his own vomit.

Source: Hattenstone, 2006

Question: How, and in what ways, is the question of identity central to Moazzam Begg's case?

References

Ahmed, S. (2004) *The cultural politics of emotion*, Edinburgh: Edinburgh University Press.

Archer, L. (2003) *Race, masculinity and schooling: Muslim boys and education*, Maidenhead: Open University Press.

Baudrillard (1993) *Symbolic exchange and death*, London: Sage.

Bauman, Z. (2000) *Liquid modernity*, Cambridge: Polity Press.

Bauman, Z. (2004) *Identity: Conversations with Benedetto Vecchi*, Cambridge: Polity Press.

Beck, U. (1992) *Risk society: Towards a new modernity*, London: Sage.

Becker, H. (1963) *Outsiders*, New York: The Free Press.

Beckford, J., Joly, D. and Khosrokhavar, F. (2005) *Muslims in prison: Challenge and change in Britain and France*, Basingstoke: Palgrave.

Bosworth, M. and Carrabine, E. (2001) 'Reassessing resistance: Race, gender and sexuality in prison', *Punishment and Society*, vol 3, no 4, pp 501–15.

Bosworth-Davies, R. (1987) *Too good to be true. How to survive the casino economy*, London: Bodley Head.

Bowling, B. and Phillips, C. (2002) *Racism, crime and justice*, Harlow: Longman.

Brah, A. (2003) 'Difference, diversity and differentiation', in J. Donald and A. Rattansi (eds) *'Race', culture and difference*, London: Sage, pp 126–48.

Braithwaite, J. (1984) *Corporate crime in the pharmaceutical industry*, London: Routledge and Kegan Paul.

Burchell, G., Gordon, C. and Miller, P. (1991) *The Foucault effect: Studies in governmentality with two lectures by and an interview with Michel Foucault*, London: Harvester Wheatsheaf.

Burnett, R. and Farrell, G. (1994) *Reported and unreported racial incidents in prisons*, Centre for Criminological Research University of Oxford Occasional Paper 14, Oxford: Centre for Criminological Research.

Burnley, J., Edmunds, C., Gaboury, M. and Seymour, A. (1998) 'Theoretical perspectives of victimology and critical research', in J. Burnley, C. Edmunds, M. Gaboury and A. Seymour (eds) *1998 national victim assistance academy textbook*, Washington, DC: Department for Justice, Office for Victims of Crime, pp 1–10.

Calhoun, C. (1994) 'Social theory and the politics of identity', in C. Calhoun (ed) *Social theory and the politics of identity*, Oxford: Blackwell, pp 9–36.

Castells, M. (2004) *The power of identity* (2nd edn), Oxford: Blackwell.

Chahal, K. and Julienne, L. (1999) *We can't all be white*, York: Joseph Rowntree Foundation/York Publishing Services.

Chesneaux, J. (1992) *Brave modern world: The prospects for survival*, Slovenia: Thames and Hudson.

Chigwada-Bailey, R. (1997) *Black women's experiences of criminal justice: A discourse on disadvantage*, Winchester: Waterside Press.

CPS (Crown Prosecution Service) (2004) *Addressing equality and diversity in the CPS: A stocktake report*, London: Equality and Diversity Unit, CPS.

Craib, I. (1998) *Experiencing identity*, London: Sage.

Croall, H. (2001) *Understanding white collar crime*, Buckingham: Open University Press.

Davie, G. (2002) *Europe: The exceptional case*, London: Darton, Longman and Todd.

Disability Rights Commission (2005) 'Latest news' (www.drc.org.uk/newsroom/newsdetails.asp?id=598&section=1).

Elias, R. (1993) *Victims still*, London: Sage.

Ewald, F. (1991) 'Insurance and risk', in G. Burchell, C. Gordon and P. Miller (eds) *The Foucault effect: Studies in governmentality*, London: Harvester Wheatsheaf, pp 197–210.

Farrall, S. and Maltby, S. (2003) 'The victimisation of probationers', *Howard Journal of Criminal Justice*, vol 42, no 1, pp 32–54.

Felsenthal, K. (2004) 'Socio-spatial experiences of transgender individuals', in Jean Lau Chin (ed) *The psychology of prejudice and discrimination: Bias based on gender and sexual orientation, volume 3*, London: Praeger, pp 201–25.

Furedi, F. (1997) *Culture of fear: Risk-taking and the morality of low expectation*, London: Cassell.

Garland, D. (1997) 'Governmentality and the problem of crime: Foucault, criminology, sociology', *Theoretical Criminology*, vol 1, no 2, pp 173–214.

Giddens, A. (1990) *The consequences of modernity*, Cambridge: Polity Press.

Giddens, A. (1991) *Modernity and self-identity*, Cambridge Polity Press.

Gilbert, P. (2005) *Leadership: Being effective and remaining human*, Lyme Regis: Russell House Publishing.

Gilroy, P. (2002) 'Diaspora and the detours of identity', in K. Woodward (ed) *Identity and difference*, London: Sage, pp 299–346.

Goffman, E. (1961) *Asylum: Essays on the social situation of mental patients and other inmates*, New York: Doubleday.

Goodwin, L. (2002) 'Time for change: A study of religious conversion and self-identity in prison', PhD thesis, Department of Sociological Studies, University of Sheffield.

Gordon, C. (1991) 'Government rationality: an introduction', in G. Burchell, C. Gordon and P. Miller (eds) *The Foucault effect: Studies in governmentality*, London: Harvester Wheatsheaf, pp 1–52.

Hall, S. (2003) 'New ethnicities', in L. Alcoff and E. Mendieta (eds) *Identities: Race, class, gender and nationality*, London: Blackwell, pp 90–5.

Hattenstone, S. (2006) 'Looking for troubles: Moazzam Begg, my years in captivity', *The Guardian Weekend*, 25 February, pp 21–8.

Health Committee (2004) *Elder abuse* (www.parliament.uk/parliamentary_committees/health_committee/hc190404_14.cfm).

HM Government (2004) *Cutting crime, delivering justice, a strategic plan for criminal justice 2004–08*, Cm 6288, London: HMSO.

HM Prison Service (2004) 'Implementing race equality in prisons: A shared agenda for change' (www.hmprisonservice.gov.uk/abouttheservice/actionplan/).

Home Office (2002) 'National policing plan 2003–2006' (http://police. homeoffice.gov.uk/national-policing-plan/policing-plan-2006.html).

Joly, P. (1995) *Britannia's crescent: Making a place for Muslims in British society*, Aldershot: Avebury.

Kemshall, H. (2003) *Understanding risk in criminal justice*, Maidenhead: Open University Press.

Lasch, C. (1980) *The culture of narcissism*, London: Sphere.

Lash, S. (1994a) 'Reflexivity and its doubles: Structure, aesthetics, community', in U. Beck, A. Giddens and S. Lash (eds) *Reflexive modernization: Politics, tradition and aesthetics in the modern social order*, Cambridge: Polity Press, pp 110–73.

Lash, S. (1994b) 'Replies and critiques', in U. Beck, A. Giddens and S. Lash (eds) *Reflexive modernization: Politics, tradition and aesthetics in the modern social order*, Cambridge: Polity Press, pp 174–215.

Lyon, D. (1999) *Postmodernity* (2nd edn), Buckingham: Open University Press.

Lyotard, F. (1984) *The postmodern condition: A report on knowledge*, Manchester: Manchester University Press.

Macpherson, Sir W. (1999), *The Stephen Lawrence Inquiry: Report of an Inquiry by Sir William Macpherson of Cluny*, London: HMSO.

McGhee, D. (2005) *Intolerant Britain? Hate, citizenship and difference*, Maidenhead: Open University Press.

McVicar, J. (1982) 'Violence in prisons', in P. Marsh and A. Campbell (eds) *Aggression and violence*, Oxford: Basil Blackwell, pp 200–14.

Myhill, A., Yarrow, S., Dalgleish, D. and Docking, M. (2003) *The role of police authorities in public engagement*, Home Office Online Report 37/03, London: Home Office (www.homeoffice.gov.uk/rds/pdfs2/rdsolr3703.pdf).

Nelken, D. (1994) *The futures of criminology*, London: Sage.

Neville, H., Oh, E., Spanierman, L., Heppner, M. and Clark, M. (2004) 'General and culturally specific factors influencing black and white rape survivors' self-esteem', *Psychology of Women Quarterly*, vol 28, pp 83–94.

Newburn, T. and Stanko, E. (1994) 'When men are victims', in T. Newburn and E. Stanko (eds) *Just boys doing business?*, London: Routledge, pp 153–65.

O'Malley, P. (1992) 'Risk, power and crime prevention', *Economy and Society*, vol 21, no 3, pp 253–75.

Punch, M. (1996) *Dirty business: Exploring corporate misconduct*, London: Sage.

Rouse, J. (1994) 'Power/knowledge', in G. Gutting (ed) *The Cambridge companion to Foucault*, Cambridge: Cambridge University Press, pp 92–114.

Saeed, A., Blain, N. and Forbes, D. (1999) 'New ethnic and national questions in Scotland: Post-British identities among Glasgow Pakistani teenagers', *Ethnic and Racial Studies*, vol 22, no 5, pp 821–44.

Simon, J. (1988) 'The ideological effects of actuarial practices', *Law and Society Review*, vol 22, no 4, pp 771–800.

Smart, B. (1992) *Modern conditions, post-modern controversies*, London: Routledge.

Spalek, B. (ed) (2002) *Islam, crime and criminal justice*, Cullompton: Willan.

Spalek, B. (2005) 'Muslims and the criminal justice system', in T. Choudhury (ed) *Muslims in the UK: Policies for engaged citizens*, Budapest: Open Society Institute, pp 253–340.

Spalek, B. (2006a) *Crime victims: Theory, policy and practice*, Hampshire: Palgrave Macmillan.

Spalek, B. (2006b) 'Disconnection and exclusion: Pathways to radicalisation', in T. Abbas (ed) *Islamic political radicalism: A European comparative perspective*, Netherlands: Brill, pp 192–206.

Spalek, B. and El-Hassan, S. (2007) 'Muslim conversion in prison', *The Howard Journal of Criminal Justice*, vol 46, no 2, pp 99–114.

Stanko, E. (1990) *Everyday violence: Women's and men's experience of personal danger*, London: Pandora Press.

Sumner, C. (1994) *The sociology of deviance: An obituary*, Maidenhead: Open University Press.

Sykes, C. (1992) *A nation of victims: The decay of the American character*, New York: St Martin's Press.

Sykes, G. (1958) *The society of captives: A study of a maximum security prison*, Princeton, NJ: Princeton University Press.

Tait, G. (2004) 'Modernity and the "failure" of crime control', in R. Hill and G. Tait (eds), *Hard lessons: Reflections on governance and crime control in late modernity*, Aldershot: Ashgate, pp 18–32.

Tatchell, P. (2002) 'Some people are more equal than others', in P. Iganski (ed) *The hate debate*, London: Profile, pp 54–70.

Taylor, G. and Spencer, S. (2004) 'Introduction'. in G. Taylor and S. Spencer (eds) *Social identities: Multidisciplinary approaches*, London: Routledge, pp 1–34.

Tupman, B. and O'Reilly, C. (2004) 'Terrorism, hegemony and legitimacy: evaluating success and failure in the war on terror', unpublished paper presented to the Political Studies Association conference, Lincoln.

Webster, C. (1995) *Youth crime, victimisation and racial harassment*, Community Studies 7 (revised edn), Ilkley: Centre for Research in Applied Community Studies, Bradford and Ilkley Community College

White, R. and Haines, F. (2001) *Crime and criminology*, Oxford: Oxford University Press.

Whitfield, J. (2004) *Unhappy dialogue, the Metropolitan Police and black Londoners in post war Britain*, Cullompton: Willan.

Williams, B. (1999) *Working with victims of crime*, London: Jessica Kingsley.

Woodward, K. (2002) 'Concepts of identity and difference', in K. Woodward (ed) *Identity and difference*, London: Sage, pp 7–62.

Young, J. (1999) *The exclusive society*, London: Sage.

TWO

Equality and diversity agendas in criminal justice

Introduction

Within the public sectors of western democratic societies like the UK, the US, Canada and Australia, substantial research attention and policy focus is generated by questions concerning equality and diversity. This is perhaps unsurprising, given that contemporary western societies are characterised by inequality (Thompson, 1998) and, moreover, are underpinned by modernity's 'imperative of order' with the concomitant belief that, with the application of the correct kinds of policies and procedures, progress can be made in relation to eliminating/reducing inequalities and oppression.

In the UK, in contrast to the US and Canada where human rights legislation has generally produced a more inclusive approach to equality so that a wide range of social groupings have been the focus of concern, 'race' and gender have traditionally been the predominant focus. However, emerging trends in the UK suggest that a broader range of social groupings are featuring more frequently in equality legislation, policy and practice. In many instances there continue to be differences in the level of protection afforded different social groupings with respect to 'race'/ethnicity, gender, class, faith, sexual orientation, disability and age; however, contemporary policy developments suggest that hierarchies of equality provisions are being levelled out so that there is growing harmonisation of protections afforded to different groupings. This reflects the emergence of 'new social movements' based on new collectivities of individuals that cut across traditional class and political affiliations, these including the feminist movement, the disability rights movement and the lesbian and gay rights movements (Woodward, 2002). New social movements have traditionally been preoccupied with building identities in opposition to mainstream society, and highlighting the oppression and discrimination that members experience.

Another emerging trend within the field of equality and diversity in the UK is that at the same time that policies are being targeted at a wide range of group collectivities in relation to 'race'/ethnicity, gender, class, faith, sexual orientation, disability and age, there is a growing sense of the artificially constructed nature of these collectivities. There is increasing awareness amongst policy makers and researchers that the distinct experiences and voices of specific communities and individuals are obscured and made invisible within the broad-based approaches to diversity that have traditionally been adopted. This critique is leading towards the pursuit of more nuanced methods and approaches in relation to promoting equality and documenting diversity, acknowledging specificities of experience and viewing clients as individuals who hold multiple identities and as individuals with multiple needs. These developments suggest that alongside the modernist agenda underpinning equality and diversity strategies, postmodern processes are also at play, involving the fragmentation of socially constructed identities, with an emphasis upon specificity of experience and individualisation. Indeed, within the new social movements themselves there has been growing concern to highlight the diversity of individuals captured within these movements, coupled with demands made by service users to be treated with sensitivity as individuals rather than as stereotypes of socially constructed social groupings.

This chapter aims to examine the trends identified above in relation to equality and diversity issues in Britain, with a particular focus upon the criminal justice system. It is argued that whereas 'race'/ethnicity has traditionally occupied a more privileged status within responses to discrimination within a criminal justice context, other social groupings are increasingly being focused upon. However, whilst a series of policies have been implemented attempting to reduce the forms of discrimination that certain social groups experience, the modernist agenda has largely failed to give sufficient voice and form to those discriminatory norms that help produce and perpetuate oppression. So, although policies are instigated to promote equality in relation to 'race'/ethnicity, gender, sexual orientation, religion, disability and age, regimes of power in relation to whiteness, patriarchy, heterosexism, secularisation, disablism and ageism remain largely intact, their invisibility helping to maintain and sustain their hegemony. Furthermore, the fragmentation of social identities, as associated with postmodern processes and the propensity for people to claim highly individualised subject positions in the absence of the dismantling of discriminatory norms that continue to be largely invisible, suggests that individuals' calls for services to be sensitive to their own specific needs are likely to be insufficient to prevent discrimination. Highly individualised service provision that is non-discriminatory in nature can only take place in a context where regimes of power have been successfully challenged. As such, it is imperative that normative knowledge constructions and power relations are made visible and then deconstructed. This discussion essentially links to wider debates around social justice. Underpinning this chapter is the idea that social justice is unachievable unless wider social systems of inequality are challenged.

First, significant pieces of legislation will be examined with respect to equality and diversity issues in the UK public sector in order to provide background material to the more focused discussions that will follow in relation to criminal justice.

British public sector legislation in relation to promoting equality and reducing discrimination

In Britain, key pieces of legislation tackling discrimination on the grounds of gender and 'race' were enacted in the 1960s and 1970s. The 1965 and 1968 Race Relations Acts recognised the discrimination experienced by minority ethnic communities in areas such as employment and housing (Thompson, 2001). The 1975 Sex Discrimination Act, applied to Great Britain but not to Northern Ireland, makes sex discrimination generally unlawful in employment, training and related matters in education, the provision of goods, facilities and services and in the disposal and management of premises. The 1975 Sex Discrimination Act also created a new body, the Equal Opportunities Commission (EOC), to ensure that the new sex discrimination laws were applied correctly (Women Equality Unit, 2007). The 1976 Race Relations Act makes it unlawful to directly or indirectly discriminate against anyone on grounds of race, colour or nationality or ethnic or national origin in employment, training and related matters in education, the provision of goods, facilities and services and in the disposal and management of premises. This piece of legislation also created the Commission for Racial Equality (CRE), the duties of which include: working towards the elimination of racial discrimination, promoting equality of opportunity, monitoring the way the Race Relations Act works, and recommending ways in which it can be improved (CRE, 2006). These legislative changes have, however, received extensive criticism, which will be raised in later chapters of this book. It is sufficient to highlight here that these changes can be construed as constituting a liberal response to discrimination, whereby more radical approaches involving changing broader social structures have not been pursued (Thompson, 2001).

As clearly shown earlier, inequalities in relation to gender and 'race' were initially targeted by policy makers. Interestingly, developments taking place in the 1990s and onwards suggest that legislation is increasingly taking into account a broader range of group collectivities, including those relating to disability, sexual orientation, age and faith. For example, the 1995 Disability Discrimination Act has provided legal rights for disabled people, covering employment, access to services, education, transport and housing. The Disability Rights Commission (DRC) was set up in April 2000 by the 1999 Disability Rights Commission Act to promote equality of opportunity for disabled people. The DRC gives advice and information to disabled people, supports legal cases, and campaigns to strengthen law. It operates in England, Scotland and Wales, whilst in Northern Ireland disability rights are overseen by the Equality Commission for Northern Ireland. New employment rights and rights of access for disabled people became law in December 2004. The 1995 Disability Discrimination Act has been amended by the 2005 Disability Discrimination Act to place responsibility on all public sector authorities to promote disability equality, which means that all public sector bodies will have a duty to promote the equalisation of opportunities for disabled people through preparing and publishing disability equality schemes (DRC, 2006).

Interestingly, equality schemes originally targeted race as a result of the implementation of the 2000 Race Relations Amendment Act, which stipulates that those providing public services ensure that their policies and services are fair. The specific duties require key bodies to prepare and publish a race equality scheme, which should demonstrate how organisations will promote race equality for staff and for the public that they serve, and this includes a focus upon arrangements for consulting on proposed policies and to monitor any adverse impact of policies on the promotion of race equality. As well as disability equality schemes, gender equality schemes have been introduced, in April 2007. These place a duty on public sector organisations to demonstrate fair treatment of women and men in the delivery of policy and services as well as in their employment (EOC, 2005).

Added to these developments, measures outlawing discrimination on the basis of religion or belief, sexuality and age have been introduced. For instance, the 2003 Employment Equality (Religion or Belief) Regulations and the 2003 Employment Equality (Sexual Orientation) Regulations outlaw discrimination on the grounds of sexual orientation, religion or belief in employment and vocational training. Thus, the 2003 Employment Equality (Sexual Orientation) Regulations, introduced in December of that year, mean that lesbians, gays and bisexuals can take action if they are the victims of harassment or discrimination at work. More recent legislation in the form of the 2006 Equality Act extends the protection afforded on the basis of religion/belief and sexual orientation from employment to the provision of goods, facilities and services in education and in the execution of public functions. Nonetheless, the Act does not include provision to extend goods, facilities, and services provision to transgendered people, although a European Union Gender Directive extends goods, facilities and services protection on the grounds of transgender status. The Act, however, does not include a general positive duty to promote equality on the basis of sexual orientation or religion/belief, so that equality schemes continue to focus on 'race', disability and gender. It is important also to note that transsexual and transgendered people are not explicitly covered by the gender equality duty since the wording here refers simply to women and men (EOC, 2005). In 2006 the 2006 Employment Equality (Age) Regulations were approved by the British Parliament. These regulations prohibit age discrimination in recruitment, promotion and training, they ban unjustified retirement ages of below 65 and remove the current age limit for unfair dismissal and redundancy rights (DTI, 2006).

The 2006 Equality Act also establishes a new single Commission for Equality and Human Rights (CEHR) that brings together all six strands of discrimination – 'race', age, gender, disability, religion and sexual orientation – into one unified organisation. The Act dissolves the EOC, the CRE and the DRC. Duties of the CEHR include the promotion of the importance of equality and diversity, the enforcement of equality law and the promotion of the understanding of the importance and the protection of human rights (EOC, 2005). The introduction of the CEHR has not been without controversy. The CRE, for instance, has opposed a single commission for equality, due to concerns that the proposals to place all equality areas under one body might dilute the focus given to 'race' issues. The British government has argued, however, that the CEHR will enable people's multiple identities and their multiple oppressions to be acknowledged in one organisation (DTI, 2003). It is important to point out, though, that despite promoting equality for a wide range of social groupings, when exercising its powers relating to its community functions, the CEHR will be required to have 'particular regard' to race, religion or belief (EOC, 2005). This suggests that in certain aspects of its functions, the CEHR will prioritise racial/ethnic/faith groupings over other social identities, and so it seems that the hierarchy of equality provisions previously alluded to will not be completely levelled out for the foreseeable future. Hierarchies of social identities also exist within the criminal justice system. Although developments in equality legislation obviously have an impact upon the criminal justice sector since agencies of the criminal justice system constitute public bodies and are therefore bound by the duties put into operation by equality laws, at different points throughout the system, at different moments in time, different identities take precedence in terms of both policy and practice.

Equality and diversity in relation to criminal justice

When exploring diversity issues in relation to the criminal justice system in England and Wales, it is important to stress the rather haphazard and unsystematic nature of research, policy and practice with respect to the social groupings of 'race'/ethnicity, gender, class, faith, sexual orientation, disability and age. It appears that, similar to public sector approaches to equality and diversity in general, there is no clear rationale underpinning criminal justice approaches to diversity and so different levels of attention are afforded different group collectivities at different points in time, at different points throughout the system, according to the political and social factors that prevail. However, bearing in mind the push towards harmonisation between group collectivities in the public sector, a fundamental question posed here is the extent to which in the foreseeable future 'race' and gender will continue to occupy a privileged status within criminal justice. Indeed, although 'race'/ethnicity has traditionally taken a special significance within hate crime legislation in Britain, there is a developing acknowledgement that other identities also merit particular attention. Originally, as the 1998 Crime and Disorder Act was being drawn up, the Home Office was resistant to including other communities in the legislation, arguing that this Act was being designed in order to send out a clear message that racial violence and prejudice is not tolerated, and including other communities would serve to weaken this message (Tatchell, 2002). Nonetheless, new specific religiously aggravated offences were later created under the 2001 Anti-terrorism, Crime and Security Act, so as to include faith communities within hate crime legislation, and, added to this, the 2003 Criminal Justice Act provides an increased sentence for offences involving or motivated by hostility based on disability or sexual orientation.

It can be argued that procedures for monitoring the level and extent of discrimination within the criminal justice system have traditionally privileged 'race'/ethnicity and gender over other social groupings, this both echoing, and being a product of, the broader public sector equality agenda. The 1975 Sex Discrimination Act and the 1976 Race Relations Act provided a powerful impetus to gender and racial/ethnic monitoring by public sector bodies,[1] and so agencies of the criminal justice system began routinely to assemble information about gender and 'race'/ethnicity to help monitor disadvantage, so as to ensure that their policies and practices were not disadvantaging women or minority ethnic communities. The more systematic monitoring of 'race' and gender, as opposed to other forms of social identity, by agencies of the criminal justice system is clearly illustrated by publications arising from Section 95 of the 1991 Criminal Justice Act. However, this allows for the monitoring of a wide variety of group collectivities since it requires the Home Secretary each year to:

> publish such information as he considers expedient for the purpose of
> (a) enabling persons engaged in the administration of criminal justice
> to become aware of the financial implications of their decisions, or
> (b) facilitating the performance by such persons of their duty to avoid
> discriminating against any persons on the grounds of race or sex or
> *any other improper ground*. (1991 Criminal Justice Act, Section 95)

In effect, 'race' and gender have been the predominant focus of concern. Whereas numerous Home Office publications can be found in relation to providing statistical information about minority ethnic groups and women, these being entitled 'Race and the criminal justice system: Statistics under section 95 of the Criminal Justice Act 1991' and 'Women and the criminal justice system: Statistics under section 95 of the Criminal Justice Act 1991', virtually no similar publications are to be found in relation to other social groupings in terms of faith, disability, sexual orientation or age. Publications under Section 95 of the 1991 Criminal Justice Act constitute a significant aspect to equality provision within the criminal justice system, since these publications comprise information that helps those working within the criminal justice system to identify and avoid inequalities and discrimination. This then raises the question of whether the movement towards the harmonisation of equality laws within the public sector might, in the future, impact upon monitoring procedures within the criminal justice system, so that information about disability, faith, sexual orientation and age will be more systematically collected and published under Section 95 of the 1991 Criminal Justice Act.

In fact, information in relation to the social identities of offenders, suspects, victims and/or witnesses, and employees in terms of disability, faith, sexual orientation and age is collected by agencies of the criminal justice system, albeit in a more arbitrary and less systematic way than in relation to either 'race'/ethnicity or gender. For example, the prison service monitors the religious affiliation of offenders as well as their ethnicity and other social characteristics such as age, partly due to the requirements of the 1952 Prison Act, which provides that members of other religious groups have the same right to practise their faith as Christian prisoners. When prisoners arrive at prison, they are therefore asked to self-classify their religion.[2] British police services, on the other hand, tend to monitor offenders and suspects through the lens of 'race'/ethnicity rather than religion. The police have collected information on ethnicity for many years at the local level, partly due to the information given by witnesses to police officers about the physical appearance of offenders. At the national level, a number of developments have led to the increased focus upon ethnic monitoring by the police, including the requirements of Section 95 of the 1991 Criminal Justice Act, the Royal Commission on Criminal Justice in 1993 – which argued that a national system of race and ethnic monitoring should be implemented in the police service in order to establish how minority ethnic communities are treated by the criminal justice system and to ensure that practices and procedures were not disadvantaging particular groups – and a joint working party with the Association of Chief Police Officers (ACPO) and the CRE in 1993 which issued a strategic policy document including the issue of how ethnic monitoring is to be covered. At the same time, the police inspectorate introduced a performance indicator requiring all forces to provide ethnicity statistics on their use of stop/search powers under the 1984 Police and Criminal Evidence Act (Fitzgerald and Sibbitt, 1997). In 1996, mandatory ethnic monitoring came into effect in all police force areas for stop and searches, arrests, cautions and homicides. The classifications were based on the police officer's visual perception of the suspect, using the four-point scale (Home Office, 2003b). In a post-11 September 2001 context, amid rising concerns that young Muslim men are being targeted by stop and search under counter-terrorism legislation, calls have been made to monitor the faith identities of those who are stopped and searched by the police (Spalek, 2005). However, this has so far been resisted by police services, which may partly be due to the logistical difficulties of monitoring religious identities since police officers will not be able to use physical appearance as a means of identifying suspects for the purposes of data collection, posing practical difficulties in a stop and search situation. This illustrates that data emerging from the criminal justice system are not only influenced by political and social factors but also by practicalities. The viewpoints of employees working for the criminal justice system are also likely to influence the collection of data. When ethnic monitoring was first introduced into the criminal justice system, there was a lack of returns within the probation service due to probation officers' concerns that this information might be used against minority ethnic groups rather than for them. In terms of monitoring religious identity, it appears that agents working for the criminal justice system have concerns about asking individuals questions regarding faith, viewing this as overly intrusive (Spalek, 2005). So the concerns that agents of the criminal justice system themselves have are likely to impact upon the extent and consistency of the monitoring of equality and diversity.

The introduction of hate crime laws has also influenced the collection of data with respect to social identities within the criminal justice system. This is because with hate crime laws, agencies of the criminal justice are required to take into consideration victims' identities and their perceptions when considering the motivation of an offender, so that crimes motivated by racial and religious, as well as other forms of hatred, are dealt with more severely. Although 'race' has traditionally taken a special significance within hate crime legislation in Britain, there is a developing acknowledgement that other identities also merit particular attention. As highlighted previously, hate crime laws now apply to religion, sexual orientation and disability as well as to 'race'. Where local partnerships between the police and other statutory and voluntary agencies are developed to encourage victims to report hate crimes, then there is likely to be increased pressure to monitor the racial/ethnic and religious identities as well as the sexual orientation and disability of victims. Clearly then, the introduction of new types of hate crime will impact upon the types of social identities that agencies of the criminal justice system collect data about. In the future, new legislation might be implemented that focuses upon abuse of older people as a type of hate crime and so, again, this will influence monitoring procedures.

Target setting within the criminal justice system and equality provision

The criminal justice system is replete with government targets, which also influence monitoring procedures. The government has introduced a number of public sector agreements (PSAs) into the system that agencies are expected to meet. The most significant PSA targets appear to be: increasing the number of crimes for which an offender is brought to justice; the need to raise public – including Black and minority ethnic (BME) communities' – confidence (and reduce the fear of crime) in the criminal justice system; and to increase year on year the satisfaction of victims and witnesses. The PSAs as outlined by government are set to remain until at least 2008. In a paper, 'Cutting crime, delivering justice: A strategic plan for criminal justice 2004–08' (HM Government, 2004), the government sets out its vision for criminal justice in 2008. The key themes that are raised here include raising the public's, as well as BME communities', confidence in criminal justice, and also ensuring that victims and witnesses are treated with respect and understanding. The government also plans to introduce local targets for increased confidence in areas where there are high BME populations, including London,

West Midlands, Greater Manchester, West Yorkshire, Thames Valley and Leicester. The National Criminal Justice Board is responsible for supporting 42 local criminal justice boards to deliver the criminal justice system PSAs. The National Criminal Justice Board was created in 2003 and has responsibility for combating inequality and discrimination in the criminal justice system, and for communication across the system (Home Office, 2003a).

Black and minority ethnic sub-targets

As can be seen in the earlier discussion, within the PSA target to boost confidence in the criminal justice system there is a sub-target of boosting BME communities' confidence. This sub-target reflects the importance with which the government views 'race' and ethnicity, particularly since the publication of the 1999 Macpherson Report, which highlighted the significance and prevalence of 'institutional racism'. Interestingly, the CRE has argued for the use of sub-targets in relation to BME communities for all relevant PSA targets, arguing that these communities represent a significant proportion of the general population (9%), claiming that without delivering to this proportion of the population, the broader mainstream targets will not consequently be achieved (Spencer, 2004). The introduction of a BME sub-target has important implications for all agencies of the criminal justice system as in the future agencies will perhaps be required to extend BME sub-targets to all PSAs that they are required to meet.

Sub-targets in relation to other identities

Given that there is currently a movement towards harmonisation of equality provision within the public sector, it is important to speculate here about future targets set for the criminal justice system by government. It is not inconceivable to suggest that government and/or agencies of the criminal justice system will bring in sub-targets for PSAs that are aimed at other group collectivities, based on gender, disability, age, faith or sexuality. For instance, representatives of lesbian, gay, bisexual and transgender (LGBT) communities have argued that they have low confidence in the criminal justice system and that there is a significant level of under-reporting of the hate crimes that are committed against them (CPS, 2004a). Introducing a sub-target to raise the confidence that LGBT communities have in criminal justice would thus help to focus agencies' attention on these issues more significantly. Similarly, as a result of anti-terrorism legislation and its likely disproportionate impact on Muslim communities (Spalek, 2005), and particularly as religious identity is increasingly being recorded by agencies of the criminal justice system, targets to boost Muslims' confidence levels may be introduced.

Gender also has a particular significance in relation to the setting of PSA sub-targets. Crime surveys consistently show that women's crime-related anxiety is higher than men's (Skogan and Maxfield, 1981, Hough and Mayhew, 1983;

Gordon and Riger, 1989; Prime et al, 2001), and women's groups argue that there is a lack of confidence in the criminal justice system by women (CPS, 2004a). As gender issues are mainstreamed into the public sector, and in light of new domestic violence initiatives being developed within the criminal justice sector, it is perhaps timely to consider introducing a sub-target to raise women's confidence in criminal justice and/or to reduce their fear of crime. Indeed, as over 50% of the general population is female (National Census, 2001), it might be argued that the only way to achieve the mainstream PSA target of boosting confidence levels is by having a sub-target specifically directed at women. Age may also increasingly feature in targets, especially when taking into consideration that older people's fear of crime is significantly higher than younger people's (Pain, 1995). A survey of fear of street crime amongst older people carried out by Age Concern in 2002, which had 4,000 returned questionnaires, shows that a third of respondents felt that fear of crime had affected their quality of life and made them feel lonely and isolated (Age Concern, 2002). The government also appears to be continually raising PSA target levels, and so it might further be argued that a greater number of sub-targets will need to be introduced by agencies of the criminal justice system, otherwise they will not be able to achieve these ever-demanding figures.

Monitoring procedures

It is important to note, however, that the introduction of a greater range of sub-targets into PSAs poses certain challenges in terms of data collection and analysis, specifically in relation to sampling size and statistical significance. Agencies of the criminal justice system will need to show a commitment towards broadening out the measurement of PSAs to include a wider range of groups of people, ensuring that adequate booster samples of target groups are obtained. For some groups of the population, where numbers are particularly low, it may be particularly problematic to get hold of sample sizes that are statistically significant, especially when cost effectiveness is likely to be an issue.

This point can be clearly illustrated by reference to the British Crime Survey, which is a national crime survey administered by the Home Office that measures, among other things, forms and extent of victimisation. From January 2001 the British Crime Survey has included an annual minority ethnic boost sample. The researchers designing and implementing the British Crime Survey have acknowledged the limitations of the minority ethnic booster, and have argued that greater disaggregation of minority ethnic groups is desirable; however, on the grounds of cost effectiveness, given the size and geographical distributions of the diverse communities, this has not happened. These researchers also argue that they would like to differentiate between Pakistani and Bangladeshi groups; however, due to the numbers being too small to support reliable statistical analysis, the two groups are combined (Clancy et al, 2001). The latter point illustrates the ways in which classificatory systems construct and impose borders upon identities. As a result, there is increasing acknowledgement of the arbitrary nature of the systems of classification that are used within the criminal justice arena and how specific communities may be subsumed within the general categories that are used to classify people, thereby obscuring significant cultural and individual differences. Indeed, more nuanced approaches to equality and diversity are being developed because of raised awareness, both within academic and policy-focused work, that the distinct experiences and voices of specific communities are obscured and made invisible within the broad-based approaches that have traditionally been used, and this will be discussed next.

Specificity in relation to equality and diversity

Alongside modernity's 'imperative of order', and the construction of social groupings at which policies in relation to equality and diversity can be targeted, postmodern processes can be discerned, challenging the unitary appearance of these groupings. It seems that within the general groupings in relation to 'race'/ ethnicity, gender, faith, sexual orientation, disability and age, 'voices claiming specificity' can be found that highlight the diversity of peoples associated with these general groupings and which argue for a greater focus upon the documentation of individual experiences and upon meeting individual needs.

In relation to 'race'/ethnicity, Phillips and Bowling (2003) propose that criminologists must place a greater emphasis upon developing a 'minority perspective' within criminology, one that articulates the experiences of specific communities and takes into account their histories and identities. Similarly, Chakraborti et al (2004) argue that within the general categories and labels, such as those relating to 'minority ethnic', 'Black' or the increasingly popular term 'BME', are a host of 'hidden peoples' and 'hidden' forms of victimisation that have rarely received attention from criminological examinations of 'race and racism', and that the often generalised, broad and unwittingly exclusive academic discussions and writing on this subject have allowed important considerations to go unnoticed.

The current system of ethnic monitoring in place in the criminal justice system actually makes it very difficult to gain information about particular ethnic groups, since these tend to be subsumed within broad, racial, categories. Until very recently, a nine-point system of race and ethnic monitoring had been used by agencies of the criminal justice system, relating to the categories used by the 1991 National Census. However, the ways in which statistics have often been collected and statistically analysed is according to a modified four-point scale relating to Black, White, Asian and Chinese and Other (Chinese and Other being one category). This focus upon racial categories makes it difficult to substantiate any claims of discrimination or bias within the criminal justice system that particular ethnic communities might be experiencing. From April 2003, a 16-point system of ethnic monitoring has been introduced, relating to the system adopted in the

2001 National Census. However, the new 16-point system of classification raises similar issues to those found under the nine-point system of race and ethnic monitoring. Although the new system enables more detailed information to be compiled, statistics in relation to offenders, suspects, victims, witnesses and employees of the criminal justice system, and any targets that are set, are likely to be presented according to a modified five-point scale relating to Black, White, Asian, Chinese and Other, and Mixed. The deputy chair of the CRE has argued that agencies of the criminal justice system like the Crown Prosecution Service (CPS) may need to acknowledge differences between Indian, Pakistani and Bangladeshi communities when considering the issue of the representation of ethnic minorities within their workforces (CPS, 2004b). This is because the latter two groups experience more social and economic deprivation than the former group. However, statistics in relation to the ethnic composition of the workforce in the criminal justice system tend to be aggregated, and so Indian, Pakistani and Bangladeshi communities are often subsumed within a general Asian category (Spalek, 2005). Whiteness as a monolithic category is also being increasingly challenged, amid rising acknowledgement of the diversities to be found within this grouping (Garland et al, 2006). Indeed, white minority groups are increasingly likely to feature in the criminal justice policy agenda, particularly in light of the expansion of the European Union (EU) that has meant that many individuals from the EU accession states have come to work in the UK. In 2005, 80,000 citizens from the group of eight central and eastern European countries that acceded to the EU on 1 May 2004 (known as the A8 countries) immigrated to the UK for a year or more (National Statistics Online, 2007). Figures produced by Scotland Yard and the Greater London Authority suggest that a southern or eastern European is eight times more likely to be the victim of a racial crime than a white European (Muir, 2005).

The issue of the multiplicity of identities subsumed within the category of gender has been raised by academics, social activists and policy makers. In terms of the category 'woman', the dominance of a white, Eurocentric perspective underpinning much feminist work has been extensively documented, illustrating how black women have been overlooked by the wider feminist movement, through 'gender essentialism' – the view that there is a monolithic women's experience (Harris, 1997: 11). Thus, feminist research looking at domestic violence against minority ethnic women suggests that there is a substantial and significant cultural context to the offending that takes place, and to victims' experiences, their understandings and their survival strategies. However, mainstream victim support services often fail to take ethnic and cultural differences into account (Choudry, 1996; Mama, 2000; Stark, 2003; Neville et al, 2004). The experiences of Muslim women in relation to domestic abuse may also be different, thereby requiring support that is sensitive and responsive to their needs (Ahmad and

Sheriff, 2003). A recent Fawcett Society report (2004), *Women and the criminal justice system*, also raises the issue of the diversity to be found amongst women, since the report highlights how lesbians and black women may be deterred from reporting crime on account of poor earlier experiences of homophobia or racism against themselves and/or the perpetrator. The Fawcett Society report also highlights that women with disabilities have particular issues, too, that need to be addressed by agencies of the criminal justice system. A study of female victims of domestic violence who have mental health issues also illustrates that these women require particularly sensitive responses to their plight (Humphreys and Thiara, 2003). Gender also includes men, and diversity amongst men is increasingly being acknowledged. For instance, researchers have argued that there is more than one kind of masculinity and so it is important to acknowledge the diversity of masculinity constructions and their hierarchical ordering, since some varieties of masculinity occupy a hegemonic position within society (Jefferson, 1994; Connell, 2005).

With respect to the social grouping of faith, this consists of a multiplicity of different religions and belief systems. However, religious identities have traditionally been overlooked by agencies of the criminal justice system as well as by policy makers and academics. This may partly be due to the secular roots of the academic discipline of Criminology, which displaced religious frameworks of understanding crime and criminality that existed in pre-modern times (Morrison, 1995). Findings from the Home Office Citizenship Survey reveal that religious affiliation may be an important aspect of individuals' self-identities, particular for those from minority ethnic communities. The 2001 Citizenship Survey reveals that religious identity is a much more fundamental aspect of the self-identity of minority ethnic groups when compared to many White Christians (Attwood et al, 2003). Moreover, for Muslims, religion was ranked second only after family in terms of the importance to their self-identity (O'Beirne, 2004). Nonetheless, ethnic rather than religious identities have traditionally been the focus of research, policy and practice. However, this scenario is beginning to change. Social scientists are increasingly questioning the omission of religious identities in contemporary policy making and research, arguing that despite the effects of the Enlightenment, religion continues to be used by people as a cultural resource (Beckford, 1996). Added to this, Britain now has a significant and growing Muslim population, which has provided added impetus towards the increasing focus upon religious identities within criminal justice.

The heterogeneous nature of the category of sexual orientation is being increasingly highlighted by representatives of LGBT peoples, who argue that agencies of the criminal justice system need to recognise differences between LGBT communities and need to respond with greater specificity and sensitivity. Furthermore, within the categories of 'lesbian', 'gay', 'bisexual' and 'transgender' is a large amount of diversity. Within the policy arena, the restricted nature of the definition of transgender used in the 2006 Equality Act has generated some controversy. The Act uses the following definition: 'proposed, commenced or completed reassignment of gender'; however, this confines the definition to those who have begun a medical process of gender reassignment, thereby excluding those individuals who might define themselves as transgendered but who may not have entered into any medical process (EOC, 2005).

Disability also is a social category that includes a wide diversity of people. Disabilities can include sensory disabilities that arise from physical impairments, psychiatric disorders or intellectual disabilities (which may also be referred to as learning disabilities) (Lonsdale, 1990). This significant level of diversity is likely to mean that different services are required to be developed, taking into consideration individuals' different physical, psychological and mental health needs.

The issue of the diversity to be found among older people is also being increasingly raised. Older lesbians, gay men and bisexuals are less likely to access services because they have lived a large part of their lives in less liberal times and encounter unique problems as they age, due particularly to the heterosexism of mainstream providers who regularly assume that all the older people they serve are heterosexual (Age Concern, 2002). Older people from minority ethnic communities also have particular needs, and so public sector organisations must come to better understand these groups of individuals as well. Indeed, a Home Office study reveals that older people from minority ethnic groups feel that the police do not take them seriously when they report crimes, and they feel that the police do not trust them (Docking, 2003).

Summary

These discussions illustrate two dominant themes that are emerging from the equality and diversity agenda within the public sector in general and more specifically within the criminal justice system. Group collectivities in relation to 'race'/ethnicity, gender, faith, sexual orientation, disability and age are the social groupings around which equality provisions are being based, and an emerging trend appears to be one of increasing harmonisation in the level and forms of protection afforded to each individual grouping. At the same time, the significant level of diversity to be found within these general groupings is being increasingly acknowledged by both researchers and policy makers, and so another important trend appears to be a focus upon specificity of experiences when documenting and responding to individuals' needs.

Invisible social norms that produce oppression and inequality

Whilst the trends discussed earlier can be applauded for the development of policies and practices that are aimed at alleviating discrimination according to 'race'/ethnicity, gender, faith, sexual orientation, disability and age, and for the development of more nuanced approaches that acknowledge specificity of experience and need, nonetheless they largely leave intact those norms that reproduce social inequalities. It seems that the claims–making activities of the new social movements have predominantly involved stressing differences from mainstream society, with the main focus of concern being to build new identities. But by placing attention upon the construction of new identities, and the building of new communities, this can serve to detract attention away from social norms in relation to whiteness, patriarchy, secularisation, heterosexuality, able-bodiedness and ageism that remain largely hidden. Within the new social movements there may be some critique of social structures including 'race', gender, heterosexism, and so forth, that serve to reproduce inequalities; however, the predominant focus is very much upon creating identities on the basis of difference in relation to 'race'/ethnicity, gender, faith, sexual orientation, disability and age rather than attempting to particularise dominant, oppressive norms, the existence of which provides the ever-present danger that differences come to be viewed as deviancies/abnormalities. Thus, for example, although minority ethnic writers and researchers have, particularly since the 1980s, produced a large volume of work about their lives, suggesting that academic disciplines must increasingly contend with the heterogeneity of people, many argue that this has had little impact upon mainstream disciplines, with white people's experiences continuing to form the basis around which norms are created and around which minorities' lives are judged (Collins, 1998; Bolles, 2001; McClaurin, 2001). Implicit within the potential to stigmatise minority ethnic communities is the notion of 'whiteness', which is rarely acknowledged in social scientific arenas, but rather is considered to be what is 'normal', 'neutral' or 'commonsense'. As a result, those individuals whose subject positions lie outside the 'white' category constitute the 'other', and their lives can be judged according to the notion of a monolithic 'white' experience that is rarely openly articulated and challenged (Garland et al, 2006).

Western scientific discourse encourages and legitimises binary, oppositional, either/or categories, so that human differences have been viewed simplistically in opposition to each other (Collins, 1998). The notion of difference is implicit within the social groupings that have emerged within equality and diversity agendas because categorisations involve marking out distinctions between the categories themselves (Woodward, 2002). This means that inter-group differences may be stressed and exaggerated, and individuals may be viewed monolithically through one predominant lens, thereby overlooking the complexity of their lives and their multiple subject positions. For example, studies reveal that for members of minority ethnic groups, religious identity is also often an important aspect of self-identity. As a result, researchers stress that religious affiliation and ethnicity should be considered together rather than separately when making policy decisions (O'Beirne, 2004). Thus, focusing exclusively upon faith can serve to omit individuals' ethnicities, which are also likely to feature significantly in their everyday lives. Similarly, by viewing individuals predominantly in terms of their sexual orientation, this may serve to typecast them as no more than sexual beings, thereby overlooking other dimensions to their lives (Stein, 1993). At the same time, the construction of social categories can exaggerate in-group sameness when in fact there may be large differences between individuals who are classified under the same social grouping. For instance, faith identities are mixed and heterogeneous, as are other identities in relation to 'race'/ethnicity, gender, sexual orientation, disability and age. Indeed, Stein (1993) argues that the differences among women who identify themselves as lesbians are often as great as, or greater than, those between lesbians and women who called themselves straight. Therefore, although social groupings may give the illusion of sameness, within-group differences may actually be more salient.

Categorisations also involve marking out distinctions from things that are silent, normative and invisible (Moreton-Robinson, 2004), and yet in reality there may be considerable overlap here as well. For example, bisexuality, although located within the minority grouping LGBT, calls into question the notion of sexuality as being consistently heterosexual or homosexual, suggesting that homosexuality overlaps and blends with the norm of heterosexism (Stein, 1993). Differences between socially constructed groupings and the wider norms against which they are contrasted can be exaggerated, with there often being little acknowledgement of how each social grouping can interact and merge with these wider norms. Thus, for example, the 'race'/ethnicity grouping may help to create an impression that minority ethnic groups stand apart from whiteness, and intense debate is often generated regarding the question of the extent to which minority groups have assimilated into the wider, dominant culture (Spalek, 2006). However, it might be argued that minority cultures are shaped by, as well as shape, the wider social norms that exist (see Young, 1999; Roy, 2004). Also, ethnic borders are constantly shifting, being 'subject to negotiation and re-negotiation' (Ratcliffe, 2004: 30), with terminology like 'mixed race' and 'dual heritage' illustrating the merging of racial/ethnic borders. Similarly, there is significant diversity within the social grouping of faith, and, in Northern Europe, overlaps between faith identities and the wider social norm of secularisation is evident. For example, some individuals may describe themselves as being 'secular Muslims' or 'secular Christians',[3] and Roy (2004) claims that young Muslims living in the suburbs of France are fascinated by western urban youth subculture, as exemplified by the way that they dress, the food that they eat and the genre of music that they listen to. Indeed, one of the suspects of the bombing attempts in London on 21 July 2005, Hussein Osman, dressed in rapper-style clothing, drank beer and his idol was US rapper Tupac Shakur; he did not eat pork, though, and so perhaps in some nominal way identified himself as being Muslim as well (Hooper, 2005).

Work that is generated in relation to social groupings of 'race'/ethnicity, gender, faith, sexual orientation, disability and age rarely involves discussions about the ways in which these groupings are themselves linked to, and can serve to reproduce and maintain, whiteness, patriarchy, secularisation, heterosexuality, able-bodiedness and ageism. Perhaps subconsciously those involved in building social movements around 'race'/ethnicity, gender, faith, sexual orientation, disability and age, as well as researchers and policy makers, set these groups apart from norms of oppression by operating according to a distorted 'oppressor–oppressed' dichotomy. This approach can serve to perpetuate further the norms of oppression that exist as this helps to maintain their invisibility and also serves to highlight differences between people rather than acknowledging commonalities. This approach also suggests that it is only white people, men, secular individuals, heterosexuals, able-bodied individuals and young people who produce universalising tendencies that cause discrimination, when in fact it might be argued that all individuals can be linked to and can serve to reproduce and maintain oppressions in relation to whiteness, patriarchy, secularisation, heterosexuality, able-bodiedness and ageism. Within feminism in particular, there has been some discussion of the ways in which women can maintain and perpetuate patriarchy. For example, a feminist text written by Roberta Hamilton (1986: 385) is entitled 'The collusion with patriarchy: A psychoanalytic account'. In Stein's (1993: xv) edited collection of lesbian accounts, it is argued that 'today we [lesbians] are discovering how much we are actually embedded in the culture from which we have tried to escape, and how important it is for us to learn to live with contradictions – while pushing up against them'. In this way, it is important to highlight the ways in which all individuals, all social groupings, are implicitly involved in constructing and reconstructing social norms of oppression.

The postmodern tendency to fragment and individualise human experience, in the absence of a thorough examination, documentation and eventual deconstruction of social norms that perpetuate and maintain oppression, will do little for social justice. As long as the universalising tendencies in relation to whiteness, patriarchy, secularisation, heterosexuality, able-bodiedness and ageism remain hidden and unchallenged, then people's claims to be treated as individuals with specific needs will do little to promote a more inclusive and less oppressive society. As a result, those making individualistic claims for respect when demanding better service provision are likely to continue to be disappointed. Attention should therefore be squarely placed upon uncovering and dismantling those hidden social norms that oppress people. Only then will it be possible to develop ways of responding to individuals' needs in a way that goes beyond the contemporary trends in equality and diversity that involve the construction of social groupings as well as the increasing fragmentation of social identities. People want to be treated with humanity,[4] but in order for this to be achieved the assumptions that construct sameness and deviance need to be challenged. Only then might it be possible to move to a point at which people's common humanity is acknowledged, as well as their uniqueness and individuality, so that social justice underpins increasingly specific responses to individuals' unique needs.

Conclusion

This chapter has examined contemporary developments within the area of equality and diversity, with a specific focus upon the criminal justice system. It has essentially identified and explored two trends that reflect those taking place in the equality and diversity agenda of the public sector in general: echoing modernity's 'imperative of order', hierarchies of equality provisions seem to be levelling out so that there is growing harmonisation of protections afforded to different social groupings in terms of 'race'/ethnicity, gender, class, faith, sexual orientation, disability and age. At the same time, postmodern processes are also at play, involving the fragmentation of social constructed identities, with an emphasis upon specificity of experience and individualisation. Both these trends mean that agencies of the criminal justice system are increasingly adopting a double-stranded approach that involves balancing the need to address the inequalities that can be found between broad group collectivities based on 'race'/ethnicity, faith, gender, sexual orientation, disability and age, and the need for a greater sensitivity and responsiveness of service delivery towards specific communities and individuals.

This chapter also highlights how, even though a series of policies have been implemented attempting to reduce the forms of discrimination that certain social groups experience, the modernist agenda has largely failed to give sufficient voice and form to those discriminatory norms that help produce and perpetuate oppression. As such, regimes of power in relation to whiteness, patriarchy, heterosexism, secularisation, disablism and ageism remain largely intact, their invisibility helping to maintain their hegemony. Furthermore, the fragmentation of social identities as associated with postmodern processes, and the propensity for people to claim highly individualised subject positions – in the absence of the dismantling of discriminatory norms that continue to be largely invisible – suggests that individuals' calls for services to be sensitive to their own specific needs are likely to be insufficient to prevent discrimination. Rather, those hidden social norms that oppress people need to be attended to and dismantled before we can develop nuanced responses to diversity that, while acknowledging individuals' common humanity, also respond to individuals' unique and specific needs. The next chapter considers approaches to researching identities and communities, where individuals' voices are given a central place as it is argued that the experiences of those individuals occupying marginalised positions in society can help to shed light on oppressive social structures and norms.

Notes

[1] Of course, the wider context within which the sex and race discrimination laws were drawn up is one of significant inequalities for women and Black communities, with both the feminist and Black civil rights movements playing

a key role in highlighting the plight of these groups and in calling for greater protection from discrimination.

[2] The prison service uses the following categories: Anglican (Anglican, Church in Wales, Church of England, Church of Ireland, Episcopalian), Roman Catholic, Free Church (Baptist, Celestial Church of God, Church of Scotland, Congregational, Methodist, Non-conformist, Pentecostal, Presbyterian, Quaker, Salvation Army, United Reformed Church, Welsh Independent), Buddhist, Hindu, Jewish, Church of Jesus Christ of Latter-day Saints, Muslim, Sikh, Other (Protestant, Jehovah's Witness, Greek/Russian Orthodox, Seven-Day Adventist, Ethiopian Orthodox, Spiritualist, Chrisadelphian, Christian Scientist), Other non-Christian religions (Pagan, Druid, Taoist, Jain), Unrecognised religions (Rastafarian, Nation of Islam), No religion (Atheist, Agnostic) (Guessous et al, 2001).

[3] The author has heard a considerable number of people describe themselves in these ways.

[4] For example, at the inquiry into the death in care of her brother, Dr Joanne Bennett stated, 'Just get the humanity right!' (Gilbert, 2005).

Chapter questions

To what extent is there a hierarchy of equality provisions within the criminal justice sector?

How, and in what ways, is acknowledging diversity within social groupings important for policy and practice?

What are the 'new social movements', and how might these be linked to the perpetuation of universalising tendencies that cause discrimination?

Case study
The Commission for Equality and Human Rights

Our mission

The Commission for Equality and Human Rights is the independent advocate for equality and human rights in Britain. The CEHR aims to reduce inequality, eliminate discrimination, strengthen good relations between people, and promote and protect human rights.

The CEHR will challenge prejudice and disadvantage, and promote the importance of human rights.

The CEHR is a statutory body established under the Equality Act 2006. It will enforce equality legislation on age, disability and health, gender, race, religion or belief, sexual orientation or transgender status, and encourage compliance with the Human Rights Act 1998.

The CEHR will work to bring about effective change, using its influence and authority to ensure that equality and human rights remain at the top of agendas for government, employers and society. It will campaign for social change and justice.

The CEHR will act directly and by fostering partnerships at local, regional and national levels. It will stimulate debate on equality and human rights. It will give advice and guidance, including to businesses, the voluntary and public sectors, and also to individuals.

The CEHR will develop an evidence based understanding of the causes and effects of inequality for people across Britain, and will be an authoritative voice for reform.

Source: CEHR website, http://www.cehr.org.uk/content/purpose.rhtm

Question
What benefits and drawbacks are there to having a single commission addressing equality and diversity issues?

References

Age Concern (2002) *Survey of fear of street crime amongst older people*, London: Age Concern, Policy Unit.

Ahmad, F. and Sheriff, S. (2003) 'Muslim women of Europe: Welfare needs and responses', *Social Work in Europe*, vol 8, no 1, pp 30–55.

Attwood, C., Singh, G., Prime, D. and Creasey, R. (2003) *2001 Home Office Citizenship Survey: People, families and communities*, Home Office Research Development and Statistics Directorate Research Study 270, London: Home Office.

Beckford, J. (1996) 'Postmodernity, high modernity and new modernity: Three concepts in search of religion', in K. Flanagan and P. Jupp (eds) *Postmodernity, sociology and religion*, Basingstoke: Macmillan, pp 30–47.

Bolles, A. (2001) 'Seeking the ancestors: Forging a black feminist tradition in anthropology', in I. McClaurin (ed) *Black feminist anthropology*, London: Rutgers University Press, pp 24–48.

Chakraborti, N., Garland, J. and Spalek, B. (2004) 'Out of sight out of mind? Towards developing an understanding of the needs of hidden minority ethnic communities', *Criminal Justice Matters*, no 58, pp 34–5.

Choudry, S. (1996) 'Pakistani women's experience of domestic violence in Great Britain', Research Findings 43, London: Home Office Research and Statistics Directorate, pp 1–4.

Clancy, A., Hough, M., Aust, R. and Kershaw, C. (2001) *Crime, policing and justice: The experiences of ethnic minorities. Findings from the 2000 British Crime Survey*, Home Office Research and Statistics 223, London: Home Office.

Collins, P. (1998) *Fighting words*, Minneapolis, MN: University of Minnesota Press.

Connell, R. (2005) *Masculinities* (2nd edn), Cambridge: Polity.

CPS (Crown Prosecution Service) (2004a) *Community engagement monitoring: An audit of communities' concerns and priorities June–September 2004*, London: Equality and Diversity Unit, CPS.

CPS (2004b) *Equalities symposium July 1–2*, London: Equality and Diversity Unit, CPS.

CRE (Commission for Racial Equality) (2006) 'What is the CRE?' (www.cre.gov.uk/about/index.html).

Docking, M. (2003) 'Public perceptions of police accountability and decision-making', Home Office Online Report 38/03 (www.homeoffice.gov.uk/rds/pdfs2/rdsolr3803.pdf).

DRC (Disability Rights Commission) (2006) 'What do we do?' (www.drc.gb.org/whatwedo/index.asp).

DTI (Department of Trade and Industry) (2003) 'Hewitt and Falconer announce crackdown on discrimination', press release 29 October, reference P/2003/537 (www.berr.gov.uk).

EOC (Equal Opportunities Commission) (2005) Parliamentary Briefing, Equality Bill, 21 November, Commons Second Reading.

Fawcett Society (2004) *Women and the criminal justice system*, London: Fawcett Society.

Fitzgerald, M. and Sibbitt, R. (1997) *Ethnic monitoring in police forces: A beginning*, Home Office Research Study 173, London: Home Office.

Garland, J., Spalek, B. and Chakraborti, N. (2006) 'Hearing lost voices: Issues in researching "hidden" minority ethnic communities', *British Journal of Criminology*, vol 46, pp 423–7.

Gilbert, P. (2005) *Leadership: Being effective and remaining human*, London: Russell House Publishing.

Gilbert, P. (2006) 'The spiritual foundation: awareness and context for people's lives in Britain today', in M.E. Coyote, P. Gilbert and V. Nicholls (eds) *Spirituality, values and mental health: Jewels for the journey*, London: Jessica Kingsley Publishers, pp 14–67.

Gordon, M. and Riger, S. (1989) *The female fear*, New York: The Free Press.

Guessous, F., Hooper, N. and Moorthy, U. (2001) *Religion in prisons 1999 and 2000 England and Wales*, Home Office Report 15/01, London: Home Office (www.homeoffice.gov.uk/rds/pdfs/hosb1501.pdf).

Hamilton, R. (1986) 'The collusion with patriarchy: A psychoanalytic account', in R. Hamilton and M. Barrett (eds) *The politics of diversity*, London: Verso, pp 385–97.

Harris, A. (1997) 'Race and essentialism in feminist legal theory', in A. Wing (ed) *Critical race feminism*, London: New York University Press, pp 11–18.

HM Government (2004) *Cutting crime, delivering justice, A strategic plan for criminal justice 2004–08*, Cm 6288, London: HMSO.

Home Office (2003a) *Improving public satisfaction and confidence in the criminal justice system*, framework document, July, London: Home Office.

Home Office (2003b) *Statistics on race and the criminal justice system: A Home Office publication under section 95 of the Criminal Justice Act 1991*, London: HMSO.

Hooper, J. (2005) 'Suspect was a Roman Romeo in love with US', *The Guardian*, 2 August (www.guardian.co.uk/attackonlondon/story/0,,1540639,00.html).

Hough, M. and Mayhew, P. (1983) *The British Crime Survey*, Home Office Research Study 76, London: HMSO.

Humphreys, C. and Thiara, R. (2003) 'Mental health and domestic violence: I call it symptoms of abuse', *British Journal of Social Work*, vol 33, pp 209–26.

Jefferson, J. (1994) 'Theorising masculine subjectivity', in T. Newburn and E. Stanko (eds) *Just boys doing business?*, London: Routledge, pp 32–45.

Lonsdale, S. (1990) *Women and disability*, London: Macmillan.

McClaurin, I. (2001) 'Theorizing a black feminist self in anthropology: Toward an auto ethnographic approach', in I. McClaurin (ed) *Black feminist anthropology*, London: Rutgers University Press, pp 49–76.

Mama, A. (2000) 'Woman abuse in London's black communities', in K. Owusu (ed) *Black British culture and society*, London: Routledge, pp 89–110.

Moreton-Robinson, E. (2004) 'Whiteness, epistemology and indigenous representation', in E. Moreton-Robinson (ed) *Whitening race*, Canberra: Aboriginal Studies Press, pp 75–88.

Morrison, W. (1995) *Theoretical criminology: From modernity to post-modernism*, London: Cavendish Publishing.

Muir, H. (2005) 'Report reveals hierarchy of hate', *The Guardian*, 7 March (www.guardian.co.uk/crime/article/0,,1431869,00.html).

National Census (2001) 'Population: gender' (www.statistics.gov.uk/cci/nugget.asp?id=431).

National Statistics Online (2007) 'Migration' (www.statistics.gov.uk/cci/nugget.asp?id=260).

Neville, H., Oh, E., Spanierman, L., Heppner, M. and Clark, M. (2004) 'General and culturally specific factors influencing black and white rape survivors' self-esteem', *Psychology of Women Quarterly*, vol 28, pp 83–94.

O'Beirne, M. (2004) *Religion in England and Wales: Findings from the 2001 Home Office Citizenship Survey*, Home Office Research Study 270, London: Home Office Research, Development and Statistics Directorate.

Pain, R. (1995) 'Elderly women and fear of violent crime: The least likely victims?', *British Journal of Criminology*, vol 35, pp 584–98.

Phillips, C. and Bowling, B. (2003) 'Racism, ethnicity and criminology: Developing minority perspectives', *British Journal of Criminology*, vol 43, no 2, pp 269–90.

Prime, D., Zimmeck, M. and Zurawan, A. (2001) *Active communities: Initial findings from the 2001 Home Office Citizenship Survey*, London: HMSO.

Ratcliffe, P. (2004), *'Race', ethnicity and difference: Imagining the inclusive society*, Maidenhead: Open University Press.

Roy, O. (2004) *Globalized Islam: The search for a new ummah*, New York: Columbia University Press.

Skogan, W. and Maxfield, M. (1981) *Coping with crime*, Beverly Hills, CA: Sage.

Spalek, B. (2005) 'Muslims in the UK and the Criminal Justice System', in T. Choudury, *Muslims in the UK: Policies for engaged citizens*, Budapest: Open Society Institute, pp 253–343.

Spalek, B. (2006) 'Disconnection and exclusion: Pathways to radicalisation?', in T. Abbas (ed) *Islamic political radicalism: A European comparative perspective*, Netherlands: Brill, pp 192–206.

Spencer, S. (2004) CPS Equalities Symposium, 1–2 July 2004, London: Equality and Diversity Unit.

Stark, E. (2003) 'Race, gender and woman battering', in D. Hawkins (ed) *Violent crime: Assessing race and ethnic differences*, Cambridge: Cambridge University Press, pp 171–97.

Stein, A. (1993) 'Introduction', in A. Stein (ed) *Sisters, sexperts, queers beyond the lesbian nation*, Harmondsworth: Penguin, pp xi–xvii.

Tatchell, P. (2002) 'Some people are more equal than others', in P. Iganski (ed) *The hate debate*, London: Profile Books, pp 54–70.

Thompson, N. (1998) *Promoting equality: Challenging discrimination and oppression in the human services*, London: Macmillan.

Thompson, N. (2001) *Anti-discriminatory practice* (3rd edn), Hampshire: Palgrave.

Women Equality Unit (2007) 'Gender equality duty' (www.womenandequalityunit. gov.uk/legislation/discrimination_act/sda-guide.pdf).

Woodward, K. (2002) 'Concepts of identity and difference', in K. Woodward (ed) *Identity and difference*, London: Sage, pp 7–62.

Young, J. (1999) *The exclusive society*, London: Sage.

THREE

Researching identities and communities: key epistemological, methodological and ethical dilemmas

Introduction

The issue of whether a focus upon identities can help us to understand the social world is one that has generated considerable attention. If, as suggested in Chapter One, social identities are fluid and forever changing, so that the narratives that people tell about themselves will only ever be partial and contingent upon broader social, cultural, political and historical factors (Imtoual, 2006), then how valid is the notion of social identity as a tool through which to accumulate knowledge about social phenomena? Hall (1995: 66; 1996) conceptualises identities as sliding; however, at the same time he argues that identities are significant as these constitute the sites at which the social world is experienced and acted upon, regardless of how temporary these points of attachment are, being influenced by discursive practices underpinned by power relations.

Taking on board Hall's (1996) affirmation of the significance of social identity, this chapter will focus upon some of the epistemological, methodological and ethical dilemmas that arise when researching identities, with crime and criminal justice constituting the background context to the issues raised here. It will be argued that engaging with the notion of identity inevitably leads to the researcher having to confront a number of important issues. It seems that it is critical that researchers, whilst documenting specificity of experience, and acknowledging differences between people, do not lose sight of power relations that generate and reproduce inequalities and injustices. Inevitably, tensions will arise between researching diversities on the one hand and claiming broader unities of experiences on the other. Making any type of generalisation is always subject to the criticism that this conceals considerable differences between individuals and can serve to perpetuate any prejudices and stereotypes that are contained within any labels that purport to describe particular groupings of individuals. Nonetheless, discourses that claim no knowledge beyond that which is local and situated cannot challenge forms of social organisation that are unjust, and localisms do not produce discourses that are absent of mentions of power, as power is inherent to all knowledge claims, no matter how nomadic they may be (Fricker, 2000).

The wider environment in which the researcher operates also needs to be considered. The information collected by state institutions regarding social groupings is likely to be incomplete and rather generalistic, so that detailed and specific information about particular social identities is likely to be absent. For example, within the criminal justice system, statistics in relation to victims, offenders and suspects tend to be collected according to 'race'/ethnicity and not religious identity, thereby making it very difficult to gain information about specific faith communities and their experiences of crime and community safety. Also, rather simplistic categories may be employed by government organisations, subsuming particular identities within their remit, thereby masking the experiences of these identities. For example, broad terms like 'Asian' can hide the specific problems and concerns of those, such as Pakistani or Bangladeshi identities, that are subsumed under such an 'umbrella' classification. Gaining access to individuals in disempowered positions can also be extremely problematic, and researchers have often relied upon formal community associations or so-called community leaders, whose views and perspectives may not reflect those of the wider population of individuals who might be conceptualised as belonging to the particular social grouping that the researcher is trying to gain information from and about.

The issue of the multiplicity of subject positions held by both the researcher and the researched also potentially raises many questions. For example, if research subjects occupy a number of subject positions and they experience multiple forms of oppression from multiple sources, then how can researchers carry out work that reflects the richness of people's experiences rather than prioritising one form of identity over another, and thereby potentially prioritising an aspect of a person's identity that they themselves do not view as being the predominant one at that particular moment in time? Also, the researcher will themselves be occupying a wide range of subject positions, all of which may influence the research design, data collection and analysis at different points within a research study. Therefore, a position that acknowledges the complexity of identities that a researcher holds calls for greater reflexivity over the research process. Exploring which aspects of self-identity become dominant during research and examining the impact that these aspects have on the study being undertaken can enhance our understanding of the relationship between self-identity and research, and can serve to highlight the micro-processes involved in perpetuating dominant knowledge constructions.

Clearly, the subject of social identities raises many important questions, and some of these will now be discussed in the paragraphs that follow.

Identities as constructed out of difference: oppositional binaries in western discourse

Identities are constituted out of difference, thus we define what we are by what we are not. As Hall states:

> Identities are constructed through, and not outside, difference. Only through the relation to the Other, the relation to what it is not, to precisely what it lacks, to what has been called its constitutive outside that the 'positive' meaning of any term – and thus its 'identity' – can be constructed. (Hall, 1996: 45)

According to Collins (1998), western scientific discourse has created the illusion of binary oppositions, so that human differences have been viewed simplistically in opposition to each other. Drawing upon the work of Derrida (1997), Taylor (2004) also argues that components of language find their meaning through the presence of an Other, an opposite that is devalued, so that differences are stressed between these antagonistic opposites and those considered to constitute the Other are often perceived as being inferior and so excluded and prevented from entering the borders of the dominant category making up the particular dichotomy. For example, it might be argued that the category White gains its meaning from its opposite Black, and that without Black, White would contain different meanings (Taylor, 2004).

According to Felsenthal (2004), oppositional binaries like male/female, straight/gay or normal/deviant underpin western culture, constructing taken-for-granted assumptions and norms about the world. However, in practice these binary oppositions are fluid, so that there is a wide range of identities and experiences that cannot be neatly conceptualised through any one element of a binary, but rather lie 'somewhere in between'. For example, in relation to the binary straight/gay, there are a myriad of social identities that defy being classified as being either straight or gay, including transgender, transsexual, transvestite or bisexual identities.

The above assertions raise a number of important research questions. As demonstrated, all unities are socially constructed and are underpinned by power and exclusion (Hall, 1996). Therefore, an ingrained difficulty when researching or writing about any so-called 'unities' in relation to 'race'/ethnicity, gender, religion, sexual orientation, disability and age is the exclusive nature of these artificial groupings and how they serve to mask differences between people and specificities of experience. At the same time, by referring to and/or using these general categories, the researcher may be complicit in reproducing binary oppositions through which an Other is constituted, devalued and stigmatised.[1] Focusing upon the side of the binary opposition that occupies the stigmatised or devalued position does not necessarily mean that the construction of a deviant Other is prevented, as this may serve to reproduce dominant stereotypes associated with the particular unity that is being focused upon, particularly if researching areas like crime and/or victimisation, where the potential to stigmatise entire communities is always present. For example, Brah (1996: 24, in Mohammad, 1999: 221–2) maintains that Asians[2] in Britain have been regarded as being 'outsiders', as 'undesirables' who practise 'strange religions', and that the use in research of the general category 'Asian', a category associated with these negative connotations, may therefore serve to reproduce, rather than undermine, these prejudices. And as Gunaratnam (2003) asserts in relation to 'race'/ethnicity, but in a comment that is equally applicable to all other social groupings, the seemingly unavoidable use by researchers of outdated or inadequate terms for racial and ethnic backgrounds can generate simplistic or – perhaps even more worryingly – deterministic assumptions about the behaviours or experiences of such groups. These assumptions can inadvertently lead to the reproduction of existing, dominant power relations between different social groups that may be the opposite of what well-meaning researchers had originally intended the consequences of their research to be. Perhaps this is partly why postmodern approaches have stressed the fragmentation and diversity of social identities, on political grounds of inclusiveness, since the use of any general category is necessarily exclusive as well as being prejudicial (Fricker, 2000).

However, postmodern perspectives that focus on the fluidity and diversity of identities can lose sight of those discriminatory norms that help produce and perpetuate oppression. By stressing the locally produced and contingent nature of any knowledge claims, regimes of power in relation to whiteness, patriarchy, heterosexism, secularism, disablism and ageism remain unchallenged and therefore largely intact. The postmodern focus upon the localised and transitory nature of any social norms suggests that such an approach cannot sufficiently challenge those wider norms that perpetuate inequalities (Fricker, 2000). As McClaurin (2001) argues, there is a materiality to identity that should be acknowledged, stemming from broader relations of power. In the context of late modernity, it is too easy to slide into a kind of particularisation that does not allow us to criticise or to tackle those forms of social organisation that are unjust. For instance, some activists in the US are seeking to encourage white people to adopt a kind of postmodern subjectivity that removes itself from the universal burden of whiteness to become a minoritised white that claims a subject position that is far removed from whiteness (Wiegman, 1999). However, it is difficult to see how this position can challenge and seek to overturn those oppressive social practices that stem from whiteness, since in disclaiming one's subjectivity from wider norms of oppression this does little to enable engagement with, and criticism of, those norms. This issue will be returned to a little later in this chapter when the question of researcher subjectivities is examined more specifically.

Perspectival realism: a social ontology of fragmentation alongside political engagement

A potentially useful epistemological position to pursue when considering conducting research through the lens of social identity is perspectival realism. This places social identities at the centre of analysis and, importantly, it contains a social ontology of fragmentation whilst also claiming a position of political engagement and, therefore, of critical discursive practice (Fricker, 2000). This links in to Collins' position: 'Theorising from outsider-within locations reflects the multiplicity of being on the margins within intersecting systems of race, class, gender, sexual and national oppression, even as such theory remains grounded in and attentive to real differences in power' (1998: 5). Perspectival realism claims that different social identities constitute different social locations through which the world is experienced and viewed, so that at any given moment, the social world can be viewed rationally in more than one perspective. However, power relations in relation to 'race'/ethnicity, gender and so forth can influence knowledge production, constraining access, as well as the legitimacy granted, to the myriad of perspectives that different social identities hold.

In particular, the perspectives of those individuals whose identities lie at the margins, occupying disempowered positions, are likely to be hidden as their claims may appear to be less rational than those claims produced by discursive practices arising from, and being constituted through, technologies that emerge from, and are established through, sites that can be linked to locations of power (Fricker, 2000). Within the perspectival realist approach it is therefore important to gain access to those people who occupy marginalised positions, as through the narratives that these individuals tell about their lives it might be argued that this provides for a critical understanding of the social world, since people in disempowered positions can bring insights into, and shed light upon, dominant social processes that serve to create and perpetuate discrimination and oppression. This epistemological position draws heavily upon feminist standpoint theory (Fricker, 2000), and indeed has close similarities with Cain's (1990: 134) notion of a 'deconstructed and reconstructed feminist standpoint epistemology' that incorporates a multiplicity of standpoints, but at the same time acknowledges the shared experiences of women under patriarchy, except that women's experiences are not, of course, the only focus of attention.

Inevitably, tensions will arise between researching diversities on the one hand and claiming broader unities of experiences on the other; making any type of generalisation is always subject to the criticism that this conceals considerable differences between individuals and can serve to perpetuate any prejudices and stereotypes that are contained within any labels that purport to describe particular groupings of individuals. Nonetheless, it is important to stress that discourses that claim no knowledge beyond that which is local and situated cannot engage politically with forms of social organisation that are unjust, nor are these localisms themselves devoid of power (Fricker, 2000). Therefore, although a plethora of work has arisen out of postmodern perspectives that claim the fragmentation of identities and the relativism of knowledge constructs, a perspectival realist position involves acknowledging the contingent nature of identities yet at the same time, and importantly, it involves a critical engagement with broader power relations with respect to whiteness/patriarchy/secularism and so forth.

Identities as multifaceted, situated and transitory

It seems that two key features of identity formations include their transitory nature and their interaction with social discourses that help shape and build them. Thus, according to Hall (1996: 6), identities are 'points of temporary attachment to the subject positions which discursive practices construct for us', and, in Wetherall's (1996) view, identity is a continuing process, identities undergo continual transformations but they have histories and are dependent upon past and current social positions. Furthermore, identities, while being transient, are necessary in enabling individuals to experience and act upon the world (Hall, 1995). At any point in time, individuals are likely to hold a number of identities, since no one identity marker is likely to define a person fully. Moreover, a person's identities will rarely fit neatly or wholly into any particular side of an oppositional dichotomy, as their subjectivities are likely to reflect the complexities of the social world rather than be built entirely through binary oppositions.

The complex, transitory and multifaceted nature of social identities poses some difficult questions for criminological research. If individuals are likely to hold a multitude of identities at any point in time, and social identity is an epistemologically valid position through which to research the social world, then how do researchers know which identities to focus upon? It might be argued that research must be open to the many different subjectivities that research participants occupy; however, this position is problematic, as an individual may occupy many different identities and so deciding which identities are most relevant to a particular piece of work can create significant difficulties. Moreover, it may not be valid to decide in advance which identity or sets of identities constitute the predominant self-concept of the research subjects as the subjects themselves may consider that other aspects of their identities are more relevant to the particular research topic or question being focused upon at that particular moment in time.

The point above can be illustrated by reference to research studies that have examined questions in relation to crime and victimisation through the lens of 'race'/ethnicity. It might be argued that this work implicitly assumes that 'race'/ethnicity is a more predominant aspect of self-identity than religious affiliation, even though the research participants themselves have not been asked which identities they consider are pertinent to the ways in which they live their lives and experience the social world. For example, the Keighley Crime Survey was carried out in 1995, exploring the crime and victimisation experiences of Asian and white youths (Webster, 1995). While generating some important findings, this work nonetheless marginalised the faith identities of the Asian youth, leading Quraishi (2005) to argue that because the majority of Webster's (1995) Asian research population were Muslim, the lack of a substantial and in-depth focus upon the role of Islam in these young men's lives is a significant weakness of this study. In a study exploring black men who engage in sexual activity with other men, Parks (2004) asks whether it is valid to make a distinction between 'gay black' and 'black gay', thereby raising the question of whether an individual whose self-concept places their sexual orientation before their 'race' will experience the world differently from a person whose concept of self places 'race' before their sexual orientation, and the implications that this has for empirical enquiry. At the same time, it is likely that in different locations different aspects of self will predominate, which suggests that it is perhaps not possible to place one aspect of self-identity above any other aspects.

Researchers in the US are increasingly focusing upon double or even triple identity positions and how these link to wider processes of discrimination and victimisation. Work carried out by Black critical feminists, for instance, illustrates very forcefully the multitudinous nature of subjectivity, showing how black women's lives are marked by a multitude of race, class and gender positions, thereby highlighting the multiplicity of subject locations and the simultaneity of oppression that can be experienced: 'Those of us who live on the margins of society have always embodied multiple roles, straddled multiple social arenas, negotiated multiple effects of power and fashioned multiple identities to survive' (McClaurin, 2001: 55).

While acknowledging that 'as yet, there have been very few empirical studies focusing on multiple minorities in the workplace', Nelson and Probst (2004: 199) refer to a study looking at the barriers that Black immigrant women experience in the workplace, which refers to the 'triple jeopardy' that these women experience in relation to their ethnicity, race and gender. Similarly, in relation specifically to criminal justice, a HM Inspectorate of Probation report (2004: 53) reveals that in the probation service (now a part of the National Offender Management Service – NOMS), one-fifth of minority ethnic staff have indicated that they experience 'dual discrimination', in relation to racism as well as other aspects of their identities.

Some research studies have examined the ways in which individuals manage the different aspects of their subjectivities in their daily lives, exploring which aspects of identity become more significant in which types of context. For example, Myers (2004) suggests that double or triple identity minority status is very difficult to manage over time and across different social settings. Myers (2004) uses the example of ethnic gay individuals who may feel that they have constantly to make a choice between their 'race'/ethnicity and being homosexual, and, depending upon the particular social context, may stress one aspect of their identity over others. Parks (2004) further maintains that holding multiple subject positions involves experiencing multiple oppressions, therefore it is important to research the cumulative impact of these multiple forms of oppression upon the individuals concerned.

Another point that needs to be highlighted here is that, as well as work exploring the multiple identities and the multiple oppressions that people may experience, greater focus should also be placed upon those individuals whose identities transgress culturally constructed dichotomies, including those whose identities may be blended and merged from a multiple of cultural and other traditions. Indeed, it might be suggested that those individuals whose identities overtly challenge the construction of binary oppositions that underpin western societies are likely to experience significant prejudice and victimisation. For instance, according to Taylor (2004), for the biracial individual, the Black/White dichotomy, which represents society's rigid conceptualisation of 'race'/ethnic identities, may have a detrimental impact upon, and interrupt, their development of a sense of self as a 'blended identity'. Garland et al (2006) argue that people of dual heritage are often overlooked by research that has failed to appreciate the extent to which such people can suffer distinct forms of victimisation as a result of the processes of non-acceptance that can operate against those who do not fall conveniently into a particular ethnic category. Members of this minority grouping can find themselves ostracised from the more recognised ethnic communities to whom they feel they belong on the basis of their 'mixed' (and therefore non-exclusive) characteristics. The white partners of minority ethnic individuals may also experience unique forms of racism, which can arise as a result of their partner's ethnicity as well as their own exclusion from (and commonly perceived 'betrayal' of) both the mainstream and minority communities, which can be very hurtful and yet are seldom acknowledged (Garland et al, 2006). Transgressing the gender dichotomy can be just as painful. Transgender people, for instance, can experience transphobic violence and abuse, so that they may limit their use of public space, remaining behind closed doors (Felsenthal, 2004).

The discussions in the paragraphs above suggest that research must be increasingly flexible, open to the many subjectivities that individuals occupy, and must feature the exploration of multiple identities and multiple forms of oppression (including their cumulative impact). At the same time, research should particularly focus upon documenting the experiences of those individuals whose identities powerfully transgress and challenge dominant binary oppositions/ dichotomies, as these persons are likely to experience high levels of violence and abuse. However, even if a researcher adopts a reflexive approach to their work and acknowledges that social identities are constructed, relational and socially located, they will still have to operate in environments where this understanding may largely be absent. When considering the wider context in which research is carried out, there are a number of difficulties involved when attempting to adopt a more open-ended approach that places identities at the centre of research, as will now be discussed below.

The wider discipline-related, political and social contexts to researching identities

Research as being skewed

The context within which research grants and funds are awarded may not be so flexible or open to the multiple subjectivities that participants occupy, and may place restrictions upon the particular lens through which to view individuals' experiences. For instance, it might be argued that placing 'race'/ethnicity as the predominant lens through which to view offenders' experiences, including other aspects of their identities in relation to, say, their faith or sexual orientation, may generate different research findings from a study that places faith or sexual orientation as the predominant lens through which to view individuals' experiences. Nonetheless, in a criminal justice context, where issues in relation to 'race'/ethnicity have traditionally generated substantial policy interest, and perhaps have generated more interest than other forms of identity, it is perhaps fair to argue that it is likely that 'race'/ethnicity will constitute the predominant lens through which social experience is documented, as this type of research is more likely to get government funding than research that focuses upon other social identities. It might therefore be argued that research is inevitably skewed towards using particular identities through which to view and understand the social world, and therefore the criminal justice context. Importantly, historical and political processes, as well as the philosophical foundations of the subject discipline of criminology itself, will also influence which identities predominate over others.

Criminology and social identities

Mirroring other social scientific disciplines, 30 years ago criminology focused upon class as the predominant social identity through which to research and analyse crime, criminality and victimisation, thereby reflecting the centrality of class as opposed to 'race', gender or other forms of social identity.[3] The work of radical criminologists like Gordon, (1973), Quinney (1980), Friedrichs (1983) and left realists, including Young and Matthews (1992), pays testament to the focus upon class. However, reflecting the emergence of women's and race equality movements, gender and 'race'/ethnic identities have increasingly generated research attention, thereby challenging dominant criminological knowledge constructions that have traditionally failed to take these identities into account. For example, Gelsthorpe (2002: 117) claims that 'feminists' challenges to criminology have come from different directions ... in forceful and unmistakable ways that question the epistemological basis and methodological processes of criminology'. Similarly, minority perspectives in relation to 'race'/ethnicity have shed light upon the dynamics of post-war immigration, and the complex relationships between ethnicity, Black cultures, crime and victimisation (Sim et al, 1987; Bowling, 1999; Bowling and Phillips, 2003).

The ability of feminist and critical race perspectives to transform criminological knowledge, epistemological positions and research methodologies raises the question of whether other social identities might have a similar effect upon criminological enquiry. Faith (including spiritual) identities, for instance, have the potential to challenge the secular underpinnings of criminology. Criminology is a discipline of modernity, and its secular roots mean that the issue of religion and people's beliefs has rarely featured as an object of study. As Morrison (1995: 5) suggests: 'Criminology claims the status of the rational and scientific attempt to study the phenomena of crime. It was born with the death of God. It was meant to aid in the journey, the construction of a secure modernity.'

Criminologists, and indeed social scientists in general, have perhaps unwittingly operated according to the binary opposition of secular/spiritual and focused largely upon the secular, so that the spiritual has constituted a deviant Other where the secular and the spiritual have been treated as two separate worlds. This is particularly surprising in relation to research stemming from 'racial'/ethnic identities, as studies reveal that religious affiliation is a much more fundamental aspect of the self-identity of minority ethnic groups when compared to many White Christians (O'Beirne, 2004: 18). Furthermore, when studying the victimising experiences of minority ethnic women, critical Black feminists in the US have introduced the concept of 'spirit injury' in order to explain and to try to understand the full impact of racism and sexism upon women's lives (Davis, 1997; Williams, 1997). Also, Shorter-Gooden's (2004: 408) study suggests that for some African American women, participation in a congregation or spiritual community is part of their coping strategies against the debilitating consequences of racism and sexism. Parks (2004) uses anecdotal evidence to suggest that white gay men, bisexuals, lesbians and trans adults perceive their religious and spiritual practices to be central to their overall sense of self. Indeed, Weatherford and Weatherford (1999) reveal that some black men and women who engage in same-sex sexual behaviour might remain invisible within the black churches that they belong to out of a fear of possible expulsion. Other churches may foster racial and sexual orientation identities, for example, the US gay affirmative church Unity Fellowship (Weatherford and Weatherford, 1999). These issues suggest that criminologists will need to engage more with the faith and spiritual identities of people when researching crime and victimisation, rather than overlooking these or relegating them to a deviant Other. This analysis suggests that work being constituted through, and arising from, the lens of social identity can significantly affect the knowledges that are constructed by social scientific disciplines. It is perhaps timely to consider the impacts that other social identities in relation to sexual orientation, disability and age might have upon the subject discipline of criminology, and indeed these are explored more fully in the chapters that follow.

State agencies and official knowledge constructions

A particular difficulty that researchers face when studying individuals' identities, and the broader communities that they may belong to, is the nomenclature employed by government agencies. Often, specific communities are subsumed within larger collectivities based on 'race'/ethnicity, gender, faith, sexual orientation, disability and age, so it is difficult to gain information about specific experiences. For instance, historically, minority ethnic populations have tended to be grouped together by criminal justice agencies and the Home Office according to broad, essentially racial, categories in a way that makes it very difficult to find accurate data on specific minority ethnic communities. There are many reasons for this. One issue relates to the practical difficulties of collecting more specific data. There has been much discussion about the system of ethnic monitoring that the police service should adopt. When the nine-point system of classification was originally introduced into the criminal justice system (see pp 47-8), it was agreed that in some instances, it would not be possible for police forces to follow this. For example, in stop and search situations the full nine-point scale might not always be practical to use as this would require police officers to ask people to classify themselves. Therefore, in these situations it was decided that a modified four-point scale should be used, consisting of Black, White, Asian and Other,[4] as it was argued that these can be determined via visual appearance (Home Office, 2003). Another reason for the use of general categories relates to the issue of obtaining sample sizes that are statistically significant and the cost effectiveness of doing this. This suggests that to enable the documentation of specificities of experience, qualitative approaches to data collection will inevitably have to be pursued, particularly if researching communities whose numbers are very low.

Another significant factor to the amount of information that is available regarding social groupings in relation to crime and victimisation relates to governmental targets that are set for agencies of the criminal justice system. As highlighted in Chapter Two, public service agreements, which have been introduced by the Home Office, refer specifically to Black and minority ethnic (BME) groups only. Not only does this means that agencies of the criminal justice system will use a general BME sub-target when monitoring and assessing their performance rather than more specific categories in relation to 'race'/ethnicity, but also, other identities in relation to gender, faith, sexual orientation, disability and age are bypassed. This point illustrates how the broader political context will influence which identities are more significant than others, so that there will be significant differences in the amount and detail of information available between different social groupings. As suggested in Chapter Two, procedures for monitoring the level and extent of discrimination within the criminal justice system have traditionally privileged 'race'/ethnicity and gender over other social groupings, this both echoing, and being a product of, the broader public sector equality agenda. Perhaps with the movement towards the harmonisation of equality laws within the public sector, this might lead to information being more systematically collected about disability, faith, sexual orientation and age.

Researcher subjectivities and social identities in the documentation of social experience

Researchers as occupying similar identities to research participants

One issue that researchers have to tackle when conducting empirical enquiry involving people is the question of researcher identities and whether these should mirror as much as possible those identities held by research participants. There may be considerable merit to being 'an insider' as a researcher, meaning that one's social identities mirror as much as possible those of the participants. Gorelick (1991: 464) observes that 'a subject population does not tell the truth to those in power', and so it might be valid to claim that research participants might not reveal the same, or as much, information to a researcher who occupies an 'outsider' status. Whilst feminist researchers call for the researcher to acknowledge that she/he may be in a position of power over the researched, as participants may be asked to reveal sensitive/intimate information about themselves (Renzetti and Lee, 1993), there may be wider political, social and cultural factors at play – which go beyond the interview situation itself – that detrimentally impact upon any trust that the researcher is attempting to generate. For example, in her study of Muslim Australian women, Imtoual (2006) argues that in the present political context where Muslims are often viewed suspiciously by wider society, and are under increasing state surveillance, her identity as a Muslim Australian woman was essential to the study. It may be the case that where the researcher's subject position means that they could not have experienced the same or similar situations as the participants, then gaining legitimate accounts of participants' lives may be extremely difficult. For example, being 'White' may be problematic if attempting to gain accounts of racism, since 'Whiteness' can provide protection from racial harassment and discrimination (Lewis and Ramazanoglu, 1999), and yet a research participant may claim that 'you can't appreciate racism unless you've experienced it' (Weller et al, 2001: 20). This is perhaps why Papadopoulos and Lees (2002) argue that as 'insiders' minority ethnic researchers are better placed to do work around racism since they have greater awareness and understanding of minority issues and so can provide accounts of experiences and perceptions that are more genuine and legitimate. Indeed, the researcher is also likely to gain access to particular populations much more easily when researching individuals who occupy similar subject positions to themselves. But it is worth bearing in mind, however, that the voices of 'outsiders' may carry more legitimacy within wider society than the voices of 'insiders', who might be perceived as being 'biased'. Therefore, 'outsiders' can not only serve to prevent insiders' discourses from being marginalised within social scientific discourses but also can help in any claims-making activities that take place in broader political and policy arenas.

Researcher identities as multiple

It is important to stress that researchers occupy multiple identities, so that while some aspects of their identities might help them to establish rapport and trust, and to gain access to research participants, other aspects to their identities may work against them. For example, Stanfield (1993: 7) argues that the professional status of a minority ethnic researcher can cause problems, even when studying those with whom they share a common ethnic background. Sometimes, a researcher can draw upon specific aspects of their multiple identities in order to help gain the trust of the research participants. For instance, in a study looking at the experiences of Muslim male prisoners in Britain, Quraishi (2003) illustrates how being a Muslim and a bilingual researcher of South Asian parentage enabled him to connect with some of the prisoners who took part in the project. A significant number of Muslims in prison are Black Caribbeans, however, and so when working with these prisoners, Quraishi (2003) emphasised common religious beliefs, as his ethnicity and linguistic skills did not correlate with these individuals. Similarly, in a study exploring the negotiation of the personal safety of a group of Muslim women who wear the hijab, Spalek (2002) drew upon her position as a woman in order to help establish rapport and trust with the participants, since Spalek's ethnicity and religious identity differed from that of the research participants. This suggests that the 'insider'/'outsider' status may itself be a culturally produced dichotomy, accentuating differences between taking an 'insider' and an 'outsider' position when in reality a researcher is likely to be both. As Bartunek and Reis state (1996: 67), 'no-one is simply or solely an "insider" or "outsider" in any particular inquiry situation'.

A perspectival realist position seeks to create knowledge that moves beyond essentialist discourses. It is therefore legitimate to suggest that it is important to move beyond an essentialist view of the researcher, and take on board the complexity of subject positions that a researcher may occupy and how these might influence the research process. This approach has in fact been a significant feature of feminist and anthropological work. Feminist research principles call for reflexivity over this process, so that the values and characteristics of the researcher are made visible. This is because it is argued that the beliefs, characteristics and behaviour of social scientists influence the design of a study, including the ways in which data is produced and analysed (Harding, 1987; Edwards and Ribbens, 1998). Work carried out by Black critical feminists particularly illustrates the multitudinous nature of subjectivity, since black women's lives are marked by a multitude of race, class and gender positions, thereby highlighting the multiplicity of subject locations and the simultaneity of oppression that can be experienced (McClaurin, 2001). The notion of 'double consciousness' has been raised, highlighting how distinct aspects of self can co-reside, and so as well as there being aspects of the self linked to marginalised positions, there may also be parts of the self that can be linked to the perpetuation of centres of power (Collins, 1998; McClaurin,

2001). This suggests that different aspects of a researcher's self-identity, such as their gender, age, 'race'/ethnicity or sexual orientation, will influence the research process at different points in a study.

Research ethics and identities

In reflecting on the research process, researchers should think critically about the ways in which aspects of their multiple identities may be linked to broader power dynamics. During a piece of work, different aspects of the researcher's self will come into play at different moments, and while some aspects of a researcher's subjectivity can be linked to marginalised, outsider positions, which can help to produce oppositional knowledge, other aspects of self-identity may maintain and reproduce dominant racial, cultural – and so forth – knowledge constructions. For example, in a study exploring Muslim women's fear of crime, Spalek (2005b) argues that while her position as 'woman' helped to gain data about women's management of their personal safety, her position as 'western researcher' may have inadvertently led to the perpetuation of dominant knowledge constructions and the production of a deviant Other. Spalek's (2005b) sampling procedure was underpinned by the binary of 'free choice' versus 'no choice' in relation to veiling when deciding which Muslim women to interview. For Spalek (2005b), 'free choice' meant that the women were under no pressure either from their families or from their wider communities to veil but, rather, had decided to do so for themselves. However, by constructing the binary opposition free choice/no choice it might be agued that this served to perpetuate dominant western misrepresentations of Islam, relegating the 'no choice' side of the binary to a deviant, oppositional Other.

A reflexive approach like the one discussed above can serve to highlight the micro processes involved in perpetuating dominant knowledge constructions and power relations. It requires openness from the researcher and is particularly powerful because it forces the researcher to engage with those power positions that they themselves may be linked to. This enables the researcher openly to acknowledge and challenge those invisible norms that serve to produce and maintain discrimination and oppression. Thus, for example, this approach might involve a 'White' or a 'heterosexual' or an 'able-bodied' researcher, through carrying out work with 'Black/minority ethnic' and/or 'gay' and/or disabled individuals, in exposing, questioning and deconstructing the norms of 'Whiteness', 'heterosexism' and/or disablism. Therefore, it should not be assumed that difference itself should be the reason for not undertaking a particular piece of work. Indeed, there might be considerable merit in carrying out work about individuals whose subject positions are quite different from one's own, as long as reflexivity over the research process takes place legitimately, involving as much disclosure as possible on the researcher's part. And, similar to claims made that those in oppressed positions may not articulate their perceptions or experiences to those who occupy oppressor positions (Gorelick, 1991; Collins, 1998), an issue that needs to be raised is whether, and in what ways, those whose identities can be linked to positions of power/domination also have understandings and perspectives about the social world that they keep hidden from those whose identities might be linked to disempowered positions. This then raises a further ethical and methodological question in relation to how, and in what ways, researchers can make visible those collective secret knowledges that are shared in private by groups located within positions of power, which may also be as subtle as body language rather than verbal expression.

Summary

The discussion above essentially suggests adopting a research approach that has a deep commitment to a personal ethic based on self-reflexivity and a critical engagement with those oppressive structures to which one's own identities can be linked. It seems that if research is to have a meaning that goes beyond any so-called results generated by studies, then it is important for the researcher to be self-reflexive and to consider the ways in which they themselves may be linked to power relations that oppress. This can then be part of a wider personal ethics that seeks to challenge discrimination and prejudice. Of course, acknowledging that as a researcher one can be 'oppressor' as well as 'oppressed' is extremely difficult, and if taking on board Hollway and Jefferson's (2000) approach of using the psychoanalytic theory of Melanie Klein to argue that the researcher, as well as the participant, is a 'defended subject', then this suggests that when reflecting upon a research project, researchers may avoid addressing the particularly difficult or uncomfortable aspects of themselves that may be linked to wider power positions, and so the nature of the researcher's subjectivity and its influence upon the research process may never be sufficiently exposed or analysed. A focus upon the emotions that are experienced by a researcher as they carry out their work may help to illuminate her/his subject positions.

An emerging body of feminist work considers emotionality to be a central part of documenting and examining the nature of the researcher's subjectivity (see Pickering, 2001). Traditionally, this form of introspection has not been pursued, amid concerns that researchers who explore their feelings might attract accusations of 'unhealthy absorption' or 'emotional exhibitionism' (Pickering: 2001: 486). Nonetheless, this work suggests that by analysing emotionality, there is the potential to reveal hidden decision-making processes which can be linked to power hierarchies inherent in research (Pickering, 2001). As part of this process, researchers examine the emotions that they experience as they carry out their work. The emotions that are identified are then used as markers that can help reveal aspects of both the researcher's and participants' biographies that have a significant, if hidden, effect upon the research process. However, it is important to stress that while potentially being a methodological avenue that is worth pursuing, there is the issue of 'emotion management', which involves the researcher pursuing reassuring feelings during the interview situation by overlooking important differences between themselves and the research participants. This would suggest caution when claiming any kind of 'rapport' or 'understanding' between the researcher and the research participants. Comfortable feelings may be the product of successful emotional management rather than any valid relationship between interviewer and interviewee (see Spalek, 2005b).

Conclusion

This chapter has raised many critical issues in relation to placing identities at the core of social research. It appears that despite the temporal and sliding nature of identities, they nonetheless constitute the sites at which the social world is experienced and the sites through which power relations are at play. However, postmodern perspectives that stress the fluidity and situated nature of identities, while highlighting the transient and multitudinous nature of subject positions, fail to engage in critical discursive practice. As a result, this chapter stresses that a potentially useful epistemological position to take is that of perspectival realism. This acknowledges the fluidity and multitude of subject positions, and takes the position that at any given moment, the social world can be viewed rationally in more than one perspective. At the same time, however, this approach also stresses and seeks to challenge those wider norms that perpetuate inequalities, thereby containing the position that there is a materiality to identity.

This chapter also stresses the many difficulties that can arise from a focus upon social identities. Increasingly, it seems, research will explore the multiple identities that research participants hold, the ways in which these are negotiated, and how double, triple or even quadruple discrimination might be experienced cumulatively. But this raises the question of how researchers should decide in advance what aspects of identity to focus on and explore, and also which framework of understanding to use to analyse participants' experiences. It might be suggested, for example, that exploring social experiences through the lens of 'race'/ethnicity already biases research results as this assumes that 'race'/ethnicity is the predominant aspect to research participants' lives. Furthermore, although a researcher might wish to adopt an approach that acknowledges that social identities are constructed, relational and socially located, they are likely to still have to operate in environments where this understanding may largely be absent. For example, research-funding bodies may implicitly function according to a 'hierarchy of identities' whereby it is easier to obtain funding for projects based on particular identities rather than others. Therefore, work that seeks to locate social experience from outside the dominant identities through which social scientific research has traditionally been carried out will struggle to find funding. At the same time, the statistics compiled by state institutions and any targets that are set by government may consist of very general social groupings, thereby subsuming specific identities, making it very difficult to obtain accurate data in relation to specific communities.

The question of researchers' identities is also addressed here. This chapter suggests that it is important to move beyond an essentialist view of the researcher, and to take on board the complexity of subject positions that a researcher may occupy and how these might influence the research process. During a piece of work, different aspects of the researcher's self will come into play at different moments, and whilesome aspects of a researcher's subjectivity can be linked to marginalised, outsider positions – which can help to produce oppositional knowledge – other aspects of self-identity may maintain and reproduce dominant knowledge constructions, including racial and cultural ones. It is argued that increasing self-reflexivity on the part of the researcher is desirable, and that, moreover, this should be framed by a personal ethic that involves critical engagement with those oppressive structures to which one's identities can be linked. If research is to have a meaning that goes beyond any so-called results generated by studies, then it is important for the researcher to be self-reflexive and to consider the ways in which they themselves are linked to power relations that oppress. The next chapter focuses upon the notion of 'community', this being increasingly a feature of criminal justice policy and practice.

Notes

[1] It is important to point out, however, that social movements have striven to resignify those identity markers that have traditionally occupied a devalued position within society. For example, the civil rights and Black rights movements have worked towards reclaiming and redefining blackness (Wiegman, 1999).

[2] The term 'Asian' can be considered to occupy Black in the White–Black dichotomy if using Mirza's (1997: 3) approach, where Black is considered to consist of the shared space of postcolonial migrants of different languages, religions, cultures and classes through the shared experience of racialisation and its consequences.

[3] Mawby and Walklate (1994) argue that while left realists have offered a much more detailed portrayal of victimisation at a local level, they have nonetheless focused predominantly upon the relationship of class to victimisation, to the detriment of race, gender and age. Thus, for example, left realists' understanding of race issues is seen to be partial and incomplete (Sim et al, 1987), and the extent to which their research methods capture women's experiences of victimisation is also questionable (Walklate, 1992).

[4] The common usage of the 'four-category' ethnic category system can be seen in a number of recent Home Office-sponsored pieces of research, including, for example, Matrix Research and Consultancy and Nacro's (2004) analysis of drug testing in the criminal justice system and Calverley et al's (2004) assessment of black and Asian offenders on probation, which uses both nine- and four-point systems. The Home Office's 2001 Citizenship Survey (Attwood et al, 2003), whilst employing the 1991 Census nine-point categorisation for some of its analysis, also often combines these categories to form a smaller five-point scale.

Chapter questions

How does perspectival realism differ from critical realism?

How valid is the notion of social identity as a tool through which to accumulate knowledge about social phenomena?

Which factors serve to limit research around identities and criminal justice?

Case study
'Taking things personally: Young Muslim women in South Australia'

My own identity as a young Muslim woman was essential in creating the necessary bonds of trust for these interviews to take place. This is particularly important given the current 'war on terrorism' context in which many Muslims feel uncomfortable about expressing any dissatisfaction with the society in which they are located for fear that this may in some way be construed as a rejection of that society, or worse, as a statement of bad intention towards that society. In particular, some narratives of harassment and the women's dissatisfaction with the behaviour of public servants and officials would not have been told to non-Muslim interviewers because the women would have felt too unsure of their research agenda and motivation. Interviewees would have wondered: what is this interviewer's attitude towards Islam? Will my stories be co-opted to tell a 'tale of oppression' or similar stereotypical narrative? What is this interviewer's relationship with governmental forms of surveillance and control? How anonymous will my stories be? Will my stories be used 'against' the broader Australian Muslim community under current regimes of surveillance and control as encouraged by the 'war on terror'? Will the interviewer respect and acknowledge my agency and personal choices or will my stories be written into a narrative of religious extremism and/or religious oppression?

Source: Imtoual, 2006: 57

Question
How, and in what ways, are researcher subject positions relevant to the research process?

References

Attwood, C., Singh, G., Prime, D. and Creasey, R. (2003) *2001 Home Office Citizenship Survey: People, families and communities,* Home Office Research Study 270, London: Home Office Research Development and Statistics Directorate.

Bartunek, J. and Reis, L. (1996), *Insider/outsider team research,* Qualitative Research Methods Series 40, London: Sage.

Bowling, B. (1999) *Violent racism: Victimisation, policing and social context* (revised edn), Oxford: Oxford University Press.

Bowling, B. and Phillips, C. (2003) 'Racist victimisation in England and Wales', in D. Hawkins (ed) *Violent crime: Assessing race and ethnic differences,* Cambridge: Cambridge University Press, pp 154–70.

Brah, A. (1996) *Cartographies of diaspora: Contesting identities,* London: Routledge.

Cain, M. (1990) 'Realist philosophy and standpoint epistemologies or feminist criminology as a successor science', in L. Gelsthorpe and A. Morris (eds) *Feminist perspectives in criminology,* Buckingham: Open University Press, pp 124–40.

Calverley, A., Bankole, C., Kaur, G., Lewis, S., Raynor, P., Sadeghi, S., Smith, D., Vanstone, M. and Wardak, A. (2004) *Black and Asian offenders on probation,* Home Office Research Study 277, London: Home Office Research Development and Statistics Directorate.

Collins, P. (1998) *Fighting words,* Minneapolis: University of Minnesota Press.

Davis, D. (1997) 'The harm that has no name: Street harassment, embodiment and African American women', in A. Wing (ed) *Critical race feminism: A reader,* New York: New York University Press, pp 192–202.

Derrida, J. (1997) *Politics of friendship,* London: Verso.

Edwards, R. and Ribbens, J. (1998) 'Living on the edges: Public knowledge, private lives, personal experience', in J. Ribbens and R. Edwards (eds) *Feminist dilemmas in qualitative research,* London: Sage, pp 1–24.

Felsenthal, K. (2004) 'Socio-spatial experiences of transgender individuals', in Jean Lau Chin (ed) *The psychology of prejudice and discrimination: Bias based on gender and sexual orientation, volume 3,* London: Praeger, pp 201–25.

Fricker, M. (2000) 'Feminism in epistemology: Pluralism without postmodernism', in M. Fricker and J. Hornsby (eds) *The Cambridge companion to feminism in philosophy,* Cambridge: Cambridge University Press, pp 146–65.

Friedrichs, D. (1983) 'Victimology: A consideration of the radical critique', *Crime and Delinquency,* vol 29, no 1, pp 283–93.

Garland, J., Spalek, B. and Chakraborti, N. (2006) 'Hearing lost voices: Issues in researching hidden minority ethnic communities', *British Journal of Criminology,* vol 64, pp 423–37.

Gelsthorpe, L. (2002) 'Feminism and criminology' in: M. Maguire, R. Morgan and R. Reiner (eds) *The Oxford handbook of criminology* (3rd edn), Oxford: Clarendon Press, pp 112-43.

Gordon, D. (1973) 'Capitalism, class and crime in America', *Crime and Delinquency*, vol 20, no 2, pp 163–87.

Gorelick, S. (1991) 'Contradictions of feminist methodology', *Gender & Society*, vol 5, no 4, pp 459–77.

Gunaratnam, Y. (2003) *Researching 'race' and ethnicity: Methods, knowledge and power*, London: Sage.

Hall, S. (1995) 'Fantasy, identity, politics', in E. Carter, J. Donald and J. Squires (eds) *Cultural remix: Theories of politics and the popular*, London: Lawrence and Wishart, pp 3–72.

Hall, S. (1996) 'Introduction: Who needs "identity"?', in S. Hall and P. du Gay (eds) *Questions of cultural identity*, London: Sage, pp 1–17.

Harding, S. (1987) *Feminism and methodology*, Milton Keynes: Open University Press.

HMIP (Her Majesty's Inspectorate of Probation) (2004) *Towards race equality: Follow-up inspection report*, London: HMIP

Hollway, W. and Jefferson, T. (2000) *Doing qualitative research differently*, London: Sage.

Home Office (2003) *Statistics on race and the criminal justice system. A Home Office publication under section 95 of the Criminal Justice Act 1991*, London: Home Office Research Development and Statistics Directorate.

Imtoual, A. (2006) 'Taking things personally: Young Muslim women in South Australia discuss identity, religious racism and media representations', PhD thesis, University of Adelaide, Department of Gender Work and Social Inquiry.

Lewis, B. and Ramazanoglu, C. (1999) 'Not guilty, not proud, just white: women's accounts of their whiteness', in H. Brown, M. Gilkes and A. Kaloski-Naylor (eds) *White? women*, York: Raw Nerve Books, pp 23–62.

McClaurin, I. (2001) 'Theorizing a black feminist self in anthropology: Toward an auto ethnographic approach', in I. McClaurin (ed) *Black feminist anthropology*, London: Rutgers University Press, pp 49–76.

Matrix Research and Consultancy and Nacro (2004), *Evaluation of Drug Testing in the Criminal Justice System*, Home Office Research Study 286, London: Home Office Research Development and Statistics Directorate.

Mawby, R. and Walklate, S. (1994) *Critical victimology*, London: Sage.

Mirza, H. (1997) 'Introduction: Mapping a genealogy of Black British feminism', in H. Mirza (ed) *Black British feminism: A reader*, London: Routledge, pp 1–28.

Mohammad, R. (1999), 'Marginalisation, Islamism and the production of the other's "other"', *Gender, Place and Culture*, vol 6, no 3, pp 221–40.

Morrison, W. (1995) *Theoretical criminology: From modernity to post-modernism*, London: Cavendish Publishing.

Myers, L. (2004) 'Black women coping with stress in academia', in Jean Lau Chin (ed) *The psychology of prejudice and discrimination: Bias based on gender and sexual orientation, volume 3*, London, Praeger, pp 133–50.

Nelson, N. and Probst, T. (2004) 'Multiple minority individuals: Multiplying the risk of workplace harassment and discrimination', in Jean Lau Chin (ed) *The psychology of prejudice and discrimination: Ethnicity and multiracial identity, volume 2*, London: Praeger, pp 193–217.

O'Beirne, M. (2004) *Religion in England and Wales: Findings from the 2001 Home Office Citizenship Survey*, Home Office Research Study 270, London: Home Office Research Development and Statistics Directorate.

Papadopoulos, I. and Lees, S. (2002) 'Developing culturally competent researchers', *Journal of Advanced Nursing*, vol 37, no 3, pp 258–64.

Parks, C. (2004) 'Black men who have sex with men', in Jean Lau Chin (ed) *The psychology of prejudice and discrimination: Bias based on gender and sexual orientation, volume 3*, London: Praeger, pp 227–48.

Pickering, S. (2001) 'Undermining the sanitized account; violence and emotionality in the field in Northern Ireland', *British Journal of Criminology*, vol 41, pp 485–501.

Quinney, R. (1980) *Class, state and crime* (2nd edn), New York: Longman.

Quraishi, M. (2003) 'Room with a view: Methodological considerations of prison research', paper presented at 'Muslims in Prison: A European Challenge' Conference, Centre for Research in Ethnic Relations and Department of Sociology, University of Warwick, 12–13 December.

Quraishi, M. (2005) *Muslims and crime*, Aldershot: Ashgate.

Renzetti, C. and Lee, R (1993) 'The problems of researching sensitive topics', in R. Lee and C. Renzetti (eds) *Researching sensitive topics*, London: Sage, pp 3–11.

Shorter-Gooden, K. (2004) 'Multiple resistance strategies: How African American women cope with racism and sexism', *Journal of Black Psychology*, vol 30, no 3, pp 406–25.

Sim, J., Scraton, P. and Gordon, P. (1987) 'Introduction: crime, the state and critical analysis' in P. Scraton (ed) *Law, order and the authoritarian state,* Milton Keynes: Open University Press, pp 1–70.

Spalek, B. (2002) 'Muslim women's safety talk and their experiences of victimisation', in B. Spalek (ed) *Islam, crime and criminal justice*, Cullompton: Willan, pp 50–71.

Spalek, B. (2005b) 'Researching black Muslim women's lives: A critical reflection', *International Journal of Social Research Methodology*, vol 8, no 5, pp 1–14.

Stanfield, J. (1993) 'Methodological reflections: An introduction', in J.H. Stanfield and R.M. Dennis (eds) *Race and ethnicity in research methods*, London: Sage, pp 3–15.

Taylor, M. (2004) 'Sociohistorical constructions of race and language: Impacting biracial identity', in Jean Lau Chin (ed) *The psychology of prejudice and discrimination: Ethnicity and multiracial identity, volume 2*, London: Praeger, pp 87–108.

Walklate, S. (1992) 'Appreciating the victim: Conventional, realist or critical victimology?', in J. Young and R. Matthews (eds) *Issues in realist criminology*, London: Sage, pp 102–18.

Weatherford, R. and Weatherford, C. (1999) *Somebody's knocking at your door. AIDS and the African-American Church*, New York: Haworth Pastoral Press.

Webster, C. (1995) 'Youth Crime, Victimisation and Racial Harassment', *Community Studies*, no 7 (revised edition), Ilkley: Centre for Research in Applied Community Studies, Bradford and Ilkley Community College

Weller, P., Feldman, A. and Purdam, K., (2001) *Religious discrimination in England and Wales*, Home Office Research Study 220, London: HMSO.

Wetherall, M. (1996) 'Life histories/social histories', in M. Wetherall (ed) *Identities groups and social issues*, Milton Keynes: Open University Press, pp 299–361.

Wiegman, R. (1999) 'Whiteness studies and the paradox of particularity', *Boundary 2*, vol 26, no 3, pp 115–50.

Williams, P. (1997) 'Spirit-murdering the messenger: The discourse of finger pointing as the law's response to racism', in A. Wing (ed) *Critical race feminism: A reader*, New York: New York University Press, pp 229–36.

Young, J. and Matthews, R. (1992) 'Questioning left realism', in R. Matthews and J. Young (eds) *Issues in realist criminology*, London: Sage, pp 1–18.

FOUR

Communities and criminal justice: engaging legitimised, project and resistance identities

Introduction

The notion of 'community' features significantly in criminal justice policy and practice. Underpinned by the principle of 'active citizenship', whereby individuals are encouraged to volunteer their services, to participate in and contribute to civil society, communities are viewed as an important resource for tackling crime and incivility, by working with local criminal justice organisations, as well as other statutory and voluntary sector organisations. Reflecting the importance that community involvement in helping to respond to crime and disorder is given by government, 'community participation', 'community engagement' and 'community scrutiny of performance' feature significantly in criminal justice policy and practice.

The emphasis placed upon community participation in criminal justice reflects broader developments in governance, whereby responsibility and accountability for crime is increasingly focused towards local levels, while at the same time centralised control in terms of resources and target setting is maintained. Also, formal responsibilities for policy implementation and service delivery are progressively being shared across statutory and voluntary agencies and community groups in the form of partnership work (Prior et al, 2006). These developments also constitute a form of institutional reflection (Lash, 1994), which, as highlighted in Chapter One, involves criminal justice institutions opening themselves up to the communities that they serve, with the lay public engaging with, as well as critiquing, rival forms of expertise. Individuals and the communities to which they belong are therefore being encouraged to identify and define the problems that they face and to put forward solutions to those problems, and to work with, and alongside, agencies of the criminal justice system.

However, the notion of 'community' is itself contentious and open to many different interpretations, particularly within the context of late modernity, where modern and postmodern processes combine and interact to create multiple forms of belongingness, including international diasporas spanning many different geographical locations, localised acts of self-identification based on ethnic or cultural allegiances, as well as local groupings that contain transnational characteristics. However, within government discourse the notion of community tends to be treated rather unproblematically, as both subject and object of policy making and intervention: as Prior et al (2006) state, 'subject because many current policies require "the community" to be an active participant in the delivery of policy outcomes; and as object, because many current policies view "the community" as a key source of needs and problems and as a target for change in itself'.

This chapter aims to interrogate the notion of community with respect to the criminal justice and community safety sectors. It is argued that the term 'community' is a catch-all phrase used by government as a way of simplifying, merging and combining complex social identities and groupings for the purposes of policy development and implementation. Furthermore, although the term 'community' gives the outward impression of neutrality, the ways in which the term is used and operationalised by government suggest that it is loaded with assumptions about the kinds of social identities that are included, as well as fostered, for the purposes of community participation, engagement and scrutiny of performance. It might be argued that legitimising identities are both encouraged and approached by agencies of the criminal justice system, rather than those that might be characterised as project and resistance identities. As a result, there is a danger that agencies do not move significantly beyond dialogue that is largely symbolic and tokenistic, since legitimising identities are the means through which government can extend its power and ideologies through social actors (Castells, 2004). Project and resistance identities can potentially have more far-reaching consequences for criminal justice policy and practice, leading to new paradigms and new ways of combating and responding to crime. However, presently, any interaction that takes place between state institutions and those communities that might be characterised as project identities is likely to consist of struggles over knowledge claims rather than engagement as such. Resistance identities are the least likely to engage with state institutions, building walls of resistance. The question that this raises for criminal justice policy is how, and in what ways, and also how far, resistance identities should be included in the policy-making process, particularly as these might contain groupings that contain elements of racism, religious fundamentalism or nationalism. The notion of community involvement in criminal justice therefore raises many burning issues, some of which will be addressed in this chapter.

Communities as multifaceted and imagined

Community is a complex, multifarious and widely debated concept. Lash (1994) argues that communities do not consist of shared interests or properties, but rather, shared meanings form the basis of community life. This understanding of community is reflected in other works. For example, Hall (1996) argues that community consists of the meanings that individuals associate with and share together, and Kennedy and Roudometof (2004: 6) offer the following definition:

'Communities are units of belonging whose members perceive that they share moral, aesthetic/expressive or cognitive meanings, thereby gaining a sense of personal as well as group identity.'

Considerable debate has arisen within academic literature regarding the extent to which global forces penetrate, and interact with, communities. Some affiliations may consist of highly localised associations between people, based on ethnic or other cultural allegiances, so that global and/or transnational processes may not be so significant (Rew and Campbell, 1999; Castells, 2004). At the same time, highly localised identities can be constructed that have a strong transnational character (Kempny, 2004), and communities can also be built around global agendas such as human rights or environmental issues. It is important to stress that the local and global are mutually dependent on each other, and so it is not possible to distinguish between solely local and transnational communities and those that are 'purely' global in character, since these 'types of communities share specific experiences that justify their inclusion into a single category' (Kennedy and Roudometof, 2004: 16). Many communities might be conceptualised as consisting of 'diasporas', which are both local and global in character (Gilroy, 2002). In diasporas individual members gain a sense of belonging, devising narratives about themselves and their origins, about how they are linked to broader global religions, nationalities and/or ethnicities as well as to localities that are 'simultaneously home and a place of exile' (Rew and Campbell, 1999: 167). Significant heterogeneity is to be found within international diasporas, with respect to factors like class, education and generational cohort, and so whilst claiming a broader group identity, individuals may also live with the fragmented and plural nature of the particular diaspora(s) with which they associate themselves (Kennedy and Roudometof, 2004).

The development of new technologies has enabled dispersed populations to interact and link together important parts of their social and cultural lives (Gilroy, 2002).[1] For instance, the internet has transformed networking amongst diasporas, as exemplified by the diaspora of more than 50 million Tamil-speaking people around the globe. Here the internet has played a crucial role in helping to hold this diaspora together, since it has enabled significant networking to take place, generating international sympathy and money for the Liberation Tigers of Tamil Eelam (Ubayasiri, 2004). Another example that can be used consists of the role of the internet in connecting the Burmese diaspora, which includes those pro-democracy Burmese activists who have been living in political exile in other parts of the world. The internet has taken a significant part in the democratic claims-making activities of this diaspora (Oo, 2004). But migrant diasporas constitute only one type of diaspora, and there are many other kinds of transnational community. For example, transnational relationships have also developed in relation to sport, leisure, clubs and associations, as well as other forms of cultural life, constituting 'communities of taste' (Kennedy and Roudometof, 2004; Lash, 1994). For instance, O'Connor (2004) documents punk as an example of a global cultural movement, which exists in different locations across the globe in the form of local scenes, and he argues that studying culture in a global era involves 'multisite ethnography'. O'Connor (2004) also illustrates how conduits for the transmission of punk and hardcore include record distribution, letters, travel and touring bands. Taste communities transgress the traditional distinction between consumer and producer, as those individuals who enjoy consuming a particular cultural genre may also at the same time be contributing to its production (Lash, 1994).

It is important to point out the transitory nature of individuals' attachments to communities. For example, Bauman (2004) writes about the fluidity of attachments in contemporary society, with people being 'constantly on the move', looking to find or establish new identities and communities of belonging. Similarly, according to Kennedy and Roudometof (2004), participation in community has become much more flexible, open and subject to negotiation. This means that it is likely that individuals participate in a wide range of communities and their affiliations with particular groupings are likely to change over time. Moreover, the diversity of the communities to which individuals attach themselves is likely to be vast, involving the negotiation of multiple identities (Kennedy and Roudometof, 2004). Added to this, all communities are likely to contain a dimension of fantasy and imagination, whereby myths of commonality may be created. Colic-Peisker (2004) argues, for instance, that within diasporas, ideological mechanisms may be at play that create imagined communities through myths of common history, ancestry and interests. Castells (2004) also suggests that all communities can be viewed as imagined if we take the position that all feelings of belongingness are culturally constructed. Indeed, if all communities work through minds, attitudes and discourses, as well as through geographical locales or through social, familial and other ties, then it is not difficult to see the significance of social engineering, whereby particular ideologies may be constructed by, and reproduced through, political institutions and apparatuses, to help construct or encourage particular forms of belongingness.

Community engagement within criminal justice

Within the criminal justice sector, the notion of 'community' features significantly in government discourse, both as the subject and object of policy making and intervention (Prior et al, 2006). The community is thereby viewed as a valuable ally in helping to prevent and respond to crime and incivility, and it is also regarded as being an object in its own right, requiring government intervention. These developments can be linked to broader changes in governance that have been taking place over the last 15 years or so.[2] At the same time that the control over resources has been increasingly centralised at a national level, and various national targets have been set by government that agencies of the criminal justice should meet, responsibility and accountability for decision making has been channelled towards local levels. Communities are therefore viewed as an important resource for tackling crime and incivility, working with local criminal justice organisations, as well as the voluntary sector.[3] Communities are also viewed as needing government help and intervention themselves and therefore as the object of governance, whereby tackling crime is not seen as an end in itself, but rather, broader goals in relation to 'civil renewal', 'community cohesion' and 'strengthening communities' are also pursued (see Prior et al, 2006).

In policy documents that are put together by the Home Office, as well as by agencies of the criminal justice system, 'community engagement', 'community participation' and 'community scrutiny of performance' are often referred to. For example, in relation to policing, the pursuit of an approach that involves local community involvement in combating crime and responding to disorder can be seen in two key policy documents: the Home Office paper (2004a) *Building communities, beating crime: A better police service for the 21st century*, and the *National policing plan 2005–08* (Home Office, 2004b). According to the former:

> A police service which is engaging effectively with the community
> will have a detailed, neighbourhood level understanding of the
> demographics of the community it serves; have a detailed – and
> regularly update – picture of the interests, needs, priorities and
> preferences of every section of that community; establish and facilitate
> an ongoing and consistent dialogue with all sections of the community
> by regularly discussing and sharing information; understand how, and
> the extent to which, different sections of the community feel most
> comfortable in interacting with the police. (Home Office, 2004a: 3)

According to the *National policing plan 2005–08*, 'neighbourhood policing extends partnerships beyond the statutory agencies and voluntary groups to bring in members of the community themselves' (Home Office, 2004b: 9). A key feature of community engagement entails an increasingly localised approach to policing, whereby police authorities and police forces should focus upon 'creating local targets to increase customer satisfaction, public confidence and feelings of public safety that reflect the priorities of their communities' (Home Office, 2004b: 14), and so 'target-setting should be a bottom–up process so that communities have local ownership of targets' (Home Office, 2004b: 9). Community engagement should also include participation and scrutiny of performance, thereby involving local communities with the design, implementation and evaluation of training packages that police officers are expected to undertake. For example, according to the *National policing plan 2005–08* (Home Office, 2004b: 17), the government is 'committed to taking forward training initiatives to increase community engagement in policing so that members of local communities are actively involved in all stages of the training cycle – from analysis to design and delivery through to evaluation'.

The above developments taking place within the police service are also reflected at other points throughout the criminal justice system. The Crown Prosecution

Service (CPS), for instance, is increasingly engaging with communities when undertaking its day-to-day activities. When drawing up policies on the prosecution of religiously and racially aggravated crime, as well as crimes motivated by hostility towards lesbian, gay, bisexual and transgender, and disabled peoples, the CPS consulted many community groups and representative bodies. Indeed, the CPS's approach to community engagement with respect to racial and religious hate crime has been recommended as a model of best practice and has been positively profiled in Whitehall (CPS, 2004). Illustrating the importance with which community engagement is viewed, the CPS has produced good practice guidance on community engagement, and the development of a strategic and sustainable approach to community engagement features in the CPS *Business strategy 2005–08* (CPS, 2005). One area that is likely to be progressively further developed by the CPS is that of community participation in the learning requirements, the design or the evaluation of CPS staff training programmes. Representatives from community and faith groups have already contributed to a national training programme on racially/religiously aggravated crime. With prosecution policies, alongside other programmes, increasingly targeted at a broader range of communities, as highlighted in Chapter Two of this book, this aspect to community participation is likely to play a growing role. Community scrutiny of the effectiveness of new CPS training procedures is also likely to take on a more significant role in the future through gaining feedback from local communities via, for example, the use of local surveys.

The probation service, now a branch of the National Offender Management Service (NOMS), has also turned significant attention towards community involvement in the work that it carries out. An important policy document was published by the National Probation Directorate in March 2003, entitled *The heart of the dance: A diversity strategy for the NPS for England and Wales 2002/2006* (NPD, 2003). Objective 5 in this document illustrates the importance with which work with communities is taken by probation, thus:

> **Priority objective 5: Communicating and connecting with local communities and working in partnership**
> **Aim:** the National Probation Service (NPS) ... to have significantly increased its profile and credibility amongst those groups;
> **Outcome:** the NPS to have built trust, confidence and close connections with diverse groups, communities and agencies, which reflect the local population;
> ...
> ... by 2006 the NPS would have established good models of consultation with minority ethnic communities. (NPD, 2003: 24-5)

The developments highlighted in the above paragraphs essentially reflect what Lash (1994) calls the pursuit of a 'representative democracy', whereby criminal justice institutions are opening themselves up to the communities that they serve, with the lay public engaging with, as well as critiquing, service priorities and provision. This approach also involves creating criminal justice agencies whose workforces represent the profile of the working population at both national and local levels, as the following section will elucidate further.

Community representation within criminal justice

A key strategy in enhancing public confidence in the criminal justice system, as set out in the government strategy document 'Cutting crime, delivering justice' (HM Government, 2004), is to create a criminal justice workforce that is diverse and more fairly represents the local community that it serves. The government's vision for 2008 is that employees working in the criminal justice system will be from a wide range of backgrounds, with high levels of job satisfaction. Given that staff surveys carried out by the CPS in 2000, 2002 and 2004 showed that action on equality, diversity and respect has a high positive impact on employee engagement and satisfaction (CPS, 2004), this clearly suggests that equality and diversity issues are central to achieving a criminal justice workforce with a high degree of job satisfaction.

The agency that has probably received most attention regarding the representation of its workforce is the police service. The government has signalled its commitment to create a police service that is representative of the general population, with a particular emphasis upon minority ethnic groups as a result of the Macpherson Inquiry into the death of Stephen Lawrence, alongside a HM Inspectorate of Constabulary report, *Winning the race: Embracing diversity* (HMIC, 2000), both of which gave heightened focus to the need for greater attention to be paid to the recruitment, retention and career development of minority ethnic police officers. In March 2003, 2.9% of officers and 5.5% of police staff were from minority ethnic communities. This represents a more than 50% increase in the number of minority ethnic officers since 1999. The government has introduced a target of 7.7% of all serving police officers in England and Wales to be drawn from minority ethnic backgrounds by 2009 (Home Office website 'Race relations and the police', www.homeoffice.gov.uk/police/about/race-relations/). Local police forces are also expected to reflect the percentage of the local minority ethnic working population in each particular area:

> It remains a fundamental challenge for the police service to ensure that the composition of its workforce is truly representative of the communities it serves. The Government's race equality targets commit police forces to achieving ethnic minority representation for officers and staff by 2009 in proportion to the economically active ethnic minority population in the force area. (Home Office, 2004a: 94)

However, in large urban conurbations such as London, Manchester, West Yorkshire and Leicestershire, where minority ethnic communities can make up a substantial proportion of the local population, and an even higher percentage of the working population due to the young age profile of these groups, police services have struggled, and continue to struggle, to meet their local targets. For example, the Metropolitan Police Service in London has argued that reaching its current target of 25.9% ethnic minority recruits is unachievable without exemptions from the current law (Harrison, 2006). This has sparked considerable debate about whether affirmative action should be pursued in order to recruit Black candidates proactively. Affirmative action is, however, illegal under racial equality laws in the UK and so new legislation would have to be introduced for this to be viable.

The CPS has been praised for the progress that it has made in terms of the make-up of its employees, which compares favourably with the Civil Service as a whole (HM Government, 2004). Of CPS staff, 13.9% are from Black and minority ethnic communities, 66% are female and 4.4% have disabilities (HM Government, 2004: 53). Nonetheless, the CPS acknowledges that at some middle-management and senior levels, the workforce is under-represented in terms of these categories of people. As a result, future plans include addressing these areas of under-representation by, for example, developing positive action programmes that target these groups (CPS, 2004). The National Probation Service has acknowledged that a disproportionately low number of Asian compared to African/African-Caribbean staff are employed, and so in *The heart of the dance* document (NPD, 2003), Objective 1.2.1 states that the National Probation Service seeks to increase the existing Asian representation by 20%.

Criminal justice agencies are also increasingly acknowledging the multiple subject positions that employees hold and the relevance of this for issues to do with staff recruitment and retainment. For example, according to a HM Inspectorate of Probation report (HMIP, 2004: 53), in the probation service, one-fifth of minority ethnic staff have indicated that they experience 'dual discrimination', meaning that they feel discriminated in ways not only related to racism but also in relation to other aspects of their identities, like their faith. A report by the Open Society Institute, *Muslims in the UK: Policies for engaged citizens*, further highlights the multitudinous nature of employee subjectivity, since the difficulties facing some Muslim women police officers are stressed, because they face competing demands and expectations in relation to their gender, ethnicity and faith identities, which might help explain their under-representation in the police service (Spalek, 2005). Promotional work undertaken by agencies of the criminal justice system aimed at encouraging under-represented groups to apply for positions is likely therefore to take further into consideration the complexity of people's identities when encouraging them to submit job applications. An increasingly sophisticated approach to recruitment is therefore likely to include a greater acknowledgement of the multiplicity of subject positions that employees hold, so that material promoting careers can more accurately reflect individuals' everyday lives.

Summary

As illustrated in the discussions mentioned previously, the notion of 'community' underpins, feeds into, and helps to build key policy initiatives within the criminal justice sector. In this way, the concept of 'community' holds significant political and ideological sway, and has had a considerable impact upon the policies and practices of all agencies of the criminal justice system, as well as other statutory bodies. Although agencies of the criminal justice system are developing policies and practices that are aimed at communities in relation to 'race'/ethnicity, gender, faith, sexual orientation, disability and age, and are increasingly acknowledging specificities within those groupings, it is important to highlight that the concept of 'community' itself is not neutral, but rather the ways in which it is constituted by government institutions and practices suggest that it is an ideologically loaded term, a form of nation building, underpinned by a particular viewpoint about the kinds of identities that should be legitimised within society, as discussed in more detail later.

Community as ideology

Hughes (2004) argues that the notion of community still has currency, despite the fact that the concept has become fractured and challenged in recent years. Indeed, according to Crawford (1997), community was the social buzzword of the 1990s. It might be argued that this is because the term 'community' constitutes a catch-all phrase, a kind of 'trump card' (Calhoun, 1994: 26), which enables policies to be developed, as this allows complex, at times fragile and unstable, and multitudinous social affiliations – which may have transnational and global dynamics – to be subsumed within its artificially constructed boundaries. As Calhoun (1994: 20) observes, 'The sheer scope and complexity of recognisable identities and competing identity schemes makes recognition problematic and in need of specific establishment in various institutional and interactional settings.'

As such, 'community' might be viewed as a kind of toolkit for central and local government, through which a whole myriad of identities can be unproblematically concealed and submerged, to help frame and achieve broader political goals. It is therefore unsurprising that community has been conceived and utilised by central government in rather an abstract way, so that specific communities are rarely mentioned or given very much detailed analysis. As Crawford (1997: 150) states, 'in policy discourse – what the community constitutes, its boundaries or the values and interests it prioritises are rarely explicated'. In policy documents issued by the Home Office the word 'community' and its plural are often used in a generic sense, and specific communities are mentioned only in passing. For example, in the Home Office (2003a) publication *Policing: Building safer communities together*, 'community' is referred to throughout, as in the following excerpt:

> We want a police service which enjoys widespread public support and
> trust, in all parts of the community, which reflects the broad diversity of
> British society … In short, we must transcend our traditional notions of
> policing by consent, and establish a new principle of policing through
> cooperation. This new methodology will only work if we empower
> local communities to engage in the common endeavour of beating
> crime. (Home Office, 2003a: 2)

According to the Home Office, civil renewal is the renewal of civil society through
the development of strong, active and empowered communities, in which people
are able to do things for themselves, define the problems they face, and tackle
them in partnership with public bodies (Home Office: 2004c: 2):

As illustrated in these examples, the word 'community' is referred to in rather
a repetitive fashion, and it might be argued that this unproblematic repetition
of an extremely complex term with multiple meanings constitutes ideological
processes at play. 'Community' itself is not questioned or explored, but rather, is
used to suggest forms of belonging, around which government policy can be
instigated and targeted.

It might further be suggested that the adoption and use of community in
government discourse can be linked to broader political concerns around creating
and symbolising nationalistic cohesion in the context of the fragmentation of
identities in late modern society. Community in this sense constitutes an imagined
community, which is created to 'fill the void left by the retreat or disintegration
or unavailability of real human communities or networks' (Hobsbawm, 1990:
46, in Colic-Peisker, 2004: 37). Added to this, the erosion of British sovereignty
and national identity, amid the mass migration of economic refugees and asylum
seekers (Betts, 2002), has created a deep anxiety within government to reinvent
notions of Britishness around which a sense of belonging can be socially
engineered.[4] So, when viewed from this broader perspective, it might be argued
that the myriad of references to 'community' scattered throughout many Home
Office policy documents and web pages constitutes ideological mechanisms
at play, taking on a symbolic role, in relation to attempting to build social
cohesion around an imagined grouping, thereby constituting a form of 'nation
building'. After all, imagery often plays a vital role in the formation of nations
and in nationalism (Smith, 1993). Indeed, it has been suggested that community
constitutes a 'feelgood word' and that it seems to carry the assumption that it is
a good thing (Hughes, 1998).

According to Edwards and Hughes (2002), in relation to crime control, the
ambiguity over what constitutes community means that in practice the strategies
of, and responsibilities for, crime control are a product of struggles between
different actors who hold different models about what constitutes community
governance, these being linked to their own particular agenda over the direction
that policies should take. At the same time, there seems to be an assumption

that more community automatically leads to less crime (Crawford, 1997), when this clearly may not necessarily be the case. Community engagement is seen as consisting of the involvement and development of partnerships between local groups and statutory and other agencies. However, partnership work can be problematic because it involves power differentials between the so-called partners, and so marginalised communities may not feel that they are actual partners in the policy process. At the same time, there are differences in the resources that are available to different groups, and different groups will have different sets of priorities so that there can be considerable tensions in partnership approaches (Crawford, 1997; Garland and Chakraborti, 2004). Furthermore, Foster (2002) argues that the capacity for communities to tackle crime and incivility can often be overstated, and so local authorities should work with community groups so as to empower them through fully taking on board their perspectives and concerns.

Community as consisting of active citizens

Community involvement in responding to crime and disorder is underpinned by the notion of 'active citizenship', initially used by the last Conservative government but then later developed by the New Labour government. Individuals, and the communities to which they belong, are being encouraged to identify and define the problems that they face and to put forward solutions to those problems. Individuals are viewed as having certain responsibilities, whereby people should be encouraged to offer their skills and knowledge to public service (Mawby and Walklate, 1994). Furthermore, all citizens, regardless of the inequalities that they may experience, can help to build safer, more tolerant communities, as the following quotation from the Home Secretary's Scarman Lecture suggests:

> I set out a philosophy of civil renewal. At the heart is a vision of strong, active and empowered communities – increasingly capable of doing things for themselves, defining the problems they face and then tackling them together. People should be encouraged to solve their problems themselves. (Home Office, 2003b: 1)

Active citizenship is an approach to governance that serves to depoliticise people because individuals are viewed as having civil citizenship rights, and not wider political, social or economic rights (Williams, 1999). Wider social and economic inequalities are often ignored so that individuals are largely viewed as being equal, and their obligations as citizens are emphasised rather than the obligations of state institutions (Mawby and Walklate, 1994; Spalek, 2006). This approach might be viewed as one that strips away collective and individual identities, as structures that produce and maintain inequalities – which will impact upon people in different ways according to the identities that they hold – are rarely acknowledged. However, if the viewpoint is taken that the social world contains powerful discriminatory norms in relation to whiteness, patriarchy and heterosexism (among others), then people's identities in relation to their 'race'/ethnicity, gender, sexual orientation, and so forth, matter. For example, in a world that privileges 'whiteness' there is little choice over the risks that a black person is exposed to in relation to race hate crime (Frankenberg, 1993; Lewis and Ramazanoglu, 1999). Similarly, in a patriarchal society, women often have to live with daily harassments and threats to personal security from male intimates, acquaintances and strangers, routinely having to engage in avoidance strategies in order to reduce their risk of being victimised (Hanmer and Stanko, 1985; Stanko, 1990). Unsurprisingly, therefore, individuals' self-identities often will influence the type of community work that they engage in. For instance, research exploring the volunteering activities of people belonging to minority ethnic groups suggests that people's ethnicities are important in the kind of work that they carry out (Britton, 2000). Similarly, it requires little imagination to suggest that faith is an important motivating factor for those individuals who undertake voluntary work through the religious communities to which they belong. However, within the notion of 'active citizenship', people's identities are largely forgotten, beyond the rudimentary acknowledgement of community, which is used as a catch-all phrase that subsumes specific identities.

The notion of active citizenship holds a powerful ideological sway as the construct of citizen as being devoid of 'race'/ethnicity, gender, faith, sexual orientation, disability and/or age identities contains assimilationist undertones, whereby all peoples are viewed as being homogeneous. Indeed, Back et al (2002) argue that in recent times public policy debate has taken on the assimilationist language of the 1960s, suggesting that although 'diversity speak' has proliferated under New Labour, the approach of building a nation through communities based on sameness rather than distinctiveness has been pursued. However, the 'active citizen', while being devoid of 'race'/ethnicity, gender, faith, sexual orientation, disability and/or age identities, is itself a constructed identity, an identity through which government can extend and rationalise control, therefore a legitimising identity through which government can formulate and propagate policy.

Community as both constituting, and being constituted through, legitimised identities

Individuals working together as active citizens thereby constitute communities of legitimised identities, so that it might be argued that the ways in which the notion of community is operated in the criminal justice system suggests that legitimising identities are actively engaged, encouraged, constructed and reconstructed, and that other, more radical, identities struggle to participate. Indeed, according to Crawford (1997), community is often seen as a homogeneous entity, silencing intra-community conflicts by marginalising those groups and individuals who voice dissent. As highlighted in Chapter One, power relations underpin all identity constructions, and so the work of Castells (2004) can be drawn upon here, proposing a distinction between three forms of identity building: legitimising, resistance and project identity. According to Castells (2004: 8), a legitimising identity 'has been constructed by the dominant institutions of society to extend and rationalise their domination vis-à-vis social actors'. Resistance identity is generated by those individuals who occupy devalued or stigmatised positions within society, who build 'trenches of resistance and survival on the basis of principles different from, or opposed to, those permeating the institutions of society'. Project identity constitutes the building of new identities that seek to transform society. For example, it might be argued that new social movements in relation to women or gay and lesbian communities have constructed project identities, since the claims-making activities of these movements has involved building new identities and challenging wider social norms, seeking to transform oppressive social structures. Castells (2004) also argues that identities that begin as resistance may bring about projects and may become dominant in the institutions of society, thus becoming legitimising identities themselves.

It might be argued that in the process of community engagement, two inter-related mechanisms are at play that suggest the construction of, and support for, legitimised identities. The first mechanism relates to the fact that within communities based on 'race'/ethnicity, gender, faith, sexual orientation, disability and age, there is considerable heterogeneity; however, community engagement is skewed so that community participation only involves certain factions whilst other groupings are almost totally overlooked. According to Crawford (1997), those groups that occupy less powerful positions or that constitute disorganised sections of society are, in particular, excluded from participation and partnership work. Indeed, those included in dialogue and participation often constitute the 'respected' and/or 'respectable' so that those groups that are seen as potentially 'troublesome' are often overlooked, marginalised or ignored (Crawford, 1997: 171).

Traditionally, dialogue has taken place with community leaders, who can, in fact, be out of touch with, or ignorant of the concerns of, those on whose behalf they are supposed to be speaking (Rowe, 2004). Community leaders are often middle-aged (or older) males who have no real comprehension of the viewpoints of younger community members or of females, whose voices may therefore remain unheard by those who are supposedly consulting them. Indeed, those individuals who are consulted may be those whose identities 'fit', that is, those individuals who largely agree with, and follow, government strategies and who do not overly or too vociferously criticise policies. An example that might be used to illustrate this point is in relation to community engagement with British Muslims. The Muslim population in Britain is very diverse. It is claimed that the Muslim community has 56 nationalities, speaks 70 languages and prays in more than 1,200 mosques, with there being about 7,000 Muslim organisations in Britain (El-Hassan, 2003; Khan, 2004). Muslim councillors, the representatives of local mosques or national organisations that claim to represent the wider Muslim community do not necessarily reflect grassroots concerns, so that there needs to be a more detailed exploration of the broader range of Muslim groups for consultation, including women's groups, which are often particularly marginalised. Women's voices may not be heard through usual consultation processes, and while men may act as a useful route into the women of their communities, they can also have a domineering influence (Todd, 2002), and so direct engagement with Muslim women's groups should be encouraged. At the same time, the voices of young Muslims are likely to be unheard and so greater attention must be paid to establishing links with Muslim youths.

When thinking about engagement with young Muslims, the issue arises of whether, how, and in what ways, should consultation and partnership work take place with those youths who are attracted to radical movements. With the British government being significantly concerned about the threat of terrorism from Islamist extremist groups, anti-terrorism provisions have been introduced banning non-violent parties that might hold viewpoints similar to those of people who engage in violence, with the Home Office creating a list of specific websites, bookshops, centres, networks and particular organisations of concern in the UK that are considered to be 'extremist'.[5] Within such a climate, it is difficult to see how engagement can take place, especially as the extent and breadth of anti-terror proposals not only might alienate the wider Muslim population, but also will significantly impede consultation with those young radicalised people who may share the same views as, and may previously have belonged to, those non-violent organisations that have been banned by government. So it is important to raise the issue of the extent to which engagement can take place with those Muslim individuals who criticise British foreign policy or who call for political unity amongst Muslims, particularly in the present political climate. It might be argued that many of those Muslim youths who are radicalised wish to engage with wider society rather than isolate themselves from it, thereby constituting 'project identities'. However, the danger of their non-participation and non-engagement is that these project identities might become resistance identities, due to government strategies that seek to isolate these groupings. It is also important to point out that project identities in general have rarely participated as partners with state institutions, rather, their interactions with government might be viewed as struggles over perceived injustices rather than community engagement as such. Radical social movements, based on 'race'/ethnicity, gender or sexual orientation (as well as other kinds of identities), are often marginalised by state officials, since they overtly criticise state agencies like the police or the prison service and seek wider social changes within society (Elias, 1993; Spalek, 2006).

For those resistance identities that are being expressed, there is little political will to engage with them, nor to encourage them to build project identities. Within notions of community engagement as practised by state agencies there seems to be little desire to engage with identities based on religious fundamentalism, white racism and various forms of nationalisms (Craib, 1998) that seek to separate themselves from wider society, perhaps because state institutions view these identities with suspicion and consider them to constitute 'a threat' to forms of togetherness that are attempting to be socially engineered. Yet it might be argued that engagement with these very groupings should be encouraged rather than to allow these identities to continue building resistance and separation from wider society. So it seems that government strategies should involve seeking ways of engaging with resistance and project identities, rather than to focus solely upon, and in this way help to reproduce, only certain kinds of legitimised identities. This leads on to the second mechanism that is at play in the process of community engagement.

The very practice of becoming involved in dialogue, and working, with state institutions may itself influence the formation and identities of those communities that are being engaged. For instance, in her study of Bosnian refugees who arrived in Britain in the 1990s, Kelly (2003) describes how access to such groups may often occur by way of organised community associations that may not, in fact, be representative of the views of such communities more generally. Importantly, Kelly (2003) argues that these associations may only be formed so as to 'conform to the expectations of the host society in order to gain the advantages of a formal community association, [although] the private face of the group remains unconstituted as a community' (Kelly, 2003: 41). This suggests that in some cases those communities that do engage with state agencies are not real communities in the sense that they consist of, and are underpinned by, shared meanings. Rather, these communities are formed to provide an appearance of unity, and to reflect legitimised identities, in the sense that those identities that are displayed are those that conform to wider societal expectations about what the nature of these communities should be. This point has also been highlighted by Prior et al (2006) and Barnes et al (2003, 2006), who argue that the ways in which 'community' is constructed for the purposes of engagement has been left largely unexamined. Also, the understandings that formal agencies themselves have of those communities that participate is a question that needs to be explored.

Critiquing community participation

Community participation can also be critiqued, particularly by drawing upon the work of Cook (2006). According to Cook (2006: 124), community participation might be thought of as consisting of five levels: information (involves telling people what is planned), consultation (involves offering some options, listening to feedback, but not allowing new ideas), deciding together (providing opportunities for joint decision making), acting together (different interests form a partnership to carry out what they decide is best to do), and supporting independent community interests (local groups are offered funds, advice or other support to develop their own agendas within guidelines). For Cook, community participation often falls short, so that the fifth level, supporting independent community interests, is rarely put into practice. Importantly, managerial imperatives and strategic decisions on what can and cannot be done influence the scope of community participation. Moreover, market research-type consultation is often used, which for Cook (2006: 125) 'masks a patronising and complacent attitude to service users'. Furthermore, it is argued that communities, particularly Black and minority ethnic communities, might experience consultation overload, and at the same time might feel let down because the issues that they have raised during consultation have not been responded or listened to (Cook, 2006).

Conclusion

The discussions presented in this chapter clearly demonstrate the complexities associated with the term 'community'. Community engagement, community participation and community scrutiny of performance are often repeated mantras to be found within criminal justice policy and practice, yet rarely is due consideration paid to the meanings associated with the concept of community. Communities are based on shared meanings, and they can be local, transnational and/or global in character. Moreover, in the context of late modernity, individuals' affiliations with communities are likely to be multitudinous, complex, fragile, as well as imagined. Nonetheless, the notion of community as conceived and operationalised within a criminal justice context tends to contain rather simplistic understandings, a kind of catch-all phrase that enables policy makers to develop and implement a range of strategies without ever having to face the difficult questions that are raised about engagement once the complexity of community is acknowledged. Indeed, this chapter suggests that the frequency with which community as an unproblematic concept, as a unity of belonging, appears in Home Office documentation suggests that this is part of a wider governmental strategy of building a national identity at a time when British sovereignty and national identity have experienced significant erosion.

It might further be argued that community participation helps to create and sustain legitimised identities, so that within the policy-making process those identities that enable government policy to be implemented, with little overt criticism, are precisely those identities that tend to be actively engaged. Project and resistance identities, on the other hand, who may seek more radical solutions to social problems and who may constitute more vociferous critics of state policies, are left out of processes of engagement altogether, and may therefore find themselves in power struggles over claims-making activities in relation to social injustices. This chapter suggests that consideration should be paid by government and state institutions to try to involve both project and resistance identities in community engagement strategies. This approach, however, raises some important questions about how, and the extent to which, it is possible to engage with resistance identities that may be based on building separation from wider society based on religious fundamentalisms, nationalisms or racisms. Despite the significant challenges that engagement with resistance identities (and indeed project identities) raises, however, it is important to stress that engagement should be actively pursued by government as a way of reducing further entrenchment and separation. It seems that within the context of late modernity, where belonging has become increasingly problematic and complex, reliance upon legitimised identities for policy implementation is too simplistic a strategy and the voices of those individuals whose sense of belongingness includes a sense of being on the margins of society should be actively sought out and included in engagement strategies. The next chapter focuses upon gender in relation to crime, victimisation and criminal justice, this being a social category that has generated substantial research and policy attention within the criminological arena.

Notes

[1] It is important to note, however, that diasporas existed long before modern technological development, as affiliations based on religion, ethnicity and transregional trading associations were commonplace before the establishment of the modern nation state (Kennedy and Roudometof, 2004).

[2] Governance here is taken to mean government institutions, structures, processes and practices, as well as objectives (Prior et al, 2006).

[3] The development of partnerships between the police service and other statutory and voluntary agencies has been a central plank of the government's approach to reducing crime. The 1998 Crime and Disorder Act gave local authorities and the police joint responsibility for the formulation of crime and disorder reduction strategies in each district, borough or unitary local authority area in England and Wales. Crime and disorder reduction strategies set out a range of objectives and targets to meet, which may include things like reducing youth offending, tackling drug-related crime and reducing the fear of crime (Spalek, 2005).

[4] For example, see the 2002 White Paper, *Secure borders, safe haven: Integration with diversity in modern Britain*, where former Home Secretary David Blunkett wrote: 'To enable integration to take place and to value the diversity it brings, we need to be secure within our sense of belonging and identity and therefore to be able to reach out and to embrace those who come to the UK' (Home Office, 2002: 1).

[5] Indeed, the Preventing Extremism Together Working Groups that were put together between August and October 2005, which held regular meetings consisting of Muslim representatives, criticised anti-terrorism provisions as excessive, badly implemented and vague (Preventing Extremism Together Working Groups, August–October 2005, ch 6: 77).

Chapter questions

How might we define 'community'?

How, and in what ways, might we view community as an ideological construct?

What difficulties does community involvement in criminal justice pose?

Case study
Engagement with Muslim communities post-11 September 2001

In an environment after 11 September 2001 and the 7 July 2005 London bombings, engagement with Muslim communities takes on particular significance, and includes an added dimension of counter-terrorism activities whereby Muslims are encouraged to work with state agencies in order to help combat extremism. Engagement strategies with Muslim communities might be conceptualised as containing both 'harder' and 'softer' approaches, involving national/federal and local dynamics, as the following diagram illustrates:

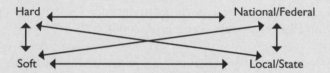

'Harder' approaches to engagement might be thought of as consisting of surveillance, policing and intelligence gathering, and therefore include the implementation of a number of anti-terrorism laws, with the expectation that Muslim communities are to work in partnership with the state in order to reduce the potential for extremism from within their own communities. 'Softer' approaches, on the other hand, might be viewed as the development of ongoing dialogue, participation and community feedback between Muslim communities, state agencies and voluntary organisations, which might serve to increase Muslims' trust of, and engagement with, state and other institutions. Such 'softer' approaches are often a direct response to a specific community need or priority and therefore are likely to have significantly higher levels of community trust and involvement than other forms of engagement. Also, policies developed to protect faith communities in general, and Muslim communities in particular, can be included here as these are designed to try and help alleviate any prejudice and violence that may be experienced by individuals.

Source: Spalek and Imtoual, 2007

Question
How, and in what ways, might 'harder' approaches to engagement with Muslim communities undermine 'softer' approaches?

References

Back, L., Keith, M., Khan, A., Shukra, K. and Solomos, J. (2002) 'The return of assimilationism: "race" multiculturism and New Labour', *Social Research Online*, vol 7, p 2 (www.socresonline.org.uk/7/2/back.html).

Barnes, M., Newman, J., Knops, A. and Sullivan, H. (2003) 'Constituting the public in public participation', *Public Administration*, vol 81, no 2, pp 379–99.

Barnes, M., Newman, J. and Sullivan, H. (2006) 'Discursive arenas: Deliberation and the constitution of identity in public participation at a local level', *Social Movement Studies*, vol 5, no 3, pp 193-207.

Bauman, Z. (2004) *Identity: conversations with Benedetto Vecchi*, Cambridge: Polity Press.

Betts, G. (2002) *The twilight of Britain: Cultural nationalism, multiculturalism and the politics of toleration*, London: Transaction.

Britton, N. (2000) *Black justice? Race, criminal justice and identity*, Stoke on Trent: Trentham Books.

Calhoun, C. (1994) 'Social theory and the politics of identity', in C. Calhoun (ed) *Social theory and the politics of identity*, Oxford: Blackwell, pp 9–36.

Castells, M. (2004) *The power of identity* (2nd edn), Oxford: Blackwell.

Colic-Peisker, V. (2004) 'Migrant communities and class: Croatians in Western Australia', in P. Kennedy and V. Roudometof (eds) *Communities across borders: New immigrants and transnational cultures*, London: Routledge, pp 29–40.

Cook, D. (2006) *Criminal and social justice*, London: Sage.

Craib, I. (1998) *Experiencing identity*, London: Sage.

Crawford, A. (1997) *The local governance of crime: Appeals to community and partnerships*, Oxford: Clarendon Press.

CPS (Crown Prosecution Service) (2004) *Addressing equality and diversity in the CPS: A stocktake report*, London: Equality and Diversity Unit, CPS.

CPS (Crown Prosecution Service) (2005) *Business strategy 2005–08* (Draft V1.3, 10 January), London: Equality and Diversity Unit, CPS.

Edwards, A. and Hughes, G. (2002) 'Introduction: the community governance of crime control', in G. Hughes and A. Edwards (eds) (2002) *Crime control and community*, Cullompton: Willan.pp 1–19.

El-Hassan, S. (2003) *A report on a consultation with individuals from the Muslim community*, London: IQRA Trust.

Elias, R. (1993) *Victims still*, London: Sage.

Foster, J. (2002) 'People pieces: The neglected but essential elements of community crime prevention', in G. Hughes and A. Edwards (eds) *Crime control and community*, Cullompton: Willan, pp 167–96.

Frankenberg, R. (1993) *The social construction of Whiteness: White women, race matters*, London: Routledge.

Garland, J. and Chakraborti, N. (2004) 'England's green and pleasant land? Examining racist prejudice in a rural context', *Patterns of Prejudice*, vol 38, no 4, pp 383–98.

Gilroy, P. (2002) 'Diaspora and the detours of identity', in K. Woodward (ed) *Identity and difference*, London: Sage, pp 299–346.

Hall, S. (1996) 'Introduction: who needs identity?', in S. Hall and P. Du Gay (eds) *Questions of cultural identity*, London: Sage Publications, pp 1-17.

Hanmer, J. and Stanko, E. (1985) 'Stripping away the rhetoric of protection: Violence to women, law and the state in Britain and the USA', *International Journal of the Sociology of Law*, vol 13, pp 357–74.

Harrison, D. (2006) 'We need positive discrimination to meet race targets say police chiefs', *The Telegraph*, 14 March (www.telegraph.co.uk/news/main. jhtml?xml=/news/2005/04/03/ncop03.xml&sSheet).

HM Government (2004) *Cutting crime, delivering justice: A strategic plan for criminal justice 2004–08*, Cm 6288, London: HMSO.

HMIC (HM Inspectorate of Constabulary) (2000) *Winning the race: Embracing diversity*, London: HMIC.

HMIP (HM Inspectorate of Probation) (2004) *Towards race equality: Follow-up inspection report*, London: HMIP.

Hobsbawm, E. (1990) *Nations and nationalism since 1780*, Cambridge: Cambridge University Press.

Home Office (2002) *Secure borders, safe haven: Integration with diversity in modern Britain*, Cm 5387, London: HMSO.

Home Office (2003a) *Policing: Building safer communities together*, London: HMSO.

Home Office (2003b) *Civil renewal: A new agenda* (based on the Home Secretary's Scarman Lecture delivered at the Citizens' Convention 11 December 2003), London: Home Office.

Home Office (2004a) *Building communities, beating crime: A better police service for the 21st century*, Cm 6360, London: The Stationery Office.

Home Office (2004b) *National policing plan 2005–08: Safer, stronger communities*, London: Home Office.

Home Office (2004c) *Impact: How community engagement is making a difference across government*, issue 2 (www.communities.gov.uk/documents/communities/ pdf/151828).

Hughes, G. (1998) *Understanding crime prevention: Social control, risk and late modernity*, Buckingham: Open University Press.

Hughes, G. (2004) 'The community governance of crime, justice and safety: challenges and lesson-drawing', *British Journal of Community Justice*, vol 2, no 3, pp 7–20.

Hughes, G. and Edwards, A. (eds) (2002) *Crime control and community*, Cullompton: Willan.

Kelly, L. (2003), 'Bosnian Refugees in Britain: Questioning community', *Sociology*, vol 37, no 1, pp 35–49.

Kempny, M. (2004) 'Cieszyn Silesia: A transnational community under reconstruction', in P. Kennedy and V. Roudometof (eds) *Communities across borders: New immigrants and transnational cultures*, London: Routledge, pp 116–28.

Kennedy, P. and Roudometof, V. (2004) 'Transnationalism in a global age', in P. Kennedy and V. Roudometof (eds) *Communities across borders: New immigrants and transnational cultures*, London: Routledge, pp 1–26.

Khan, H. (2004) 'Unite but follow me: The tragic comedy of Muslim representation', *Q News*, March.

Lash, S. (1994) 'Reflexivity and its doubles: Structure, aesthetics, community', in U. Beck, A. Giddens and S. Lash (eds) *Reflexive modernization: Politics, tradition and aesthetics in the modern social order*, Cambridge: Polity Press, pp 110–73.

Lewis, B. and Ramazanoglu, C. (1999) 'Not guilty, not proud, just white: Women's accounts of their whiteness', in H. Brown, M. Gilkes and A. Kaloski-Naylor (eds) *White? Women*, York: Raw Nerve Books, pp 23–62.

Mawby, R. and Walklate, S. (1994) *Critical victimology*, London: Sage.

NPD (National Probation Directorate) (2003) *The heart of the dance: A diversity strategy for the National Probation Service for England and Wales 2002-2006*, London: NPD.

O'Connor, A. (2004) 'Punk and globalization: Mexico City and Toronto', in P. Kennedy and V. Roudometof (eds) *Communities across borders: New immigrants and transnational cultures*, London: Routledge, pp 143–55.

Oo, Z. (2004) 'Mobilising online: The Burmese diaspora's cyber strategy against the junta', in S. Gan, J. Gomez and U. Johannen (eds) *Asian cyberactivism: Freedom of expression and media censorship*, Bangkok: Friedrich Naumann Foundation, pp 514–53.

Preventing Extremism Together Working Groups, August–October 2005, (www.communities.gov.uk/pub/16/PreventingExtremismTogetherworkinggroupreportAugOct2005_id1502016.pdf).

Prior, D., Farrow, K., Spalek, B. and Barnes, M. (2006) 'Can anti-social behaviour interventions help to contribute to civil renewal?', in T. Brennan, P. John and G. Stoker (eds) *Re-energizing citizenship: Strategies for civil renewal*, Hampshire: Palgrave Macmillan, pp 91–111.

Rew, A. and Campbell, J. (1999) 'The political economy of identity and affect', in J. Campbell and A. Rew (eds) *Identity and affect: Experiences of identity in a global world*, London: Pluto Press, pp 1–36.

Rowe, M. (2004) *Policing race and racism*, Cullompton: Willan.

Smith, A. (1993) 'The nation: Invented, imagined or reconstructed?', in M. Ringrose and A. Lerner (eds) *Re-imagining the nation*, Buckingham: Open University Press, pp 9–28.

Spalek, B. (2005) 'British Muslim communities and the criminal justice system', in T. Choudhury (ed) *Muslims in the UK: Policies for engaged citizens*, Budapest: Open Society Institute, pp 254–338.

Spalek, B. (2006) *Crime victims: Theory, policy and practice*, London: Palgrave Macmillan.

Spalek, B. and Imtoual, A. (2007: forthcoming) '"Hard" approaches to community engagement in the UK and Australia: Muslim communities and counter-terror responses', *Journal of Muslim Minority Affairs*, vol 27, no 2.

Stanko, E. (1990) *Everyday violence: Women's and men's experience of personal danger*, London: Pandora Press.

Todd, S. (2002) *Seen but not heard – Women's experiences of the police: Report of a collaboration between Thames Valley Police, Todd Consulting and the University of Surrey*, London: Thames Valley Police.

Ubayasiri, K. (2004) 'A virtual eelam: Democracy, internet and Sri Lanka's Tamil Struggle', in S. Gan, J. Gomez and U. Johannen (eds) *Asian cyberactivism: Freedom of expression and media censorship*, Bangkok: Friedrich Naumann Foundation, pp 474–512.

Williams, B. (1999) *Working with victims of crime*, London: Jessica Kingsley.

FIVE

Gender, crime, and criminal justice

Introduction

Gender in relation to crime, victimisation and criminal justice has stimulated much research interest and policy attention. Empirical evidence appears to show that sex is a key variable in relation to criminality, with most crimes being committed by men, and certainly with serious and violent crimes being predominantly carried out by men. Much debate has therefore been generated regarding women's criminality, whether the empirical evidence can be taken at face value or whether perhaps other processes are at play that serve to conceal women's true criminality. For example, some commentators have suggested that the crimes that women commit do not come to the attention of the authorities (Pollak, 1950). Whilst some studies have suggested that women are dealt with more leniently by the courts, others have indicated that women are treated more severely (Walklate, 2001). However, sex discrimination as a phenomenon has proved to be elusive to establish.

Criminology, a discipline of modernity, has very much been dominated by Enlightenment philosophy and the utilisation of science to explore crime and victimisation. However, when applied to women, apparently neutral, objective scientific research has been found to be underpinned by sexist assumptions, thus being a far cry from value-free research. Indeed, within criminology, offenders have been assumed to be male rather than female so that women offenders' experiences have been ignored, misrepresented and/or misunderstood. As a result, feminist researchers have challenged gender-biased distortions by using the voices of female offenders, and by focusing upon their experiences, to provide a more accurate picture of women offenders, their characteristics, their motivations and their contact with, and experiences of, agencies of the criminal justice system. However, this work has been criticised for viewing female offenders predominantly through a victimological rather than a criminological lens, for example, by viewing women as the victims of patriarchal institutions, so that women have constituted the criminological Other and their lawbreaking has not been viewed as real offending. Therefore, more recent positions have pursued an active engagement with the notion that women can be the perpetrators of crime, even violent crimes such as murder and infanticide (Davies, 2007).

Turning to the issue of victimisation, feminist work has questioned some of the male-orientated assumptions underpinning traditional victimological work, which has led to women's behaviour being judged and implicated in the crimes that have been committed against them. At the same time, the survey method as a way of capturing women's victimisation has been questioned, with many feminist researchers arguing that the survey method cannot capture women's everyday lives in relation to men (Walklate, 2001). The concept of a continuum of violence has been introduced by feminist researchers, whereby women's experiences of violence are perceived as consisting of a series of events that pass into one another so that each separate event is not distinguishable from the other (Kelly, 1988). This includes the wide range of abuse, intimidation, coercion, intrusion, threat and force that frames many women's lives, thereby highlighting the difficulty of approaching women's victimisation through a survey-based approach that tries to measure discrete events. Indeed, according to Walklate (2001), both national and local crime surveys incorporate a middle-class, male-based perspective in viewing crime as a clear, distinct event. As a result, both local and national victim surveys insufficiently capture the intricate nature of women's victimisation and the negotiation of their personal safety. For this reason, feminist researchers have carried out their own work on women's victimisation, using methods that have been underpinned by feminist research principles. This chapter highlights how feminist perspectives have helped to redefine violence as something that can happen in private spaces, between persons who know each other, so that women's experiences of domestic and sexual violence have been documented and used to influence policy-making processes. It is important to highlight, however, that a focus upon women, rather than men, as victims has helped to create the female as the norm through which to view victimisation, constituting men as the victimological Other (Walklate, 2003; Davies, 2007), thereby ignoring or marginalising their experiences as victims. More recently, research has documented men's experiences as the victims of crime, illustrating how men's experiences of crime can be gendered so that 'doing masculinity' can be an important aspect to the process of victimisation (Stanko and Hobdell, 1993).

A further issue raised in this chapter is that of there being significant diversity amongst women, this being an issue that reflects growing reflexivity within academia, paralleled by, and linked to, postmodern processes relating to fragmentation and fluidity of knowledge claims. Western feminism has been criticised for insufficiently taking into consideration differences between women, since a white, Eurocentric perspective has underpinned much feminist work, so that Black women have been overlooked through 'gender essentialism', the view that there is a monolithic women's experience (Harris, 1997: 11). The interconnected sources of women's oppression, relating to structures of race, gender and class, have not thereby been traditionally examined by white feminism. Nonetheless, diversity amongst women is increasingly being acknowledged by researchers, policy makers and practitioners. As a result, this chapter also includes some discussion of diversity amongst women, drawing upon research generated from work with minority ethnic women in particular.

This chapter also examines criminal justice responses to sexual and domestic violence. In particular, legal changes to the issue of consent in cases of rape are looked at, as well as the implementation of initiatives aimed at supporting victims of domestic and sexual violence. Community safety issues will also be highlighted in this chapter, where women's fear of crime and the management of their personal safety will be explored.

Gender and crime

A number of authors argue that crime statistics, alongside other empirical evidence, appear to show that sex is a key variable in relation to criminality (Heidensohn, 1985; Levi, 1994; Walklate, 2001; Davies, 2003). The vast majority of crimes are committed by men, and serious and violent crimes are also carried out predominantly by men (Heidensohn, 1985). Crime statistics produced by the Home Office, for example, show that in 2002 only 19% of known offenders were women (Home Office, 2003: iii). Self-report studies, in which people are asked if they have ever committed particular offences, show that fewer females than males admit to ever committing an offence. For example, according to a 1998/99 youth lifestyles survey, males were around two-and-a-half times more likely to have offended in the past year than females (26% compared with 11%) (Home Office, 2003: 3). Crimes that feature a high proportion of women are fraud and forgery (with 27% of those arrested being female) and theft and handling (with 22% of those arrested being female) (Home Office: 2003: iii). According to Davies (2003: 289), the economic crimes that women carry out include theft from shops, handling of stolen goods, welfare frauds and forgeries. The most common offences for women sentenced to custody in 2002 include theft from shops, wounding, robbery and burglary (Home Office, 2003: iii).

The number of women who are in prison is also much lower than the number of men. For instance in May 2007 whereas the male prison population was 75,940 the female prison population was only 4,400 (National Offender Management Service, 2007). However, it is important to note that between 1992 and 1995 the number of women prisoners rose by 57% (Carlen, 1998: xi), and that it seems likely that this rise is due to the increase in the number of women who are socially and economically deprived, who are more likely to receive custodial sentences; also, it seems likely that there has been an increased punitiveness shown by courts towards women (Carlen, 1998).

The small number of female offenders compared to male offenders has stimulated discussion about whether or not women are less prone to crime than men. Pollak (1950) suggested that women's offending is often hidden from view, consisting of crimes that are rarely recorded, such as prostitution, shoplifting and abortion. This claim has, however, been refuted, with researchers claiming that women do indeed commit less crime than men, particularly when considering violent crime (Box, 1983). According to Walklate (2001), while some studies suggest that women are treated more leniently by courts, other studies suggest that there is no chivalry but rather, women are treated more severely. For Walklate (2001: 42), 'such contradictory conclusions point to the complex way in which factors such as age, class, race, marital status, and previous criminal record interact with each other'. Thus, women's social and psychological characteristics, in terms of their class, race, mental health and family status, can influence judicial and sentencing processes. Carlen (1998) argues, for example, that women who have mental health issues, or who are socially and economically excluded, are especially likely to be imprisoned for non-violent types of crime that should not necessarily be responded to in this way. Therefore, professionals who work in the criminal justice system may morally judge women, particularly as female offenders have broken values that are associated with femininity in terms of women being perceived as being nurturing and caring individuals.

The finding that most crimes, particularly violent crimes, are committed by men has led some researchers to focus upon the construction of masculinity in order to try and explore why men in particular exhibit violent behaviour. Men have been conceptualised as acting out a range of masculinities, so that the notion of a single masculinity that all men aspire to has been challenged. According to Connell (1987: 87, in Jefferson, 1994: 12), 'hegemonic masculinity is always constructed in relation to various subordinated masculinities as well as in relation to women'. This approach captures both the variety of masculinities and their hierarchical ordering. According to Messerschmidt (1997), in contemporary western society hegemonic masculinity is defined through the paid-labour market, the subordination of women and heterosexism, which value authority, control, competitive individualism, independence and aggressiveness. Violence can therefore become a way of claiming or asserting one's masculinity (Connell, 1995). Indeed, according to Polk (1994), the largest grouping of male-on-male murders consists of killings that are the result of confrontations between men that begin as a contest over honour or reputation. Confrontational homicide is the product of men's willingness to carry out physical violence as a way of responding to threats to their manhood, where violence can also be used as a means of conflict resolution (Polk, 1994).

Masculinity in relation to white-collar crime has also been explored, as statistics also suggest that most white-collar deviance is committed by men. According to Levi (1994: 236), in England and Wales in 1990 the male-to-female ratio for those convicted in all courts was 3:1 for thefts by employees (mainly till thefts from shops), 9:1 for thefts from the mail and 4:1 for frauds generally. It may be that because women have achieved few senior positions within companies they have had fewer opportunities to commit white-collar offences (Messerschmidt, 1997). Corporate crime might also be considered as the product of masculinist values such as ambition, shrewdness and competitiveness. Many business texts and biographies of takeover battles include the metaphors of war so that intense social competition is transmitted via peer culture and then reinforced by training (Levi, 1994; Punch, 1996).

Feminists' critiques of criminology

In the 1970s and 1980s, feminists increasingly criticised criminology for its predominant focus upon men. Women writers like Smart (1977), Heidensohn (1985) and Carlen (1987) argued that while a significant amount of research had been conducted around male delinquency and criminality, only a limited amount of work had focused upon the area of women and crime. Moreover, where women were included, this work often contained gender-biased assumptions. For example, classical work in relation to Lombroso and Ferrero (1895), featuring female offenders, and then later work by Pollak (1950), contained hidden biases which meant that the experiences of women offenders had been sexualised and distorted (Smart, 1977; Heidensohn, 1985).

Female criminality has often been viewed as being determined by biology, women's hormones, their reproductive role, their emotionality or their deviousness. For instance, Pollak (1950) put forward a view that women are vengeful and deceitful, and aided by men's besotted chivalry. Women are driven to commit crimes by their physiology and their hormonal cycles. Pollak (1950) also argued that women are more devious than men, while men's criminality can be explained by greater strength and aggression. According to Heidensohn (1985), the experiences of female prostitutes have traditionally been misrepresented. Women have been portrayed as sexually deviant even though it would appear that in many cases female prostitutes are behaving rationally in that they are using sex as a way of providing financial support for themselves and their children. Indeed, Worrall (1990: 31) has argued that the economic and/or ideological dimensions to women's offending have been overlooked because criminality has been viewed as a masculine trait so that female criminals have been perceived as being 'not women' or 'not criminals'.

It is important to highlight that the sexist underpinnings of traditional work around female offenders can be linked to a positivist, scientific tradition that gained ascendancy during modernity. This tradition involved using the principles of evolution to create an evolutionary scale that placed males above females. This meant that women generally were viewed as being less advanced than men, and women offenders, in particular, were viewed as degenerate beings (Walklate, 2001). Heidensohn (1985) has argued that biased perceptions about women in terms of their criminality have proved to be powerful and long lasting. Furthermore, although the concealment of women, and indeed the distortion of women's experiences in social scientific research, has not been confined solely to criminology, as other subject disciplines have also marginalised gender issues and contained biased assumptions about women, feminist researchers have argued that the omission of gender from criminology is particularly significant because of the policy focus of the discipline. Thus it is important for researchers to turn a critical gaze towards the treatment of women by agencies of the criminal justice system, including the police, the courts and the prison system, particularly in light of the prejudices and discrimination experienced by women in these contexts (Smart, 1977).

More recently, Davies (2007) has suggested that feminists' portrayal of women as offenders has often been underpinned by an ideology of victimhood, whereby female offenders have been viewed as the victims of biased, sexist and patriarchal institutions, which 'encourages views of women as vulnerable and socially and culturally victimised'. This does not allow for a full acknowledgement of women as being the perpetrators of crime, including economic crimes and violent, interpersonal, offences. Davies (2007) argues that traditional feminist examinations of female offenders constitute a pro-women, rather than properly gendered, approach. This issue will be discussed more fully in the next section.

Female offenders

As highlighted earlier, traditionally, female offenders have received little research interest and female criminality has been viewed as the result of the actions of 'abnormal' women whose biology or psychology and/or rejection of feminine roles has led them to commit crime (Gelsthorpe, 1989). Female offenders have been viewed either as 'not women' or as 'not criminals' (Worrall, 1990). Since the 1970s, researchers have striven to challenge the assumptions and prejudices underpinning work about female offenders, and some of this work suggests that women can commit crime for similar reasons to men. For example, women who commit welfare claims fraud or robbery might be motivated by poverty and inequality; maintaining drug habits may also be a motivating factor behind women's offending (Carlen, 1990; Worrall, 1990). However, within criminological discourse and research the category of male has been conflated with the category of offender so that male offenders have constituted the norm through which deviance is viewed, thereby consigning women to the category of the Other (Davies, 2007). As such, few studies have explored women who have engaged in violence, whether this consists of stranger violence, domestic violence or infanticide, and, indeed, it has been suggested that focusing upon women who commit violence may have negative consequences for the feminist movement, and could lead to an anti-woman agenda (Davies, 2007).

Nonetheless, some work has involved an exploration of women as offenders where women's criminal activities have been fully acknowledged. For example, Davies (2003) has explored economic crimes as perpetrated by women, and has suggested that some women's motivations may be related to greed rather than to economic need. Other research here includes work in relation to women who have carried out robberies, and girls who have behaved violently (see Davies, 2007 for more details). Women are located within sites of relationships of trust that straddle society, for example as teachers, nannies or mothers, which can easily be exploited (Shapiro, 1990), suggesting that women's criminality should be taken more seriously. Furthermore, relationships of trust also underpin modern economic life (Fukuyama, 1996), and so women can also be engaged in white-collar crime, which involves an abuse of trust by the offender; however, little research has been carried out in relation to this issue. Therefore, Davies (2007) argues that: 'It remains a huge challenge to feminist criminological scholarship to consider women seriously as doers of crime rather than as the "criminological other" and to take on the subject of women as perpetrators.'

Gender and victimisation

Similar to early work on female offenders, research focusing upon women as victims has traditionally been underpinned by prejudicial assumptions about women. The founder of the (sub-)discipline of victimology was Von Hentig (1948) (see Mawby and Walklate, 1994; Zedner, 1994), who adopted a positivist (scientific) perspective, which included the discovery of factors that influence a non-random pattern of victimisation, a focus upon interpersonal crimes of violence, and the examination of how victims contribute to their victimisation (Miers, 1989). Positivist victimology was applied to women's experiences of rape, where it led to the suggestion that women are to blame in some way for the sexual violence that they experience. For example, when Amir examined police reports on forcible rape in Philadelphia, he categorised 19% of his sample of 646 rapes as cases where the victim precipitated the event (1971: 259). Amir (1971: 260) devised a typology of victim behaviour from the 'accidental victim' to the 'consciously' or 'unconsciously seductive' victim. He further suggested that his study refutes the belief that victims are not responsible for their victimisation, since he found that either consciously or by default some victims of rape precipitate the crimes committed against them (Amir, 1971: 335). These types of judgements about female victims can also operate in the criminal justice system. A 1982 documentary by Roger Graef called *Police* provoked a public outcry when it showed a woman who had reported a rape being interrogated by police officers, who asked her questions like 'Have you ever been on the game? How many times have you had sex? How many men have you had sex with? Can you count them on the fingers of one hand?'(Lees, 1999). Furthermore, domestic violence has not traditionally been viewed as constituting the 'crime problem', as it involves violence between intimates, and so victims have in the past received little, if any, help or protection from a male-orientated criminal justice system.

Feminist work has challenged mainstream perceptions of women as victims, highlighting the severity of the violence that may be experienced by women, helping to change work practices and the prejudicial assumptions underpinning agencies of the criminal justice system. Illuminating women's experiences of sexual and physical violence, abuse and harassment has been part of a wider feminist struggle to make visible women's experiences within social scientific discourses that have traditionally been gender blind (Cain, 1990; Kelly et al, 1994). Violence committed against women may not be reported to the police, nor relayed in generic national and local victimisation surveys. In an interview situation, women may not reveal the full extent of the violence committed against them because there may be children present at the time, or the abusive partner may be there; also it may be too distressing to talk about it to the interviewer, particularly where the interviewer is male (Hall, 1985). According to Walklate (2001), both national and local crime surveys incorporate a middle-class, male-based perspective in viewing crime as a clear, distinct event. As a result, both local and national victim surveys insufficiently capture the intricate nature of women's victimisation and the negotiation of their personal safety.

An important aspect of feminist work, seen as crucial to improving women's lives, has been the articulation of women's experiences of male violence. Women's lives are framed by the social structure of patriarchy, which might be viewed as consisting of male economic and social power, underpinned by the use of, or threat of, violence (Radford, 1992). By utilising research methods that are sensitive to women's needs and experiences, feminist work has thus uncovered previously hidden forms of victimisation, and men's power to define abuse has been challenged. The concept of a continuum of violence has been introduced by feminist researchers, whereby women's experiences of violence are perceived as consisting of a series of events that overlap and merge with each other (Kelly, 1988). This includes the wide range of abuse, intimidation, coercion, intrusion, threat and force that frames many women's lives. Another distinctive element of feminist work has been a focus upon women's agency, in other words, how women resist and manage their lives around violence.

Feminist researchers have criticised those traditional approaches to women's victimisation that view women themselves as precipitating the violence committed against them, arguing that these studies naturalise men's sexual violence. In feminist research, women are viewed as not just 'victims' who have violence committed against them; rather, they are seen as actively struggling against their material conditions, attempting to mitigate the harms caused by physical and sexual danger. For example, according to Dobash and Dobash (1979), battered women strive to improve their relationship with the abuser, particularly at the start of a violent relationship. Women also argue and defend themselves. Indeed, Stanko (1985) clearly illustrates how the avoidance of danger is an integral part of the everyday lives of most women. The notion that women resist and manage their lives around violence is thus a common theme in feminist research. This is why many feminist researchers have questioned the term 'victim', as this carries connotations of passivity. Although some women are killed by men, and some feel that some parts of their lives have been ruined by violence, many women nonetheless manage to reconstruct their lives, physically, emotionally and psychologically, and so it is argued that this aspect of the process of victimisation should be acknowledged through use of the word 'survivor' rather than 'victim' (Kelly, 1988; Lamb, 1999).

Of course, the predominant focus upon women as victims has meant that only a small amount of work has been carried out researching male victims. In so far as women's experiences have generated much more research interest, and the category 'female' constitutes the norm through which processes of victimisation are viewed, it appears that men as victims have been overlooked and consigned to the category of the victimological other (Walklate, 2003; Davies, 2007). The few research studies that exist suggest that men display gendered responses to crime (Newburn and Stanko, 1994). For example, in a study exploring the experiences of male victims of physical assault, male victims often articulated the need to be able to take care of themselves and their families. The victimising experience thus caused them to feel vulnerable, and this might be interpreted as an affront to their masculinity. At the same time, these men's responses to crime included fear, the development of phobias, a disruption to routine sleep and social patterns, hypervigilance and exaggerated startle responses, with some men indicating that they felt that the assault had radically altered their lives and, to some extent, their personalities (Stanko and Hobdell, 1993). Masculinity can also influence the support that is provided to male victims, and also how men relate to this support. Newburn and Stanko (1994: 163) have argued that the needs of male victims have often been neglected by service providers and this may be linked to an assumption that men do not need such support, as a result of the propagation of stereotypes around masculinity in terms of 'resilience', 'strength' or 'emotional independence'.

Davies (2007) suggests that more research is needed to explore gender and victimisation. This might include a focus upon different settings and the ways in which gender interacts with victimisation here, for example in the workplace, on the street, in school and so forth. Davies (2007) also argues that a gender agenda should take on board more fully the issue of men being victims, whether of street crime, domestic violence, stalking or sexual violence.

Gender and the fear of crime

The fear of crime is an area that has generated a substantial amount of research interest over the last 40 years. Data from national surveys, such as the British Crime Survey, consistently shows that while men are more likely to experience street crime than women (Mayhew et al, 1993; Mirrlees-Black et al, 1997), women nonetheless report significantly higher levels of the fear of crime. According to a 2001 Home Office Citizenship Survey, women were five times as likely as men to say that they never went out after dark (15% of women as opposed to 3% of men). Women were also more than three times as likely to say that they felt very unsafe if they did go out after dark (10% of women as opposed to 3% of men) (Prime et al, 2001: 2). The lack of a fit between risk of victimisation and fear of crime levels has led to the rationality of women's fear of crime being questioned, with researchers attempting to provide explanations for women's apparently high levels of fear, the so-called 'fear of crime paradox'.

One explanation that has been proposed for the high levels of fear measured among women is that women are physically and socially more vulnerable than men and so the impact of crime upon them is greater, hence their higher levels of fear (Skogan and Maxfield, 1981). According to Warr (1984), women's fear of crime is really a fear of rape, since many kinds of crime might contain an underlying dread that rape will also occur. Another reason for the different fear levels found between men and women is data bias, whereby there might in reality be very little difference between the fear levels of men and women, only that men might hesitate to admit to being afraid to survey interviewers (Maxfield, 1984: 39). The influence of the media has also been implicated, since some studies suggest that stories of victimisation have the effect of increasing fear levels among those persons who perceive themselves to be similar to those victims portrayed by the media (Skogan and Maxfield, 1981). Many crime stories feature women as victims since this has sensationalist appeal to the general public, and thus it is argued that these stories raise fear among women (Gordon and Riger, 1989). Similarly, crime reportage in the local press may induce fear in the local population, since local newspapers provide a rich source of information for local communities regarding the nature and extent of crime in their locales (Home Office Standing Conference on Crime Prevention, 1989). However, there is no conclusive evidence that mass media reports of crime have a significant impact on levels of fear of crime (Skogan and Maxfield, 1981; Shapland and Vagg, 1988).

The above explanations regarding women's fear levels are underpinned by the belief that women have irrational levels of fear because their fears do not correspond with their risks of being the victims of crime as portrayed in national victim surveys. Quite apart from wider debates around the ways in which fear of crime has been conceptualised and operationalised, and the questionable validity of making claims about the rationality or irrationality of fear levels (see Smith, 1986; Sparks, 1992; Taylor, 1996; Walklate, 2001), radical feminist perspectives have claimed that statistics in relation to victimisation do not reflect the true extent of women's experiences of violence, as crime surveys do not reveal the true extent of the daily harassments and threats to personal security that women have to live with from male intimates, acquaintances and strangers (Hanmer and Stanko, 1985). The extent to which women are attacked or harassed by men, both in public and private spaces, has led some radical feminist researchers to redefine fear of crime in terms of it being a fear of men for many women, thus: 'So how are we to interpret women's fear of crime? It is, we argue, an indication of women's fear of men' (Hanmer and Stanko, 1985: 369). It might be argued, therefore, that the 'irrationality' of women's fear is merely an assumption that gender-blind researchers have made. Once women's experiences are understood, it might be argued that it becomes apparent that their levels of fear are quite an accurate reflection of the extent of their victimisation and risk from crime (Stanko, 1987). However, according to Davies (2007), a number of writers have challenged the notion that all women are afraid and fearful of crime, with some studies finding that as well as there being fearful men, there are also fearless women.

A further dimension to women's fear levels may be anxiety concerning the responses that they receive from agencies of the criminal justice system when they report crimes. Feminist literature has highlighted the inadequacies of the criminal justice system in dealing with women's experiences of violence, particularly those relating to domestic violence and rape (Lees, 1999), and this has helped to give greater policy focus to women's victimisation, as the next section will elucidate further.

Gender and criminal justice policy and practice

Rape

National crime surveys such as the British Crime Survey undercount sensitive crimes, especially those that involve sexual violence, like rape. Victims may be unwilling to disclose details of very traumatic incidents to interviewers, especially when other people (the perpetrator even) may be present in the same room. Studies have found that women are much more likely to disclose sensitive information when the interviewer is female and specially trained, yet it is often too expensive to gender-match interviewers with interviewees when conducting national crime surveys (Myhill and Allen, 2002). Therefore, any attempts to count the extent of rape among the general population will only be approximations, and will under-represent the true prevalence of sexual violence.

According to statistics produced by the 2001 British Crime Survey interpersonal violence module (IVM), 7% of the women sampled had suffered rape or serious sexual assault at least once in their lifetime (Home Office, 2006). Furthermore, statistics from the 2001 British Crime Survey IVM suggest that 54% of rapists are current or former partners or boyfriends with only 17% being stranger rapes. Men's experiences of sexual violence are particularly undercounted, and research by Coxell et al (1999) suggests that almost 3% of men experience non-consensual sexual experiences as adults, and over 5% of children also experience such crimes.

Rape leaves a devastating psychological, emotional and physical impact upon victims. For example, women who have been raped commonly fear death at the time of the violence (Burgess and Holmstrom, 1974; Katz and Mazur, 1979). After the rape, many women will then fear being raped again and they may also have a fear of all men in general; there may also be a subsequent fear of sexual intercourse, a fear of pregnancy, a fear of venereal disease or of contracting AIDS (Burgess and Holmstrom, 1974; Katz and Mazur, 1979). Women who have been raped may suffer irritation to the throat as a result of forced oral sex, also vaginal injury or rectal pains and bleeding. Headaches, nausea and fatigue are also symptoms that have been documented (Burgess and Holmstrom, 1974). A study of 153 women who attended a sexual assault service in Newcastle, Australia between 1997 and 1999 reveals that non-genital injuries were found in 46% of the women examined (although these were mostly minor injuries) and genital injury was found in 22% of women (Palmer et al, 2004: 55). Women who have been raped may become pregnant as a result and this may lead them to undergo abortions or place their babies into adoption (Katz and Mazur, 1979; Russell, 1990).

Although most rapes are not reported to the police, the number of rapes being reported in Britain is, nonetheless, increasing. However, the conviction rate for rape has been falling, from 33% of cases reported to the police in 1977, to 7.5% in 1999, to 5.29% in 2004 (Home Office: 2006: 8). The low conviction rate is due to a number of reasons; for example, in rape cases where the offender is known to the victim there may be little, if any, physical or forensic evidence and no witnesses, and so the outcome of a trial may largely be the result of one person's word against another. Victims may also decline to cooperate with the investigative process due to a fear of being cross-examined or in some cases having the subject of their past sexual behaviour raised in court (Home Office, 2006).

Due to rising concern about the low conviction rate and also the low rate of reporting of rape, new policies and initiatives have been introduced into the criminal justice system over the last few years. These are double-stranded, consisting of changes to the law that increase the likelihood of gaining convictions in court, as well as providing victims with greater support. Researchers have documented the often-harrowing experiences of victims in court, particularly when being cross-examined by defence lawyers, because under an adversarial justice system, the victim is a witness to an alleged crime, a crime that is regarded as having been committed against the state. This work has highlighted how secondary victimisation is a common aspect of the experience of going to court for many victims, dissuading them from proceeding with their allegations, particularly in cases of domestic violence, sexual assault and rape (Ellison, 2000; Lees, 1999).

In June 1998, a report was published by the government, entitled *Speaking up for justice* (Justice, Victims & Witnesses Unit, 1998). This contained a series of recommendations for the treatment of vulnerable or intimidated witnesses in the criminal justice system, including those individuals who have experienced domestic violence and those who have made an allegation of criminal conduct that constitutes a sexual offence. Under the 1999 Youth Justice and Criminal Evidence Act, some of the recommendations in the *Speaking up for justice* report have been implemented. These include a ban on defendants conducting the cross-examination in person in rape and sexual assault trials (under Section 41), the installation of equipment into the courts to enable vulnerable or intimidated witnesses to give evidence via TV links, and the publication of further guidance to agencies of the criminal justice system, such as the police, to help reduce the burden upon witnesses (Home Office: 2001: 2). However, it seems that applications under Section 41 of the 1999 Youth Justice and Evidence Act are not made according to court rules and so an application is often made at trial rather than before a trial, meaning that victims will not know in advance whether or not they will be asked about their sexual history (Fawcett Society, 2004). At the same time, initiatives under the 1999 Youth Justice and Evidence Act to help vulnerable witnesses can be patchy, with victims highlighting that they arrive at court without the special measures having been put into place, causing them great distress (Fawcett Society, 2004).

In 2003, the Sexual Offences Act came into force, which contains for the first time a definition of consent as 'a person consents if s/he agrees by choice and has the freedom and capacity to make that choice'. Prior to this piece of legislation, if an offender could argue in court that they had an honest belief in the consent of the victim, even if such a belief was unreasonable, then they had to be found not guilty. The 2003 Sexual Offences Act sets out the circumstances whereby it is most unlikely that consent was given, for example where the victim was sleeping or was unconscious. In March 2006 the government launched a publicity campaign focusing upon the issue of consent in rape cases. The campaign was targeted primarily at men aged between 18 and 24, to raise awareness that there is a clearer legal definition of consent so that the consequences for individuals who do not ensure that they have the other person's consent before having intercourse with them might be significant. The Crown Prosecution Service has also implemented new rules on handling rape cases so as to try and secure more convictions, and specialist staff have received further training.

Wider-ranging changes have also been introduced into the criminal justice system aimed at helping the victims of rape. The public concern that Roger Graef's documentary aroused about the handling of rape cases led to a series of initiatives being implemented into police forces to handle rape victims with greater sensitivity, such as, for example, better police training, the appointment of more female police surgeons and the introduction of rape suites into many areas (Lees, 1999). According to Lees (1999), while these changes have improved rape victims' experiences, sexist attitudes nonetheless continue to operate within the police service, so that police officers may still wrongly believe that rape victims make false allegations more commonly than other kinds of victim, and police officers may 'no crime' cases, particularly in situations where the victim knows their attacker (Gregory and Lees, 1998). This example illustrates that new procedures and policies aimed at being more responsive to rape victims may not be sufficient to address their concerns, but rather, wider changes need to be made to the occupational culture of the police as well as other agencies of the criminal justice system.

Another important initiative to help rape victims is that of the setting up of sexual assault referral centres (SARCs). The first centre was established in 1986 in Manchester and in the early 2000s the British government funded the development of some more SARCs, which can be found in a variety of locations, including hospital settings. In the UK, SARCs focus primarily upon providing services needed in the aftermath of a recent rape. These services might include forensic and medical examinations (carried out by women), one-to-one counselling, screening for sexually transmitted diseases, HIV counselling, post-coital contraception and pregnancy testing and a 24-hour telephone information and support line (Lovett et al, 2004). Victims can be referred to SARCs by the police or they can also self-refer. In an evaluation study of SARCs carried out by Lovett et al (2004: 66), the majority of individuals using SARCs were women (93% of service users), and, moreover, most service users found the contact useful and positive. However, there are still too few SARCs available to victims and so not all victims of rape have access to the services that these centres provide.

Domestic violence

Domestic violence is a devastating and common crime. Results from the 2001 British Crime Survey self-completion module reveal that 21% of women and 10% of men have experienced at least one incident of non-sexual domestic threat or force since they were 16. Moreover, the presence of children in the house can almost double the risk of domestic violence for women (Parmar et al, 2005: 1). Domestic violence can be physical, psychological, emotional, financial or sexual and can leave devastating impacts upon victims. For example, victims may blame themselves for the violence that they are experiencing, and where there are inadequate institutional responses, and/or a cultural norm that stresses that women are largely responsible for the success or failure of human relationships, self-blame may be particularly acute (Dobash and Dobash, 1979; Hoff, 1990). Domestic violence also elicits a high level of fear in victims, with women reporting fearing their husbands and the likelihood of experiencing violence in the future. Women thus become nervous and expect future incidents (Dobash and Dobash, 1979). Victims of domestic violence who leave their homes may be thrust into poverty due to no longer having the partner's wages to rely upon. This is particularly acute when children are involved, since the woman will have to pay for childcare facilities if she goes to work.

In the 1990s policy makers became increasingly concerned with the issue of domestic violence and so the British government instigated a number of initiatives. In 1994 an inter-departmental working party on domestic violence was set up to promote a coordinated response to the problem at national and local level, and a ministerial group was also established to take forward the issue of domestic violence. A document, *Living without fear – An integrated approach to tackling violence against women*, was published in June 1999 (Home Office, 1999), setting out the government's strategy in relation to violence against women. A key aspect to the government's response to domestic violence is the development of a multi-agency approach, as it is recognised that victims have a wide range of social, economic, accommodation, safety, criminal and civil justice needs that require inter-agency cooperation between agencies like the police, housing associations, local authorities and victim support groups. The government has also launched a publicity campaign to raise awareness of domestic violence, which included the publication of a leaflet, 'Break the chain', which sets out the sources of help that are available to victims. Also, over 200 groups have been set up around Britain, operating different models of how to tackle domestic violence, which have been evaluated by researchers. These evaluations appear in a series of Home Office briefing papers under the heading of 'Reducing domestic violence: What works?' An example of one project that was evaluated here is that of the Merseyside Domestic Violence Prevention Project. This issued quick response pendant alarms to vulnerable women as identified by the crime prevention officer and the domestic violence prevention worker. At the same time, domestic violence victims/survivors were offered greater support. The evaluation concludes that the pendant alarms increased the physical and psychological safety of women and children. The alarms worked by preventing imminent assaults by women activating them; alarms also alerted the police for the removal of the perpetrator, and they also had a deterrent effect on the offender (Pease, Lloyd and Farrell, 1994).

Many victims/survivors of domestic violence are reluctant to cooperate with the prosecution of cases. Research shows that victims/survivors of domestic violence are often frightened of appearing in court and giving evidence against the abuser, especially when the abuser may be intimidating them physically or mentally in order to try and prevent them from pursuing a criminal prosecution (Bennett et al, 1999, in Ellison, 2000: 849). Rarely have offenders been prosecuted without the involvement of victims/survivors, even though the 1988 Criminal Justice Act allows prosecutions to proceed without the witness being in court. So, while the number of recorded domestic violence offences has increased in recent years, this has not been matched by a proportionate increase in prosecutions. Some police forces are beginning to pursue enhanced evidence-gathering activities in cases of domestic violence, particularly where the complainant is not likely to give evidence. This might involve obtaining detailed witness statements alongside photographic evidence. However, this approach is itself controversial, since it may be seen as disempowering victims (Ellison, 2000). A wide range of intervention projects aimed at assisting women to access information and advice, and also to help them to take legal action, have been developed (Parmar et al, 2005). Advocacy might involve representing the interests of women and negotiating on their behalf in a legal context (whether that is criminal or civil); it might also involve providing information and advice and safety planning. Specialist practitioners, referred to as advocates, support workers, victim workers, outreach workers or navigators, carry out a number of tasks, including raising awareness of the issue of domestic violence within local communities, liaising with partner agencies, building up trusting relationships with victims/survivors, and providing practical and emotional support, including supporting individuals through the court process (Parmar et al, 2005).

The 2004 Domestic Violence, Crime and Victims Act introduced new powers for the police and courts to deal with offenders and to support victims more effectively. This Act contains a number of provisions, including providing stronger legal protection to victims by, for example, enabling courts to impose restraining orders when sentencing for any offence (previously these orders could only be imposed on offenders convicted of harassment or causing fear of violence), making common assault an arrestable offence, and putting in place a system to review domestic violence homicide incidents, which draws upon key agencies in order to find out how to prevent future deaths (HM Government, 2006). The 2004 Domestic Violence, Crime and Victims Act also provides a victims' code of practice, which sets out the service standards that victims can expect to receive from agencies of the criminal justice system working in England and Wales. This Act also allows victims to take their cases to the Parliamentary Ombudsman if they feel that the code has not been followed by criminal justice agencies.

Women practitioners in the criminal justice system

According to Home Office figures, women practitioners make up 50% of probation officers, Crown Prosecution Service lawyers, magistrates, Crown Court, Home Office, Forensic Science Service, Department of Constitutional Affairs and Criminal Injuries Compensation Authority staff (Home Office, 2003: v). However, women are particularly under-represented in the police and prison services and in the judiciary, and they are under-represented in senior management positions. Women make up just 7% of the senior judiciary and only 7% of senior police officers (BAWP, 2006). While making up approximately 44% of the economically active population, women represent only 22% of police strength (BAWP, 2006: 3). According to a report by the Fawcett Society's Commission on Women and the Criminal Justice System, women police officers are concentrated in the lowest ranks; only five out of the 43 chief constables in England and Wales were women in 2004 (Fawcett Society, 2004: 9). A report by the British Association of Women Police (BAWP), *The gender gap*, highlights many ways in which the police service might become more inclusive of women officers in general, and minority ethnic women officers in particular (BAWP, 2001). Recommendations include the need for fully funded mentoring schemes for women police officers, the need to challenge lengthy residential training courses, and a greater use to be made of IT and distance learning packages, so that home study can be pursued. In conjunction with the BAWP, the Home Office launched a number of advertisements in the national press, designed to challenge misunderstandings about policing that women might hold, in terms of height limits, age and fitness requirements. Advertisements also appeared in several women's magazines, such as *Marie Claire, Cosmopolitan, Red* and *She*. These also featured female police officers discussing their careers and experiences (BAWP, 2001).

Spalek (2005) highlights the experiences of a group of Muslim women police officers. Muslim women police officers are, effectively, balancing a number of often competing demands and expectations placed upon them as a result of the multiple subject positions that they occupy, these being linked to their gender, ethnicity, faith, identity and professional roles. Interviews with Muslim women police officers suggest that within their own communities there exist cultural expectations about the type of work women should do, with policing carrying little status. This is further exacerbated by the low progression rates for minority ethnic women (BAWP, 2001). Out on the streets, Muslim women police officers face abuse from many angles. They report experiencing abuse from members of Muslim communities, whereby their loyalty to the community is questioned, because of a perception that they have 'betrayed' them by joining what is perceived to be a racist and Islamophobic police service. They also experience racist, sexist and Islamophobic abuse from members of the wider general public. They are also likely to be harassed for being police officers as they carry out their duties. While Muslim women police officers accept that this is an inevitable aspect to their work, the sexist, racist and Islamophobic abuse that they face from some of their own colleagues is intolerable. Women also report being discriminated against in terms of career opportunities and promotion. However, they are unlikely to proceed with formal disciplinary procedures as there is a low level of confidence in the effectiveness of these and there is the added fear that this might further stigmatise them. Other, more informal, types of support have been pursued through networks such as the Black, Asian and Muslim Police Association, as well as through networks for women specifically, such as the BAWP. In addition, alliances have been made with white senior police officers who are regarded as being 'sympathetic' to race and gender issues, whose help and advice has been sought. Some police services have introduced a policy whereby Muslim women can wear the hijab when in uniform carrying out their duties. However, interviews with Muslim women police officers suggest that they are unlikely to opt to wear a hijab in a working environment where they encounter sexist, racist and Islamophobic harassment. Indeed, allowing women police officers to wear the hijab may, in the absence of any adequate training about British Muslim identities in the police service, only serve to 'demonise' Muslim women further, as there is unlikely to be an in-depth understanding amongst police officers of the role of veiling (Spalek, 2005).

Policy, practice and diversity amongst women

The foregoing discussion highlights the importance of considering diversity issues in relation to women and criminal justice policy and practice. Indeed, western feminism has been criticised for insufficiently taking into consideration differences between women, since a white, Eurocentric perspective has underpinned much feminist work, so that Black women have been overlooked through 'gender essentialism', the view that there is a monolithic women's experience (Harris,

1997: 11).The interconnected sources of women's oppression, relating to structures of race, gender and class, have not thereby been traditionally examined by white feminism.

Nonetheless, diversity amongst women is increasingly being acknowledged by researchers, policy makers and practitioners. Population movements resulting from war, globalisation and economic deprivation can have a substantial impact upon practitioners' work as women arriving from different countries with different cultural traditions may have different needs and sets of experiences that need to be taken into account. For example, in a detailed survey of domestic violence as experienced by black women, conducted by Mama between 1987 and 1988, it was found that some men might invoke 'tradition' or 'religion' to justify their violent actions, and that some women were also battered through justifications that they were too western (Mama, 2000).Women also often referred to 'tradition', in that they had tried to conform to idealised notions of a dutiful wife. Extended families are likely to have a more significant role in minority ethnic women's experiences of victimisation, and these may sometimes intervene positively, although they can also make the situation worse (Mama, 2000). Choudry's (1996: 1) study of Pakistani women's experiences of domestic violence further reveals that the Pakistani women who took part in this project felt they faced dishonour and rejection within their own community if their marriages failed, and that language difficulties and restrictions of their personal freedom outside the family home made it very difficult for women to seek help from external agencies. Women with an uncertain immigration status may be prevented from accessing services and they may be hesitant to carry out any legal action against the offender out of anxiety that their right to remain in a particular country will be removed. At the same time, if a woman is new to a country then she will be unfamiliar with the systems of support that are available (Parmar and Sampson, 2005). According to the Fawcett Society (2004), women trafficked from another country for sexual or domestic slavery often are isolated and will fear having any contact with the authorities. Women in prostitution are also likely to have negative experiences with policing and so often will endure much violence without reporting this to the police.

Secular women's refuges may not be able to provide adequate support to individuals for whom religious frameworks of understanding may constitute a core part of their everyday lives. Ahmad and Sheriff (2003) argue that Muslim women may choose to remain in their abusive domestic environments rather than seek help from organisations that may view their religion with suspicion. Indeed, Muslim welfare organisations have found that the fact that they cater to individuals' religious and spiritual needs means that there is a large demand for their services from, for example, secular women's refuges, as spiritual support and guidance, including Islamic counselling, can be a huge comfort to victims (Ahmad and Sheriff, 2003). Mama (2000) cogently argues that cultural analysis is largely missing from work on domestic violence, yet the dynamics of race, class and culture frame women's experiences. A study by Neville et al in 2004 revealed that race and cultural factors contribute to post-rape recovery. Cultural attributions about why they were attacked were stronger in Black women than their white counterparts. The Jezebel image, a race–gender stereotype of Black women as sexually loose, which has been identified by Black feminist academics, appeared to be internalised by the Black women taking part in this study and identified as a reason why they were raped. Neville et al (2004) argue that the more powerfully that this image was internalised, the greater was the victim's self-blame, and the lower the level of their self-esteem.

Clearly, diversity amongst women is a key issue, and one that is only now beginning to be taken more seriously. Although this chapter focuses largely upon cultural and religious diversity amongst women, other differences also exist in terms of women's age, sexual orientation and so forth. Indeed, the Fawcett Society report (2004), *Women and the criminal justice system*, particularly highlights how women with disabilities have particular issues that need to be addressed by agencies of the criminal justice system, yet they are often marginalised. In Liverpool, an innovative project specifically helping vulnerable witnesses with learning disabilities has been developed, suggesting that disability issues will feature increasingly in criminal justice policy and practice; however, this area will be returned to in a later chapter on disability (see Chapter Nine).

Conclusion

This chapter has focused upon exploring gender issues in relation to crime, victimisation and criminal justice. The discussions developed here clearly show the relevance of gender to criminal justice policy and practice. Although traditionally, in terms of criminality, gender has been viewed through the lens of masculinity, and women have constituted the criminological Other, more recently, feminist work has included research and discussion regarding women as the perpetrators of a wide range of crimes. Similarly, although gendered work on victimisation has traditionally focused upon women as victims, more recently, men as victims have been acknowledged by researchers; however, much more work still needs to be done here.

With respect to the criminal justice arena, sexual and/or domestic violence has generated considerable policy attention. Crime statistics suggest that victimisation from sexual and/or domestic violence is extensive, and leaves a significant impact upon victims, and so in recent years policy makers have increasingly turned their attention towards these forms of victimisation. In Britain, the implementation of the 1999 Youth Justice and Criminal Evidence Act, the 2003 Sexual Offences Act, as well as the 2004 Domestic Violence, Crime and Victims Act, have led to a number of developments in relation to the treatment of victims by agencies of the criminal justice system as well as in court processes. However, a number of issues remain, including the extent to which policy developments have a positive impact upon victims, and whether more broad-reaching changes need to be developed. In particular, it seems that the identities and working cultures exhibited by agencies of the criminal justice system need to be further focused upon, as, despite the legislative changes that have been developed, criminal justice agencies may continue to operate according to somewhat rigid frameworks of understanding that contain gender-biased assumptions. Moreover, the lack of women holding senior positions within the judiciary and the police service should be further scrutinised and addressed. Diversity among women is also a key issue. Policy makers and practitioners are increasingly acknowledging differences amongst women, in terms of their 'race'/ethnicity, religious identity, their sexual orientation, disability or age. In future, this work is likely to take increasing precedence. The next chapter examines 'race'/ethnicity in relation to crime, victimisation and criminal justice where the relevance of 'race'/ethnic identities to criminal justice policy and practice will be highlighted.

Chapter questions

To what extent can chivalry help explain the low number of female offenders?

What contributions has feminism made to understanding female criminality?

In what ways is the criminal justice system inadequate when dealing with women's experiences of violence?

Case study
Kiranjit Ahluwalia

Kiranjit Ahluwalia, an Asian woman, set fire to her husband Deepak in May 1989 after suffering his brutality for 10 years. She was charged with murder and imprisoned for life. Her tariff was 12 years. It was at the request of her probation officer that Southall Black Sisters (SBS) got involved. SBS felt strongly that a miscarriage of justice had occurred and were given leave to appeal in September 1991 on the basis of the misdirection ground. At the appeal in July 1992, which was presided over by the then Lord Chief Justice, Taylor, the defence argued both provocation and diminished responsibility, both partial defences to murder.

Although the Appeal Court judges rejected provocation, they made a significant concession in the way in which provocation had been traditionally interpreted. They accepted the notion of cumulative provocation, which was an important plank in the defence of most battered women, and also accepted that the period of time that lapsed between an act of provocation and the defendant's response was not necessarily a cooling-down period but could be seen as a boiling-over period. However, Kiranjit won her appeal on the grounds of diminished responsibility. In the course of the SBS investigation it was discovered that a psychiatric report that had been commissioned by Kiranjit's original team had not been produced at her trial. The report clearly stated that she had suffered from endogenous depression at the material time. A retrial was ordered. However, the Crown commissioned its own psychiatric reports and decided to accept her plea on the basis of diminished responsibility. Kiranjit Ahluwalia was released in September 1992, three years and three months after she had first entered prison, to scenes of jubilation from the large number of supporters who had gathered outside the court.

Source: Southall Black Sisters Campaigns 2007 (www.southallblacksisters.org.uk/campaigns. html#kirinjit)

Question
In what ways does this case study serve to illustrate the power of feminist activity?

References

Ahmad, F. and Sheriff, S. (2003) 'Muslim women of Europe: Welfare needs and responses', *Social Work in Europe*, vol 8, no 1, pp 2–10.

Amir, M. (1971) *Patterns in forcible rape*, Chicago: University of Chicago Press.

Bennet, L., Goodman, L. and Dutton, M. (1999) 'Systematic obstacles to the criminal prosecution of a battering partner', *Journal of Interpersonal Violence*, vol 761, pp 10–36.

Box, S. (1983) *Power, crime and mystification*, London: Routledge.

BAWP (British Association of Women Police) (2001) *The gender gap*, London: BAWP.

BAWP (2006) *Gender agenda*, London: BAWP (www.bawp.org/assets/file/gaz%20mark2.pdf).

Burgess, A. and Holmstrom, L. (1974) *Rape: Victims of crisis*, Bowie, MD: Brady.

Cain, M. (1990) 'Realist philosophy and standpoint epistemologies or feminist criminology as a successor science', in L. Gelsthorpe and A. Morris (eds) *Feminist perspectives in criminology*, Buckingham: Open University Press, pp 124–40.

Carlen, P. (1987) 'Out of care and into custody', in P. Carlen and A. Worrall (eds) *Gender, crime and justice*, Buckingham: Open University Press. pp 126–60.

Carlen, P. (1990) 'Criminal women and criminal justice: The limits to, and potential of, feminist and left realist perspectives', in R. Matthews and J. Young (eds) *Issues in realist criminology*, London: Sage, pp 51–69.

Carlen, P. (1998) *Sledgehammer: Women's imprisonment at the millennium*, London: Macmillan.

Choudry, S. (1996) *Pakistani women's experience of domestic violence in Great Britain*, Home Office Research Findings 43, London: HMSO.

Connell, R. (1995) *Masculinities*, Berkeley, CA: University of California Press.

Connell, R.W. (1987) *Gender and power: Society, the person and sexual politics*, Cambridge: Polity Press.

Coxell, A., King, M., Mezey, G. and Gordon, D. (1999) 'Lifetime prevalence characteristics and associated problems of non-consensual sex in men: cross sectional survey', *British Medical Journal*, vol 318, pp 846–50.

Davies, P. (2003) 'Is economic crime a man's game?', *Feminist Theory*, vol 4, no 3, pp 283–303.

Davies, P. (2007: in press) 'Lessons from the Gender Agenda', in S. Walklate (ed) *Handbook of victims and victimology*, Cullompton: Willan.

Dobash, R. and Dobash, R. (1979) *Violence against wives: The case against patriarchy*, New York: Free Press.

Ellison, L. (2000) 'Prosecuting domestic violence without victim participation', *Modern Law Review*, vol 65, no 6, pp 834–58.

Fawcett Society (2004) *Women and the criminal justice system*, London: Fawcett Society.

Fukuyama, F. (1996) *Trust: The social virtues and creation of prosperity*, London: Penguin.

Gelsthorpe, L. (1989) *Sexism and the female offender*, Aldershot: Gower.

Gordon, M. and Riger, S. (1989) *The female fear*, New York, NY: The Free Press.

Gregory, J. and Lees, S. (1998) *Policing sexual assault*, London: Routledge.

Hall, R. (1985) *Ask any woman*, London: Falling Wall Press.

Hanmer, J. and Stanko, E. (1985) 'Stripping away the rhetoric of protection: violence to women, law and the state in Britain and the USA', *International Journal of the Sociology of Law*, vol 13, pp 357–74.

Harris, A. (1997) 'Race and essentialism in feminist legal theory', in A. Wing (ed) *Critical race feminism*, New York: New York University Press, pp 11–18.

Heidensohn, F. (1985) *Women and crime*, London: Macmillan.

HM Government (2006) *National Plan for Domestic Violence* (www.crimereduction. gov.uk/domesticviolence51.htm).

Hoff, A. (1990) *Battered women as survivors*, London: Routledge.

Home Office (1999) *Living without fear: An integrated approach to tackling violence against women* (www.womenandequalityunit.gov.uk/archive/living_without_ fear/index.htm).

Home Office (2001), *Measures to assist vulnerable or intimidated witnesses in the criminal justice system,* London: HMSO.

Home Office (2003) *Statistics on women and the criminal justice system: A Home Office publication under section 95 of the Criminal Justice Act 1991*, London: HMSO.

Home Office (2006) *Convicting rapists and protecting victims – Justice for victims of rape*, London: Office for Criminal Justice Reform.

Home Office Standing Conference on Crime Prevention (1989) *Report of the working group on fear of crime*, London: HMSO.

Jefferson, T. (1994) 'Theorising masculine subjectivity', in T. Newburn and E. Stanko (eds) *Just boys doing business?*, London: Routledge, pp 32–45.

Justice,Victims & Witnesses Unit (1998) *Speaking up for justice* (www.crimereduction. gov.uk/victims/victims30.htm).

Katz, S. and Mazur, M. (1979) *Understanding the rape victim*, New York: John Wiley and Sons.

Kelly, L. (1988) *Surviving sexual violence*, Cambridge: Polity Press.

Kelly, L., Burton, S. and Regan, L. (1994) 'Researching women's lives or studying women's oppression? Reflections on what constitutes feminist research', in M. Maynard and J. Purvis (eds) *Researching women's lives from a feminist perspective*, London: Taylor and Francis, pp 27–48.

Lamb, S. (ed) (1999) *New versions of victims*, New York: New York University Press.

Lees, S. (1999) 'The accused', *The Guardian*, 1 March.

Levi, M. (1994) 'Masculinities and white-collar crime', in T. Newburn and E. Stanko (eds) *Just boys doing business?*, London: Routledge, pp 234–52.

Lombroso, C. and Ferrero, W. (1895) *The female offender*, London: Fisher Unwin.

Lovett J., Regan, L. and Kelly, L. (2004) *Sexual assault referral centres: Developing good practice and maximising potentials*, Home Office Research Study 285, London: HMSO.

Mama, A. (2000) 'Woman abuse in London's Black communities', in K. Owusu (ed) *Black British culture and society*, London: Routledge, pp 89–110.

Mawby, R. and Walklate, S. (1994) *Critical victimology*, London: Sage.

Maxfield, M. (1984) *Fear of crime in England and Wales*, Home Office Research Study 78, London: HMSO.

Mayhew, P., Aye Maung, N. and Mirrlees-Black, C. (1993) *The 1992 British Crime Survey*, London: HMSO.

Messerschmidt, J. (1997) *Crime as structured action*, London: Sage.

Miers, D. (1989) 'Positivist victimology: A critique', *International Review of Victimology*, vol 1, no 1, pp 3–22.

Mirrlees-Black, C., Mayhew, P. and Percy, A. (1997) *The 1996 British Crime Survey*, London: HMSO.

Myhill, A. and Allen, J. (2002) *Rape and sexual assault of women: The extent and nature of the problem. Findings from the British Crime Survey*, Home Office Research Study 237, London: HMSO.

National Offender Management Service (2007) *Prison population and accommodation briefing* (www.prison.hmprisonservice.gov.uk/assets/documents/ 10002A7218052007_web_report.doc).

Neville, H., Oh, E., Spanierman, L., Heppner, M. and Clark, M. (2004) 'General and culturally specific factors influencing black and white rape survivors' self-esteem', *Psychology of Women Quarterly*, vol 28, pp 83–94.

Newburn, T. and Stanko, E. (1994) 'When men are victims', in T. Newburn and E. Stanko (eds) *Just boys doing business?*, London: Routledge, pp 153–65.

Palmer, C., McNulty, A., D'Este, C. and Donovan, B. (2004) 'Genital injuries in women reporting sexual assault', *Sexual Health*, vol 1, no 1, pp 55–9.

Parmar, A. and Sampson, A. (2005) *Tacking domestic violence: Providing advocacy and support to survivors from black and minority ethnic communities*, Home Office Development and Practice Report 35, London: HMSO.

Parmar, A., Sampson, A. and Diamond, A. (2005) *Tackling domestic violence: Providing advocacy and support to survivors of domestic violence*, Home Office Development and Practice Report 34, London: HMSO.

Pease, K., Lloyd, S. and Farrell, G. (1994) *Preventing repeat domestic violence: A demonstration project on Merseyside*, Crime Prevention Unit Series 49, London: HMSO.

Polk, K. (1994) *When men kill: Scenarios of masculine violence*, Cambridge: Cambridge University Press.

Pollak, O. (1950) *The criminality of women*, New York: AS Barnes.

Prime, D., Zimmeck, M. and Zurawan, A. (2001) *Active communities: Initial findings from the 2001 Home Office Citizenship Survey*, London: HMSO.

Punch, M. (1996) *Dirty business: Exploring corporate misconduct*, London: Sage.

Radford, J. (1992) 'Womanslaughter: A licence to kill? The killing of Jane Asher', in J. Radford and D. Russell (eds) *The politics of killing*, Buckingham: Open University Press, pp 253–66.

Russell, D. (1990) *Rape in marriage*, Indiana: Indiana University Press.

Shapiro, S. (1990) 'Collaring the crime, not the criminal: Reconsidering the concept of white-collar crime', *American Sociological Review*, vol 55, pp 346–65.

Shapland, J. and Vagg, J. (1988) *Policing by the public*, London: Routledge.

Skogan, W. and Maxfield, M. (1981) *Coping with crime*, Beverly Hills, CA: Sage.

Smart, C. (1977) *Women, crime and criminology: A feminist critique*, London: Routledge.

Smith, S. (1986) *Crime, space and society*, Cambridge: Cambridge University Press.

Spalek, B. (2005) 'Muslims and the criminal justice system', in T. Choudhury (ed) *Muslims in the UK: Policies for engaged citizens*, Budapest: Open Society Institute, pp 253–340.

Sparks, R. (1992) 'Reason and unreason in left realism: Some problems in the constitution of fear of crime', in J. Young and R. Matthews (eds) *Issues in realist criminology*, London: Sage, pp 119–35.

Stanko, E. (1985) *Intimate intrusions: Women's experience of male violence*, London: Routledge.

Stanko, E. (1987) 'Typical violence, normal precaution: Men, women and interpersonal violence in England, Wales, Scotland and the USA', in J. Hanmer and M. Maynard (eds) *Women, violence and social control*, London: Macmillan, pp 122–34.

Stanko, E. and Hobdell, K. (1993) 'Assault on men', *British Journal of Criminology*, vol 33, no 3, pp 400–540.

Taylor, I. (1996) 'Fear of crime, urban fortunes and suburban social movements: Some reflections from Manchester', *Sociology*, vol 30, no 2, pp 317–37.

von Hentig, H. (1948) *The criminal and his victim*, New Haven, CT: Yale University Press.

Walklate, S. (2001) *Gender, crime and criminal justice*, Cullompton: Willan.

Walklate, S. (2003) *Understanding criminology: Current theoretical debates* (2nd edn), Buckingham: Open University Press.

Warr, M. (1984) 'Fear of victimisation: Why are women and the elderly more afraid?', *Social Science Quarterly*, vol 65, pp 681–702.

Worrall, A. (1990) *Offending women*, London: Routledge.

Zedner, L. (1994) 'Victims', in M. Maguire, R. Morgan and R. Reiner (eds) *The Oxford handbook of criminology*, Oxford: Clarendon Press, pp 1207–46.

SIX

'Race', crime and criminal justice

Introduction

Issues in relation to 'race' and racism have generated substantial, and ever-growing, interest from and within a multitude of academic, policy and research contexts. Within criminological and criminal justice arenas, issues in relation to 'race'/ ethnicity have attracted much attention, particularly in the aftermath of the Macpherson Inquiry into the racist murder of Stephen Lawrence, which found the police service to be 'institutionally racist'.

The over-representation of Black people in prison, particularly those of African/ Caribbean heritage, has generated much research attention, under the so-called 'race and crime' debate. Here, questions have been raised about Black people's offending rates and any discriminatory treatment that they might experience at various points throughout the criminal justice system. Racial discrimination has, however, proved to be an elusive phenomenon to investigate and measure empirically, with a number of criminologists arguing that statistical evidence can never conclusively establish this (Reiner, 1989; Holdaway, 1997). Indeed, many researchers have highlighted the difficulties involved when collecting data about 'race', arguing that this is a social construct that is influenced by historical, social and political contexts that attach particular labels to particular groups of individuals at particular points in time. Information in relation to 'race' is therefore partial and incomplete and subject to many inherent biases.

The fluidity of 'race' as a concept has helped to fuel debate abut whether people's oppression must have a material basis, particularly in relation to class relations, or whether culture in relation to 'race' can constitute the material from which to experience oppression and from which to build resistance. For example, for Miles (1982), 'race' is viewed as an ideological construct that obscures economic relations of power (in Back and Solomos, 2000) so that class, rather than 'race', relations constitute the material basis of people's oppression. This position is largely reflected in the work of the left realists, who have argued that when looking at criminality amongst Black communities, social deprivation and a lack of political power are key factors (Lea and Young, 1993). On the other hand, for writers such as Gilroy (1993) and Hall et al (1978), 'race' can be viewed as a cultural resource through which social life is experienced and from which identities are built. According to Chigwada-Bailey (1997), African and Caribbean peoples have mobilised around their collective experience of racist treatment by agencies of the criminal justice system, particularly from the police and the courts. Asian groups, on the other hand, have been more involved in protecting their communities from racist, and other forms, of violence.

When examining criminal justice issues in relation to 'race'/ethnicity, it becomes apparent that there are many different knowledge claims about minority groups' experiences, and that, moreover, some claims predominate over others. Within official and administrative discourses, underpinned by an Enlightenment project, scientific methods of enquiry are pursued, involving the construction and the identification and the overcoming of the social problem of 'racism'. Knowledge claims that lie outside a scientific paradigm, such as those coming directly from individuals and communities themselves, based on individual and/or collective experiences, are of themselves judged to be less valid than those claims that are derived from scientific paradigms of enquiry. As such, communities' claims, if they are to be taken seriously by government representatives, need to be legitimised,[1] by translating their concerns into social science representations (which are likely to convey only partially these concerns as meaning may be lost in the process of translation), or when senior establishment figures highlight the concerns raised by communities themselves.

A deeper debate that runs through contemporary theorising and research around issues of 'race' relates to rising criticism of an Enlightenment project, as modernity itself is viewed as producing the suffering of wide-ranging peoples, including the Black diaspora. At the same time, growing reflexivity within academia, paralleled by and linked to postmodern processes relating to fragmentation and fluidity of knowledge claims, produces increasing concern about the limitations – as well as criticism – of contemporary knowledges about 'race' and racism. Widely used general categories, such as Black or Asian, have been criticised for being essentialist, grouping together individuals who may have little in common, thereby serving to obscure the experiences of particular groups of individuals. At the same time, the issue of the nature of the researcher's subjectivity has been raised and how this might help or hinder knowledge production around issues of 'race'. Whiteness studies have emerged, where researchers have reflected upon their subject positions in relation to whiteness and how this might impact upon the research process. Reflexivity can also be seen at an institutional level, in relation to the criminal justice system, whereby agencies such as the police, probation and prison services reflect upon, and engage with, issues of 'race', particularly following high-profile cases such as the racist murder of Stephen Lawrence and the racist killing of Zahid Mubarek in an English jail.

As can be seen above, there are many dimensions to 'race' issues in relation to crime and criminal justice. These will now be addressed in more detail in the discussions that follow. First, a short account of 'race'/ethnicity in relation to victimisation will be provided, as minority ethnic communities can experience significant amounts of crime, including burglary, assault, racial harassment and abuse.

Victimisation and 'race'/ethnic identities

Data in relation to the extent and impact of racist victimisation is generated through a number of different sources, including official crime statistics, national crime surveys, local crime surveys, local monitoring, action and support groups, and public inquiries. In Britain, under the 1998 Crime and Disorder Act, race hate crime legislation was enacted, which introduced higher penalties for offences that are racially aggravated. While the maximum sentence for common assault is six months and/or a £5,000 fine, the maximum for racially aggravated common assault is two years and/or an unlimited fine. Within this approach, the definition of a racist crime as proposed by *The Stephen Lawrence inquiry* (Macpherson, 1999 – 'the Macpherson Report') is used, this being, 'any incident which is perceived to be racist by the victim or any other person'. This indicates a significant shift in terms of police crime-recording practices, as police officers have traditionally used an evidential approach that seeks to corroborate allegations rather than automatically accepting victims' accounts. This approach might be viewed as having the potential to address widespread concerns that police officers can deny incidents that are motivated by racism, acting as gatekeepers, even though victims and witnesses are certain of their racist components (Rowe, 2004). According to Phillips and Bowling (2002: 583), police-recorded racist incidents have risen by 523% between 1988 and 1998/99, and this may be due to improved recording practices or greater confidence to report crimes to the police as well as the introduction of a victim-defined approach to racist crime. It is important to point out, however, that the definition of racist crime as an incident is problematic as this views racial violence as a one-off event rather than as an insidious feature of people's everyday lives, so that people are seen to lead largely crime-free lives that may, intermittently, be affected by violent or non-violent offences. Racist victimisation might be conceptualised more accurately as a process rather than an incident because it might be argued that victims of racist violence are often repeat victims, and so individuals' everyday lives are framed by actual, or the perceived threat of, racist acts of abuse and violence (Bowling and Phillips, 2003).

It is important to note that although there has been a significant increase in the number of racist incidents that are recorded by the police, recorded crime levels under-represent the actual extent of victimisation. National crime surveys are considered to constitute a more accurate reflection of the extent of victimisation since these surveys directly target households so that individuals may reveal experiences of crime that they have not necessarily reported to the police. It has been estimated, for instance, that the British Crime Survey (www.homeoffice.gov.uk/rds/bcs1.html) counts almost four times more incidents than police recording procedures (Koffman, 1996: 65). National crime surveys use minority ethnic booster samples since a sample of the general population will not contain a sufficiently large number of individuals of minority ethnic identity. National crime surveys suggest that people belonging to minority ethnic groups experience high levels of victimisation. For example, findings from the British Crime Survey show that Pakistanis and Bangladeshis are significantly more likely than white people to be the victims of household crime. They are also significantly more likely to be the victims of racially motivated attacks than Indians, Blacks or Whites (Clancy et al, 2001: 2). Findings from the British Crime Survey also indicate that more than one third of assaults directed against Asians and Blacks are considered to be racially motivated by respondents (Bowling and Phillips, 2003). Perhaps the high levels of risk of victimisation account for individuals' high anxiety levels about crime. Findings from the British Crime Survey 2001/02 and 2002/03 indicate that people from Black and minority ethnic (BME) backgrounds were more likely to have high levels of worry about burglary, car crime and violence than White people (Salisbury and Upson, 2004: 1). The impact of racist crime is particularly severe. Findings from the British Crime Survey 2000 indicate that a much larger proportion of victims of racial incidents said that they had been very much affected by the incident (42%) than victims of other sorts of incident (19%) (Clancy et al, 2001: 37). According to Bowling (1999), who carried out a study in North Plaistow in the London Borough of Newham, the victims of racial harassment reported feeling anger, shock and fear. Bowling (1999) further describes how victims might move house, might avoid certain places (for example, football matches, the pub), and they might invest in crime prevention techniques such as shatterproof glass and fireproof mailboxes. Collective responses to victimisation from within communities may also occur, such as the emergence of social groupings opposing racist organisations like the National Front or the British National Party.

'Race and crime': racial discrimination and the criminal justice system

Since the Home Office began monitoring for 'race'/ethnicity, statistics have consistently shown that Black, particularly African Caribbean, men and women are over-represented in prison (Shute et al, 2005). For example, on 30 June 2005 the prison population stood at 76,190, with 25% of prisoners identifying themselves as belonging to Black or minority ethnic (BME) groups. Of the male prison population, 14% were Black, 6% were Asian, 3% mixed and 1% Chinese and Other. Furthermore, 8.1% of the male prison population were Black Caribbean. Of the female prisoners, 19% were Black, 2% were Asian, 5% were mixed and 2% Chinese and Other; 9.5% of women prisoners were Black Caribbean. Foreign nationals also make up a significant proportion of the prison population, so that in June 2005, foreign nationals accounted for 36% of the BME prison population (Home Office, 2006: 86–7). This is a substantial proportion and suggests that foreign nationals charged or sentenced for importing drugs significantly influence the disproportionate number of BME prisoners. According to Kalunta-Crompton (2004), this is particularly the case for female prisoners. Thus, in June 1997, Black foreign nationals made up 80% of the UK's female foreign nationals serving a prison sentence for drug offences (Kalunta-Crompton, 2004: 13).

The high numbers of Black men and women in prison has inevitably led to questions being raised about the extent and nature of criminality amongst Black communities, and whether, and the ways in which, Black individuals might be discriminated against at various stages of the criminal justice process, as the following sections will explain.

Offending within Black communities

The contentious issue of offending among Black groups has generated much debate as well as social, political and media interest. As relations between the police and Black communities deteriorated during the 1970s, police statistics showed higher arrest rates, particularly among African Caribbean youth in London (Phillips and Bowling, 2002). A moral panic around 'mugging', underpinned by police perception of the Black population as being a potential threat to order and stability as potential trouble makers, fed into the aggressive and intimidating policing of Black communities, as vividly documented and portrayed in *Policing the crisis* by Hall et al (1978). More recently, attention has been turned towards Asian communities, with research focusing particularly upon young Asian men. While Asian men have traditionally been viewed by the authorities, as well as by wider society, as law-abiding and peaceful, more recently, and particularly in the aftermath of the attacks on the World Trade Center on 11 September 2001, young Muslim men have been viewed as constituting a 'problem group' (Alexander, 2000), as 'evil' and a 'fifth-column enemy within' by media, politicians, the security services and the criminal justice system (Poynting and Mason, 2006). The criminalisation of Muslim minorities is an area that will be addressed more fully in the next chapter, Chapter Seven, when faith identities in relation to crime and criminal justice are explored.

The issue of crime rates within Black communities has generated much research interest. In the literature, two positions can essentially be found here: critical and realist. According to the critical position, linking crime to the 'race'/ethnicity of the offender is damaging as this helps to propagate racist stereotypes that view Black communities as disorganised both politically and socially, since high arrest rates are due to police prejudice rather than high criminality (Bridges and Gilroy, 1982). Moreover, the police are to be viewed as an agency of imperialism, so that some members of Black communities are to be viewed as being engaged in an anti-colonialist struggle with the authorities (Sivanandan, 1981). On the other hand, taking a realist position, Lea and Young (1993) have argued that crime rates within Black communities must be taken seriously, because much crime is intra-class and intra-racial so that crime has a very real impact upon Black communities. Social deprivation and unemployment, as well as racial discrimination, can lead to a minority engaging in crime. For Lea and Young (1993: 124), 'the notion that some sort of cultural Geist accompanies immigrants from the colonies to the imperialist city and is directly available to the second-generation sons and daughters of immigrants born in the city is profoundly idealist'. According to Pitts (1993), higher levels of offending are associated with communities that feature the following characteristics: poverty, low educational attainment, and unemployment, as well as having a young age profile, and so 'race'/ethnicity may not be a significant factor. Critical and realist positions therefore differ according to the prominence given to issues of class or 'race'. Critical race perspectives firmly place 'race' as the primary framework through which to view experience and oppression, while realist perspectives, on the other hand, use class as the main framework of understanding, which itself can be criticised for having an understanding of 'race' issues that is partial and incomplete (Sim et al, 1987).

More recently, Phillips and Bowling (2002) have stressed that any statistics generated by criminal justice agencies only provide partial information about the nature of offenders because individuals who have been diverted from the criminal justice system are not likely to feature in any statistics generated here. Indeed, the vast majority of people who commit crime are never processed by the criminal justice system. As a result, arrest statistics, or indeed any other kinds of criminal justice-generated statistics, do not provide conclusive evidence that Black individuals are prone to greater criminality than their White counterparts, even though individuals from Black communities might be over-represented in these statistics. According to Phillips and Bowling (2002), self-report delinquency studies, in which individuals are shown a list of dishonest or criminal activities and are asked to indicate which activities they have engaged in, show rather mixed results. Some studies indicate that Black and White young people have similar rates of offending, whilst Asian people report lower rates (Bowling et al, 1994; Graham and Bowling, 1995; Ramsay and Percy, 1996; Ramsay and Spiller, 1997, in Bowling and Phillips, 2002). Other studies suggest that individuals from minority ethnic backgrounds might be more likely to conceal their offending; however, these studies have been criticised for their conceptual and methodological underpinnings (see Bowling and Phillips, 2002, for more discussion). Hence it would appear that although crime has undergone a process of racialisation, bearing testimony to the highly politicised and emotionally charged context underpinning issues of 'race' in relation to crime and criminal justice, no conclusive evidence exists that links 'race' to criminality.

Racial discrimination and the criminal justice system

The issue of racial discrimination in the criminal justice system has generated substantial research attention over the last 30 years or so. Racial discrimination has, however, proven to be an elusive phenomenon to establish. Some researchers argue that this is a result of methodological limitations in terms of using small sample sizes or grouping together different communities within broad classifications (Shute et al, 2005). Within this approach, therefore, is the implicit assumption that with the utilisation and adoption of better research methods, racial discrimination can perhaps be uncovered. Other researchers, on the other hand, argue that racial discrimination can never be conclusively established (Reiner, 1989; Holdaway, 1997). This is because it is argued that any statistical analysis is limited because the assumption that 'race' is a discrete factor – which underpins studies carried out here – is questionable (see Holdaway, 1997).

One study that appears to have proved racial discrimination in the sentencing process is a much-publicised project carried out by Hood (1992), who examined the sentencing decisions of all minority ethnic men appearing before five Crown Courts in the West Midlands and compared these with an equivalent sized sample of white men, consisting of 2,884 cases. 433 minority ethnic and white women offenders were also focused upon (Hood, 1992: 35). Hood's findings reveal that African Caribbeans made up 21% of those found guilty at Birmingham and 15% at Dudley Courts, although they accounted for less than 4% of the general male population in the age range 16–64. Asian males were convicted only slightly more often than would be expected in the population at large. Moreover, there were significant variations between the proportions of minority ethnic individuals sentenced to custody at different Crown Courts (Hood, 1992: 194). When factors such as the offender's previous criminal record or the seriousness of the offence were taken into account, Hood (1992: 199–200) found that the probability of a black male defendant being given custody was 5% higher than for a white male, with the probability in one Crown Court being substantially larger, amounting to an increased probability of 23%. Furthermore, Asian defendants who had pleaded not guilty received longer sentences than white defendants. Hood's (1992) study, therefore, points towards there being racial discrimination in the sentencing process.

Summary

The discussions above provide a snapshot of the kinds of debates that have taken place in relation to 'race and crime'. Critical race perspectives viewing Black criminality as being linked to colonialism and racist state institutions have been criticised as idealist by scholars taking a so-called 'left realist' perspective. However, left realists have also been criticised for focusing predominantly upon class issues and for their partial and incomplete understanding of race (Sim et al, 1987; Mawby and Walklate, 1994).

A large number of empirical enquiries have been undertaken to examine whether, and at which points, racist practices operate within the criminal justice system. The inability to 'prove' racial discrimination conclusively in the vast majority of studies has led to debates about whether or not racial discrimination as a phenomenon is open to statistical investigation. It might be argued that the adoption of statistical analyses and procedures to investigate racial discrimination reflects, and can be linked to, a positivist, scientific tradition, which gained ascendancy in the 17th century, under the social conditions associated with modernity (Walklate, 2003). Critical race scholars view modernity problematically, partly because modernity is a social era that caused the suffering of millions of Black people around the world. At the same time, Enlightenment philosophy underpinning modernity not only imposes borders upon knowledge but also legitimises some knowledge claims over others, as will be discussed in more detail below.

Minority experiences, knowledge claims and the project of modernity

The multitude of studies statistically exploring racial discrimination as a phenomenon bear testimony to the power of Enlightenment philosophy transcending the modern pursuit of, and claims to, knowledge, the implication here being that by using (better and more sophisticated) scientific methods so as to conceptualise and measure racial discrimination, then it might be possible to implement strategies that can be used to reduce and ultimately eliminate this phenomenon. It might be argued that this viewpoint, that racism and racial discrimination can be scientifically explored and then reduced, improved or eliminated, transcends criminal justice policy and practice. The use of race and ethnic monitoring procedures within the criminal justice system, the targets that agencies are expected to meet in terms of minority ethnic employee representation or in relation to boosting minority ethnic communities' confidence in criminal justice, and the search for uncovering and documenting direct and indirect forms of racial discrimination bear testimony to the belief that progress can be made in terms of reducing 'race effects', including racial discrimination, through the application of logical procedures that are underpinned by social scientific approaches and rationale.

Legitimising knowledge claims

It might be argued that the dominance of Enlightenment philosophy in policy – as well as in academic – arenas serves to legitimise those knowledge claims that arise from scientific approaches, as these are associated with the characteristics of objectivity and impartiality (Walklate, 2003) and therefore seen as 'real knowledge'. Claims that come from other sources, like personal experience, for example, are thereby delegitimised and consigned to the category of the 'Other'. In relation to the race and crime debate, criminological data has been unable to establish racial discrimination conclusively, even though individuals belonging to minority ethnic communities claim, on an individual or group/collective basis, that they experience discrimination and oppression (Philips and Bowling, 2002). Importantly, however, the dominance of the scientific paradigm within policy-making arenas means that communities' claims are somehow deemed to be less valid and less rational, and partisan in nature, than claims that arise from social scientific exploration.

In relation to racial discrimination, claims made by individuals or groups are in and of themselves judged to be insufficient for policy-making purposes. Claims must therefore be legitimised. One way in which claims are legitimised is when these are taken up by senior establishment figures such as those in the judiciary or members of Parliament. An example that might be drawn upon here is that of the Stephen Lawrence Inquiry, which heard accounts from local monitoring groups, churches and activists regarding experiences of racist violence, the weakness of the police response and oppressive policing practices (Phillips and Bowling, 2002). The claims of these groups/individuals were legitimised when Sir William Macpherson, a high-ranking judge who headed the inquiry, published his report (the Macpherson Report) in which he concluded that the criminal justice system is perceived by minority ethnic communities as biased against them, and that moreover, the police are institutionally racist. So it would appear that individuals' accounts can be legitimised when their claims are taken up by those who hold positions of power or respectability, who, it might be added, are often White.

It might be suggested that senior figures, in the form of senior members of the judiciary or the police or Crown prosecutors, represent and embody dispassionate, impartial, detached 'truths' so highly valued in western thinking. Claims that are made by communities themselves, on the other hand, are likely to be more emotionally charged, using graphic language that serves to convey the sense of human suffering that has been, and continues to be, experienced (Spalek, 2006). However, these claims are deemed as being partisan in nature so that it is the voices of so-called establishment figures that are more likely to be taken on board by policy makers and state agencies. These senior figures symbolically stand a long distance from the communities on whose behalf they speak, since in representing and speaking about communities' concerns, communities' emotions are largely filtered out and their experiences are represented in a detached manner; the 'figure in a suit' thereby symbolises and stands for the conquering of reason over emotion, thereby representing the Enlightened stance. As Walklate (2003: 35) observes: 'It is usual to associate positivistic "scientific" knowledge with that knowledge which is seen to be dispassionate, disinterested, impartial and abstract. These are values that are seen to be transcendent, that is, uncontaminated by the context of time and space.'

Indeed, a study of the civil service by Puwar (2000) illustrates how senior civil servants are represented as the pinnacle of rationalism and impartiality and how Black individuals lie largely outside the (White) norm. Furthermore, although communities themselves may directly try to assert their claims through forming so-called representative bodies or other organisations that try to influence policy-making processes, not all groups have equal access to those in positions of power. It might further be argued that those groups that adopt 'legitimate identities', where these conform to the wider expectations that government departments and other statutory bodies have of the communities that they supposedly represent, have better access to those sites where policies are debated and decided upon.

Another way of legitimising individuals'/communities' claims is through the use of social scientific discourse, in the form of written research reports, which may include statistical analyses. However, in the process of fitting individuals' accounts into social scientific frameworks of understanding it may be the case that certain knowledges are lost, misunderstood, reshaped or redefined (Edwards and Ribben, 1998). At the same time, social scientific discourse can serve to disempower people's claims through producing 'mixed' results that fail to substantiate their claims conclusively, which may be a reflection of the difficulty of applying a social scientific paradigm in trying to understand the social world rather than a reflection of the validity of individuals' claims. The discussion about the difficulty of establishing racial discrimination within the criminal justice system, as featured earlier in this chapter, bears testimony to the problematic nature of using statistical analyses to validate people's claims. It seems that people's claims are deemed legitimate in so far as these are substantiated by (mostly quantitative) research studies that show differences between the ways in which Black and White people are treated by agencies of the criminal justice system. However, it seems that individual or group claims can never be fully substantiated because although there will be studies that support their claims there will also be studies that do not support them, so that individuals' voices thereby become lost in a kind of empirical 'black hole'. The inability to measure objectively and conclusively to establish racial discriminatory processes has helped to move attention towards perceptions. People's perceptions are therefore emerging as the subject of policy attention. For example, a recent study carried out for the Department for Constitutional Affairs focused on investigating whether, and the ways in which, members of minority ethnic communities who had appeared in the criminal courts had perceived their treatment to be unfair or discriminatory and how this might have affected their trust or confidence in the criminal courts (Shute et al, 2005: 15). Among this study's outcomes, it was found that between a quarter and a third of minority ethnic defendants believed that their treatment by the criminal courts had been in some way unfair (Shute et al, 2005: 129).

Black critiques of Enlightenment

The above paragraphs suggest that individuals' voices and experiences cannot be viewed separately from the dominance of a positivist, scientific tradition, which historically gained ascendancy as modernity gained increasing ground. To be taken seriously by policy makers, as well as by agencies of the criminal justice system, individuals' accounts have to be legitimised through the construction of supposedly objective, if partial, 'truths', as represented by the voices of those symbolically representing Enlightenment (that is, senior establishment figures) or by being represented within social science research knowledge constructions. While it might be argued that improvements in data collection and analysis are needed so as better to reflect and represent minority communities' experiences and concerns (Bowling and Phillips, 2003), this position fails to engage critically with, and to deconstruct, the dominance of Enlightenment values, which serve to delegitimise individual and group, collective, claims. Moreover, the use of frameworks of understanding derived from, and being underpinned by, values associated with modernity is deeply problematic when researching Black (and other) communities. The application, and predominance, of a (social) scientific approach to 'race' is problematic when viewed from a perspective that actively engages with, and acknowledges, the harms caused under the guise of Enlightenment philosophy and the so-called 'civilising' process of modernity. Modernity has been linked to the creation of racial hierarchies that helped to institutionalise slavery through dehumanising those classified as 'racial others'. Indeed, although slavery ended in Britain in 1807 and in the US in 1833, the legacy of racist Enlightenment theories and approaches lived on through imperialism and colonial practices as constituted within Asia, Africa and the West Indies, and indeed stretched to white working-class groups in Ireland and England (Phillips and Bowling, 2002). Agozino (2003) highlights that classicism emerged at the height of the slave trade; however, although it challenged the arbitrary nature of punishment in medieval Europe, its principles and insights were not used to challenge the slave trade. Moreover, although the Enlightenment challenged the privilege of divine right, it denied that those colonised possessed the moral capabilities to reason about what is wrong and what is just (Agozino, 2003).

Not only have Black communities historically occupied a subordinate status – the 'Other' – in relation to Whiteness within and discourses linked to Enlightenment and the Age of Reason, but, moreover, as vividly portrayed by Gilroy (1993) in *The black Atlantic*, individuals belonging to the African diaspora have critiqued and rejected modernity and have used their own discourses, separate from modern western thinking, from which to practise resistance, and from which to account for their actions. Indeed, Wilmore (1999) argues that the Black Church has played an instrumental role in striving for Black people's liberation and for justice. According to Gilroy (1993: 68), a 'discourse of black spirituality' has been used to legitimise and choose death over slavery, which would appear to be at odds with logic and reason characteristic of western thinking in modernity, thus: 'The repeated choice of death rather than bondage articulates a principle of negativity that is opposed to the formal logic and rational calculation characteristic of modern western thinking and expressed in the Hegelian slave's preference for bondage rather than death' (Gilroy, 1993: 68).

Gilroy (1993) asks many important and interesting questions, including questions about the morality of the Enlightenment and the development of Black consciousness beyond Marxist relations. In the context of this chapter, Gilroy's (1993) work raises issues about the knowledge claims arising from, and being located within, paradigms endemic to modernity. These purport to be 'neutral' and 'value free' but are actually far from being these things and are, in fact, laden with assumptions about the world, which, under the guise of 'objectiveness', are underpinned by White perspectives despite giving the impression of being 'colour blind'. Within criminological discourse, characterised increasingly by self and discipline reflexivity, critical questions about the nature of knowledge claims are also being raised. For example, the emergence of pan-African issues in crime and justice as an area of study has included a critique of criminology as being orientalist. The next section will therefore focus upon contemporary criminological enquiry in relation to 'race'/ethnicity from a perspective of reflexivity.

Self and discipline reflexivity: 'Race'/ethnicity, crime and criminal justice

Reflexivity is becoming a characteristic feature of criminological discourse. Although the notion of reflexivity is often associated with feminist research, as feminists have played a leading role in highlighting the fallacy of so-called value-neutral or objective research so that feminist researchers have striven to articulate the often-hidden values and characteristics of the researcher and their impact on the research process (Harding, 1987; Edwards and Ribbens, 1998), reflexivity is evident in other research arenas. In the area of 'race'/ethnicity and crime/criminal justice, reflexivity takes on many dimensions. At one level, the usage of the terms 'Black', 'Asian' and, more recently, 'Black and minority ethnic' for the purposes of political action or as administrative and/or research tools when attempting to gain an understanding of 'race'/ethnicity in relation to crime and criminal justice, has been criticised for subsuming (and therefore overlooking the experiences of) many different identities and minority groupings. Reflexivity in relation to 'race'/ethnicity has also involved a focus upon researchers' subjectivities and how these interact with, and constitute a fundamental part of, the research process. Reflexivity has further included debates about the nature of criminological knowledge claims and the extent to which 'race'/ethnic identities are excluded from dominant discourses. Each of these dimensions to reflexivity will now be examined in more detail below.

Critiquing racial/ethnic categories

During the 1980s, 'blackness' as a concept referring to common political participation by non-white people gained hegemony within social and political contexts. In 1994, Modood critiqued the notion of 'blackness', claiming that this overlooked the needs and the distinctive experiences of Asian communities. Modood (1994) argued that 'Black' evokes people of African origins, thereby serving to exclude and 'otherise' Asian minorities. More recently, and specifically within, although not exclusively to, criminology – paralleling postmodern processes that stress the fluidity, fragmented nature and diversity of identities – the use of broad, 'catch-all' 'race'/ethnic classifications has been criticised. Terms like 'Black', 'Asian' or 'Black and minority ethnic'[2] when researching 'race'/ethnicity in relation to crime and victimisation have been criticised for serving to obscure the distinct experiences of specific groups. For example, Garland et al (2006) have argued that within widely used categories and labels, such as 'minority ethnic' or the increasingly popular term 'BME', are a host of 'hidden peoples' and 'hidden' forms of victimisation that have rarely received attention from criminological examinations of 'race and racism'. Phillips and Bowling (2003) have contested the term 'black criminology' as they argue that minorities in Britain are so diverse that they cannot be unified within this nomenclature. Phillips and Bowling (2003: 272) further advocate the formulation of minority perspectives in criminology that 'recognises and emphasises the marginal and excluded status of both visible and other racial and ethnic minorities. The term also allows a consideration of other minority groups' experiences as gay, lesbian, bisexual, transsexual or transgendered people'.

The use of very general categories in relation to 'race' and ethnicity within the criminal justice system has also been criticised for its potential to construct the lives of minorities as deviant. It has been argued that certain prejudices and stereotypes are contained within the labels 'Asian', 'Black' or the widely used term 'BME', with the implication that researchers should break down these categories and focus upon specific communities in order to dispel monolithic assumptions about minority ethnic groups. Thus, Phillips and Bowling (2003: 271) argue that a core component of the development of a minority ethnic perspective within criminology is the documentation of difference, consisting of a movement away from 'essentialist categorisations of racial and ethnic minorities'. However, this position is not unproblematic. One issue that researchers confront when carrying out work with hidden minorities is how to articulate the specific experiences of individuals who belong to wider minority ethnic groups without adopting a wholly relativistic position that loses the political power contained within umbrella terms such as 'Black' or 'minority ethnic', terms that highlight shared experiences of oppression that can help to generate anti-discriminatory policies and practices. Phillips and Bowling (2003) have advocated adopting a method that documents people's specific experiences but which acknowledges that aspects of these can be shared by other minorities due to broader structures of 'race', class, ethnicity and so forth – so-called 'unities within diversity'. Similarly, Maynard (2002) suggests that a cross-cultural approach should be encouraged, which has the advantage of enabling researchers to document how certain experiences are shared across communities, as well as allowing for differences to be acknowledged. It is important to stress, however, that when researching minority ethnic experiences, focus should also be placed upon the notion of whiteness, as 'Black' has traditionally been devalued and viewed as constituting the Other in relation to 'White' within western thinking, as well as in social and political practices (Collins, 1998; Bolles,

2001; McClaurin, 2001). This issue is linked to another aspect to reflexivity that can be found in criminological discourse: researcher subjectivities and how these can influence knowledge production about 'race'/ethnicity in relation to crime, victimisation and criminal justice, as the next section will explain further.

Researcher subjectivities

The question of whether minority ethnic researchers are best placed to understand the lived experiences of minority ethnic communities has been repeatedly raised by social scientists. Some argue that, even as 'outsiders', white researchers can legitimately study such issues, but that this requires active involvement with minority ethnic organisations and individuals in order to understand and portray their world-views and lifestyles (Gelsthorpe, 1993). Others, such as Papadopoulos and Lees (2002), argue that as 'insiders' minority ethnic researchers are better placed to do this work since they have greater awareness and understanding of minority issues and so can provide accounts of experiences and perceptions that are more genuine and legitimate. Nonetheless, to prevent minority ethnic discourses from being marginalised within social scientific disciplines, it is also maintained that white researchers should be encouraged to carry out work with minority ethnic groups (Russell, 1992; Rhodes, 1994). These positions, however, fail to take into account the multitudinous nature of subjectivity, so that it can be argued that researchers hold many different, sometimes conflicting, subject positions, and at different points in a research study different aspects of subjectivity may become more prominent and influence the research process.

Increasingly in criminological accounts of studies of minority ethnic groups some discussion of the multitudinous nature of the researcher's subject positions, and their epistemological influence, can be found. For example, Quraishi's (2005) work shows the complex ways in which different aspects of the researcher's self are routinely negotiated while a study is being conducted. Quraishi (2005) carried out research looking at the experiences of Muslim male prisoners in Britain, and showed that being a Muslim and a bilingual researcher of South Asian parentage enabled him to connect with some of the prisoners who took part in the project. A significant number of Muslims in prison are Black Caribbeans, however, and so when working with these prisoners, Quraishi (2005) emphasised common religious beliefs, as his ethnicity and linguistic skills did not correlate with these individuals. But when highlighting the different aspects of a researcher's subjectivity and their role in the research process, it is also important to examine critically those aspects that serve to perpetuate dominant knowledge constructions and power relations. This point has been developed by critical black feminists, within their notion of 'double consciousness' (Collins, 1998; McClaurin, 2001). This suggests that while some aspects of a researcher's subjectivity can help to document the previously hidden experiences of minority communities, other aspects of a researcher's subjectivity can lead to the misrepresentation of those experiences.

At any stage of a project, from the initial phase of articulating a research question and deciding on the sampling strategies and methods to be used, through to the analysis and writing-up phases, different aspects of a researcher's self-identity will influence the outcomes. Exploring which aspects of self-identity become dominant during research and examining the impact that these aspects have on the study being undertaken can enhance our understanding of the relationship between self-identity and research, and can highlight the micro-processes involved in perpetuating dominant knowledge constructions. Spalek (2005), for example, has explored her 'white' subject position when researching Asian Muslim women's lives in relation to the fear of crime; she argues that whiteness can place the researcher in a position of racial privilege, and can influence the way in which data is generated in a research study.

Critiquing dominant knowledge constructions within criminology

A focus upon 'race'/ethnicity has helped to fuel broader concern about the nature of criminological knowledge claims and the extent to which these reflect mainstream experiences and understandings, thereby serving to marginalise those perspectives and experiences of groups whose subjectivities lie outside dominant norms. For instance, Chigwada-Bailey (1997) has argued that feminist perspectives within criminology have not fully taken on board issues concerning Black women, who are over-represented in prison. Indeed, Black feminists have raised the issue of whiteness as a dominant, and largely hidden, norm that underpins research approaches and knowledge constructions. The invisibility of 'whiteness', whereby being white is not regarded as being a racial identity and a particular lens through which the world is viewed and experienced, but rather, is considered to be what is 'normal', 'neutral' or 'commonsense', has led to accusations that researchers have often ignored, misrepresented and misunderstood Black people's, particularly women's, lives (hooks, 1990; Harris, 1997). 'Whiteness' is thus seen as universal and devoid of any particularity, thereby serving to legitimise white power and privilege. As a result, academic discourse is increasingly featuring a focus upon, and making visible, 'whiteness' (Wiegman, 1999).

Another emerging area within criminology is that of pan-African issues in relation to crime and justice. Here, a critique of criminology as orientalist can be found, where orientalism is viewed as the tendency to negativise or idealise the practices of non-western nations (Cain, 2000). Kalunta-Crompton (2004: 5) further argues that 'mainstream criminological knowledge as we know it is reflective of a western view of the social world. It represents a hegemonic position of western conceptualisation of crime, criminality and criminal justice'. Kalunta-Crompton (2004) maintains that the voices of Africans are marginalised from criminological discourse. African perspectives not only have much to offer criminological knowledge, but, moreover, concepts developed within criminological discourse are not necessarily applicable to an African or Caribbean context, yet may be exported because of the hegemony of western criminology. Therefore, more attention should be paid to the significance of cultural relativity as well as 'the existence of a strong African cultural base from which alternative theorising can emerge' (Kalunta–Crompton, 2004: 18). A further critique of criminological discourse appears to be emerging from some researchers who have carried out work concerning Muslim communities in relation to crime and criminal justice, who stress the difficulties of including a focus upon faith identities within a secular discipline. For instance, Quraishi (2005) has placed Muslim identities at the centre of his comparative analysis of the crime and victimisation experiences of South Asians living in Haslingden, Yorkshire, and Karachi in Pakistan. According to Quraishi (2005: 116), there is a shared sense of victimisation amongst the South Asian Muslims taking part in his study, this being linked to the concept of the ummah, which consists of the individual, community and global Muslim population, so that religious oppression and Islamophobia constitute important aspects to Muslims' perceptions as oppressed minorities. This work highlights the relevance of faith identities, and more specifically Muslim identities, to experiences of crime and victimisation. The emergence of Muslim identities poses some key issues in relation to knowledge constructions for criminology, potentially heralding new areas of research and novel ways of carrying out research. This area will be returned to in more detail in Chapter Seven, where faith communities are specifically focused upon.

Institutional reflexivity, 'race'/ethnicity and criminal justice

Reflexivity can also be seen within the criminal justice system, whereby agencies are increasingly reflecting upon their policies and practices in order to attempt to minimise those harms, and to intervene on issues, relating to 'race'/ethnicity. This aspect to the work that agencies of the criminal justice system undertake is large and ever-expanding, and includes: the racial/ethnic monitoring of policies/ practices; the acknowledgement of racial (both individual and institutional) discrimination and the implementation of new policies and procedures aimed at reducing this; a focus upon the minority ethnic/racial composition of the criminal justice workforce; a focus upon the promotion and retention of minority ethnic staff and a concern to engage with members of minority ethnic groups.

Reflexivity as a feature of the criminal justice system can be evidenced by the ways in which the police, prison, probation and Crown Prosecution services are regularly monitored and inspected for their performances in relation to 'race'/ ethnicity. For instance, the HM Inspectorate of Constabulary report (HMIC, 2000), *Winning the race*, gave heightened focus to the need for greater attention to be paid to the recruitment, retention and career development of minority ethnic police officers. In relation to probation, the HM Inspectorate of Probation report, *Towards race equality* (HMIP, 2004: 41) highlighted that by 2001 the minority representation on probation boards was 16% of the total board membership.

This report also referred to the selection of 18 minority ethnic probation board members to act as diversity advisers to all probation boards. According to the Crown Prosecution Service (CPS) *Addressing equality and diversity in the CPS* report (2004a: 50), most community engagement to date can be described as public relations and the provision of information, with there being less evidence of active community involvement in CPS work. These kinds of reports can often be directly downloaded from the internet and they illustrate how criminal justice agencies reflect upon the part that they may play in perpetuating direct and indirect racial discrimination.

Policing

When discussing institutional reflexivity in relation to race/ethnicity and policing, probably the single most important event which added political impetus to the implementation of new policies and practices is the racist murder of 18-year-old Stephen Lawrence on 22 April 1993, in Eltham, South London. Stephen was walking home with his friend, Duwayne Brooks, when they were attacked, without provocation, by white youths, one of whom shouted racist chants as he approached. Stephen Lawrence received two serious stab wounds and died before an ambulance managed to arrive at the scene. Two police officers who arrived at the scene did not offer Stephen any first aid treatment. A public inquiry, led by Sir William Macpherson, found the police to be institutionally racist, which was defined as:

> The collective failure of an organisation to provide an appropriate and professional service to people because of their colour, culture or ethnic origin. It can be seen or detected in processes, attitudes and behaviour which amount to discrimination through unwitting prejudice, ignorance, thoughtlessness and racist stereotyping which disadvantages minority ethnic people. (Macpherson, 1999: 6.34)

Institutional racism might be considered as distinct from individual racism as this places more emphasis upon the outcomes of procedures rather than focusing upon individual intent. Therefore, the focus here is upon police service practices rather than the actions of racist police officers (Rowe, 2004). Rowe (2004) argues that the Macpherson Report, which stemmed from the inquiry, is significant because it provided the political impetus through and from which to develop a wide range of policies and initiatives, including improving minority ethnic communities' trust and confidence in the police service, reducing racism within the police service, establishing a greater representation of minority ethnic police officers, looking at retention and promotion issues of minority ethnic staff, and increased and improved race relations training for officers (see Rowe, 2004 for more details). However, there has been some criticism and questioning of these policy developments. For example, there seems to have been an assumption that better police–community relations will flow from an improved representation of minority ethnic groups within the police service. However, police occupational culture may transcend the ethnic (or other) identity of police officers and so minority ethnic police officers may not necessarily employ different tactics from those of their White counterparts (Holdaway, 1996; Rowe, 2004). In relation to police stop-and-search patterns, the continued over-representation of minority ethnic groups, in spite of the Macpherson Report, might suggest that the recommendations stemming from the report have had a negligible impact upon police officers' behaviour. At the same time, however, it is important to point out that some studies appear to indicate that when the ethnic composition of the available population rather than the residential population of a particular area is taken into account then there appears to be no general pattern of racial bias in stop-and-search tactics. Of further note, Fitzgerald (1999) has argued that minority ethnic people are perhaps more likely to be outside in public spaces and therefore more visible to the police because of school exclusion or unemployment or due to a greater tendency to socialise in public space (see Rowe, 2004 for a further discussion of these issues).

Probation

Issues in relation to 'race'/ethnicity have gained increasing prominence within the probation service (now a part of the National Offender Management Service). Following the inquiry into the murder of Stephen Lawrence, HM Inspectorate of Probation published a thematic report entitled *Towards race equality* in June 2000 (HMIC, 2000). The report examined the extent to which the probation service promoted and achieved race equality in employment practices and work with offenders. It contained 19 recommendations that addressed policy development, improving the quality of service delivery to offenders, the recruitment and training of staff and performance monitoring. Its publication led to the formulation of a national action plan. Other important developments include: the National Probation Directorate's publication of *A new choreography*, which was issued in August 2001, the 2000 Race Relations Amendment Act, the publication of *The heart of the dance* by the National Probation Directorate in March 2003 (NPD, 2003) and, more recently, the 2004 follow-up inspection by the HM Inspectorate of Probation, *Towards race equality* (HMIP, 2004), which examined the extent to which the recommendations of the early report (HMIP, 2000) had been implemented. The pursuit of race equality issues has led to the development of a number of important initiatives, such as the implementation of specialist projects for Black and Asian offenders, the promotion of examples of good practice for race equality and the development of links with local minority ethnic communities.

Prisons

Racism within prisons has attracted growing concern amongst policy makers and academics (Genders and Player, 1989; Penal Affairs Consortium, 1996; Bryans and Wilson, 1998). Racism in prison can include racial harassment, abusive language and assault, and both prisoners and members of staff are involved. In a study by Burnett and Farrell (1994: 9), more minority ethnic prisoners indicated that they had experienced racial incidents than white inmates. In this study, one-third of Asians and nearly half of Blacks said they had been racially victimised by staff. These incidents included assault, bullying, theft, verbal abuse and harassment.

In March 2000, Zahid Mubarek, a 19-year-old young offender serving a three-month sentence at Feltham Young Offenders Institution, was attacked and murdered by his racist cellmate, Robert Stewart, who clubbed Zahid several times over the head with a wooden table leg. Robert Stewart was obsessed with symbols of fascism and had a deep-seated hatred of black and Asian people and he had a violent past, which immediately raised the question of why he had been sharing a prison cell with Zahid. Following Zahid's murder, alongside other highly publicised incidents at other penal institutions, the Commission for Racial Equality (CRE) conducted a formal investigation into the prison service. It published its report, *The murder of Zahid Mubarek*, in July 2003 (CRE, 2003). The CRE found the prison service to be guilty of racial discrimination in its dealings with Zahid and Stewart, and the director general of the prison service, Martin Narey, announced that the service was institutionally racist and admitted that Zahid's death was preventable. In 2004, a public inquiry was held into the murder of Zahid Mubarek. The recommendations stemming from this inquiry included that attempts should be made to match prisoners with cellmates with whom they will be more at ease and that the prison service should publish guidelines to assist officers in allocating those prisoners who have to share a cell; and better training for prison officers, including a focus upon how the role of the prison officer can be improved (*Report of the Zahid Mubarek Inquiry*, 2006).

The prison service has also instigated a five-year action plan in relation to race, working in partnership with the CRE, with the CRE monitoring the extent to which race equality is being implemented in prisons. In December 2005 HM Inspectorate of Prisons conducted an investigation into race relations within prisons, the results of which were published in a report highlighting the key areas that needed to be developed in order to implement the action plan more effectively. This report was entitled *Parallel worlds: A thematic review of race relations in prisons* (HMIP, 2005). Key findings in this report include that there is no shared understanding of race issues within prison, there are instead a series of parallel worlds inhabited by different groups of prisoners and staff. For example, visible minority prisoners reported that they did not believe that their needs were met, believing that there is racism in the prison regime that manifests itself in differential access to the prison regime and different treatment by staff. While safety was the predominant concern for Asian prisoners, respect was the predominant issue for Black prisoners. Governors and white race relations liaison officers have the most optimistic, managerial, view that the regime operates fairly, although at the same time acknowledging that more work needs to be done. Minority ethnic staff were much less likely than white staff to believe that their prison was tackling race issues effectively, with many complaining of subtle racism by staff (HMIP, 2005: 6). Differences in perceptions between white and visible minority ethnic employees have also been found at other points in the criminal justice system, and will be discussed more fully later.

'Race'/ethnicity and employees of the criminal justice system

The government has placed a significant emphasis upon improving the representation of minority ethnic communities within the workforce of the criminal justice sector. This is partly due to the belief that creating a criminal justice system that more accurately reflects local communities will improve public confidence in criminal justice. Thus, in the HM Government strategy document (2004) *Cutting crime, delivering justice*, it is stated that a key strategy in enhancing public confidence in the criminal justice system is to create a criminal justice workforce that is diverse and more fairly represents the local community that it serves. The government's vision for 2008 is that employees working in the criminal justice system will be from a wide range of backgrounds, with high levels of job satisfaction. It has to be stressed, however, that statistics in relation to employee representation in the criminal justice system are very general, whereby employee representation is discussed in terms of broad categories like White or BME (Spalek, 2005). This means that specific communities are subsumed within these all-encompassing categories, and so it is not possible to know exactly which communities are under-represented, this point being particularly problematic if government is striving to achieve a workforce that represents the local community that it serves. For example, within the general category of Black, other communities are hidden, such as Black Caribbean and Black African, including Black British. As a result, agencies of the criminal justice system may, in the future, consider introducing greater specificity into workforce statistics and minority representation. A good start here might be to separate Pakistani and Bangladeshi employees from Indian employees from any overall Asian category. Indeed, this approach has already been suggested by the deputy chair of the CRE (CPS, 2004b). In this way, any targets that are set can be aimed more specifically at particular groups.

Police services

Much emphasis has been placed upon improving the minority ethnic representation of police officers, particularly in light of recommendations of the Macpherson Report, which stated that the Home Office and police services should facilitate the development of initiatives to increase the number of qualified minority ethnic recruits. Moreover, the Scarman Report, which was published in the aftermath of the Brixton urban disturbances in 1981, highlighted the under-representation of minority ethnic communities in the police (Rowe, 2004: 20). Over the last decade or so, there has been a rise in the percentage of minority ethnic police officers. For example, in March 2003, 2.9% of officers and 5.5% of police staff were from minority ethnic communities (Home Office website, www.homeoffice.gov. uk/police/about/race-relations/). Although this constitutes a rise of more than 50% in the number of minority ethnic officers since 1999, this figure is regarded as being too small and the Home Office has set a target of 7.7% of all police officers in England and Wales to be drawn from minority ethnic backgrounds (Home Office website, www.homeoffice.gov.uk/police/about/race-relations/). Furthermore, although the percentage of minority ethnic officers in senior ranks has increased, this has increased at a very slow rate. For example, whereas minority ethnic officers constituted 0.2% of superintendents in 1992, minority ethnic officers made up 1.8% of superintendents by 2002 (Rowe, 2004: 31). Although following the Macpherson Report police services have sought to improve the retention and progression of minority ethnic staff, by rooting out racism and creating an environment in which racist attitudes and behaviour are freely and openly challenged, racism continues to be a feature of minority ethnic police officers' working lives, detrimentally impacting upon recruitment strategies. The proportion of Black and minority ethnic officers within the 43 police forces of England and Wales as at 31 March 2005 was 3.5%, an increase over the prevous year (3.3%). The BME officers comprised 3.8% of all constables, 2.4% of sergeants, 2.3% of inspectors and chief inspectors and 2.3% of superintendents and above (Home Office, 2006). At the same time, cultural factors may be at play; for example, a career in policing may not be viewed as sufficiently respectable amongst some minority ethnic communities. Affirmative action, which is illegal under race equality laws, has been considered as a way to help boost the number of minority ethnic police officers, with the National Black Police Association national executive having voted to lobby government for this. The first Black Police Association (BPA) was established in 1994 in the Metropolitan Police Service 'to improve the working environment of Black personnel within the Metropolitan Police Service with a view to enhancing the quality of service to the public' (Rowe, 2004: 58). Most police services now have BPAs, which include those individuals of African, African Caribbean or Asian descent. According to Holdaway (1996, in Rowe, 2004), the establishment of BPAs provides the opportunity for improving the recruitment of minority ethnic staff.

The Crown Prosecution Service

The Crown Prosecution Service has been praised for the progress that it has made in terms of the make-up of its employees, which compares favourably with the civil service as a whole (HM Government, 2004). Thus, 13.9% of staff are from Black and minority ethnic communities, 66% are female and 4.4% are disabled (HM Government, 2004: 53). Nonetheless, the CPS acknowledges that at some middle management and senior levels, the workforce is under-represented in terms of these categories of people. As a result, future plans include addressing these areas of under-representation by, for example, developing positive action programmes that target these groups (CPS, 2004a). The CPS conducts staff surveys, for example, surveys in 2000, 2002 and 2004 produced data on employees' perceptions and satisfaction. The staff survey shows that action on equality, diversity and respect has a high positive impact on employee engagement and satisfaction (CPS, 2004a), and so, bearing in mind the government's intention of having a criminal justice workforce with high levels of job satisfaction (HM Government, 2004), equality and diversity issues are central to achieving this broader aim. The survey results reveal some differences between perceptions of being treated fairly and with respect between different groups of people. There is a gap between the perceptions of female, disabled, lesbian and gay, BME staff and the white male group, who consistently feel more satisfied. Also, staff from a Chinese ethnic background respond less favourably than other groups do on almost all key questions (CPS, 2004a).

The probation service

Home Office statistics indicate that minority ethnic groups are proportionately represented in the probation service, although there is concern about the lack of minority ethnic individuals occupying senior positions (Home Office, 2006). Moreover, the HM Inspectorate of Probation follow-up report *Towards race equality* highlighted marginalisation amongst minority ethnic staff, particularly those working in predominantly white areas (HMIP, 2004). According to Heer (2007: 2–3), using statistics from a Home Office report, on 31 December 2005 minority ethnic groups made up 11.79% of probation staff, nine out of ten regions have improved minority ethnic staff recruitment over the last 12 months, 7.06% of staff define themselves as 'Black', 2.79% as Asian; 1.48% as of 'mixed heritage', and 0.46% define themselves as 'other'. Of Asian staff, 53.17% are Indian, 30.63% are Pakistani, 4.12% are Bangladeshi and 12.08% are 'other'. However, there is insufficient representation of minority ethnic groups in senior positions. Less than 1% of senior probation officers are from minority ethnic groups; there are no minority ethnic chief officers or deputy chief officers, although there has been an increase in the percentage of minority ethnic middle managers, for example, 2.77% of area managers are from minority ethnic groups (Heer, 2008:

in press). Staff within the probation service are supported by the Association of Black Probation Officers and the National Association of Asian Probation Staff (NAAPS), which were set up in order to improve the working conditions of minority ethnic employees. According to Heer (2008), the NAAPS arose out of a need for Asian staff to assert themselves as separate from Black groups, attempting to address and dismantle stereotypes associated with Asian culture.

A study undertaken in 2004 investigating the experiences of Asian employees in the probation service, which included a sample size of 140 Asian staff, indicates that some respondents thought that their religious practices, including wearing cultural dress to work, had an effect upon their promotional prospects. At the same time, some respondents indicated that they had experienced racist comments or behaviour based on stereotypical views of Asians. Many also indicated that they felt prejudice in relation to their faith, language, dress and culture, causing them to feel marginalised within the workplace (Heer, 2007). This latter finding illustrates the multiple sites from which prejudice can be experienced, and indeed, according to the HM Inspectorate of Probation follow-up report, *Towards race equality* (HMIP, 2004: 53), one-fifth of minority ethnic staff have indicated that they experience 'dual discrimination', meaning that they feel discriminated in ways not only related to racism but also in relation to other aspects of their identities, like their faith. This point links to an issue raised in Chapter Four about the multiplicity of subject positions and how employees can experience multiple forms of discrimination. Government stresses the need for positive outreach work in order to promote working in the criminal justice system for a diverse range of communities (HM Government, 2004). The multiplicity of subject positions that employees hold suggests that agencies of the criminal justice system will need to adopt an increasingly sophisticated approach to recruitment, which takes into account the complexity of identities and the multiple sites at which prejudice can be experienced.

Conclusion

'Race'/ethnicity issues in relation to crime and criminal justice are multifaceted and include theoretical, methodological and policy dimensions. A central debate here appears to be in relation to the extent to which, and the reasons why, Black people are over-represented in police arrest and prison statistics and the methodological difficulties involved in establishing racial discrimination. The 'race and crime' debate not only illustrates the limitations, and difficulties, of employing statistical analyses, and using various racial/ethnic classificatory systems, to explore 'race' issues, but it also raises deeper questions about Enlightenment philosophy and the applicability of work underpinned by this to researching Black communities. Critical race perspectives have linked Enlightenment philosophy to practices that created racial hierarchies that helped to institutionalise slavery. At the same time, individuals belonging to the African diaspora have used their own discourses, separate from modern western thinking, from which to practise resistance, including a discourse of Black spirituality.

Reflexivity is increasingly a characteristic feature of criminological discourse. The usage of the terms 'Black', 'Asian', and more recently, 'Black and Minority Ethnic' (BME), for the purposes of political action or as administrative and/or research tools, has been criticised for subsuming many different identities and minority groups. Reflexivity can also be seen in the growing focus upon researchers' subjectivities and how these interact with, and constitute a fundamental part of, the research process. Reflexivity has further included debates about the nature of criminological knowledge claims and the extent to which 'race'/ethnic identities are excluded from dominant discourses. Reflexivity is also clearly evident within the criminal justice system, whereby agencies are reflecting more upon their policies and practices in order to attempt to minimise those harms, and to intervene on issues, relating to 'race'/ethnicity. While the years following the publication of the 1999 Macpherson Report have witnessed an upsurge in the levels of interest that policy makers have shown towards issues of ethnicity and 'race', an outstanding issue that needs increased and sustained focus is the validity of 'progress' as a concept that seems to underpin many approaches to 'race' and racism, and the dominance of scientific methods of enquiry when researching issues in relation to 'race'/ethnicity. Increasingly, it seems, minority voices will include a critique of modernity, and other frameworks of understanding will feature progressively more in social science disciplines. Indeed, in the next chapter, which looks at faith identities in relation to crime and criminal justice, the challenges posed to dominant knowledge constructions by the voices of religious minority groupings are highlighted.

Notes

[1] Notwithstanding the difficulty of verifying claims in the light of 'mixed' results that are often generated by empirical research that fail to establish anything conclusively.

[2] 'Black and minority ethnic' is a 'catch-all' term that has found currency amongst many statutory and voluntary organisations in England since the late 1990s.

Chapter questions

What factors might help account for the over-representation of Black people in prison?

In what ways is shedding light on modernity and an Enlightenment project helpful when taking a critical perspective on 'race' issues?

How, and in what ways, are agencies of the criminal justice system involved in 'institutional reflection' in relation to 'race'/ethnicity?

Case study
Zahid Mubarek

At 3.35am on 21 March 2000, an alarm sounded in an office on Swallow Wing at Feltham Young Offenders Institution. Malcolm Nicholson, a guard, thought it was the usual night-time request from inmates for toilet paper, so went to cell number 38 armed with a roll.

The cell had been shared for six weeks by Zahid Mubarek, 19, who was due to be released later that day, and Robert Stewart, who was so dangerous that he should have been incarcerated on his own. The prison officer opened the flap on the cell door to see Robert Stewart holding what appeared to be a stick. Lying on a bed, covered in blood, was Zahid Mubarek. Stewart said Zahid had had an accident and Mr Nicholson, realising Zahid was seriously injured, returned to his office to raise the alarm.

Stewart, from Manchester, had broken a leg off a table and bludgeoned Zahid to death. He was covered in Zahid's blood, and was taken to another cell, where he used the heel of his boot to scrawl a swastika and the words 'Manchester just killed me padmate'. Staff told the inquiry that Stewart was calm, and within half an hour of the murder was sound asleep.

Mr Justice Keith concluded that chance after chance to spot the danger that Stewart posed was missed or not acted on. The inquiry identified 186 failings that led to Zahid's 90-day sentence turning into a death sentence. The failings, the inquiry found, were either institutional or by 19 named individuals.

Stewart, 19 at the time of the murder, had a deep-seated personality disorder that 'deprived him of all sense of conscience', the report found. He had been in and out of prisons and young offender institutions, displaying bizarre behaviour such as swallowing batteries, flooding his cell and talking to walls.

In Hindley Young Offenders Institution, near Wigan, he was friends with inmate Maurice Travis. On 22 November 1997, three years before Zahid was murdered, a nurse wrote that the pair could 'endanger' the lives of others, but her warning was not acted on. Two years before Zahid's death, Travis was convicted of stabbing a fellow prisoner to death while he and Stewart were inmates at Stoke Heath Young Offenders Institution at Market Drayton, Shropshire. Mr Justice Keith said that Stewart had been present when Travis committed that murder and may have been involved.

Stewart was in and out of prisons, being moved around the system, with no one appearing to realise how dangerous he was. Mr Justice Keith said: 'Because of a pernicious and dangerous cocktail of poor communications and shoddy work practices, prison staff never got to grips with him.' Stewart was finally moved to Feltham Young Offenders Institution, Middlesex, where chance led him to be housed with Zahid. Feltham was overstretched, with poor industrial relations and a demoralised staff. The report branded it a transit camp. Mr Justice Keith concluded: 'Feltham was being asked to do too much with too few resources. It did not have the number of staff it needed to keep pace with its increasing population.'

The significance of letters that Stewart wrote, in which he fantasised about racial violence and even killing his cellmate, was missed. The inquiry found he was so dangerous he should never have shared a cell with anyone, let alone an ethnic minority prisoner. The prison was blighted by institutional racism, and by a failure to tackle overt racism. Procedures were poor, and some were just not followed by staff.

Source: Dodd, 2006

Question
To what extent is institutional racism in the prison service responsible for the murder of Zahid Mubarek?

References

Agozino, B. (2003) *Counter-colonial criminology: A critique of imperialist reason*, London: Pluto Press.

Alexander, C. (2000) *The Asian gang*, Oxford: Berg.

Back, L. and Solomos, J. (2000) 'Introduction: Theorising race and racism', in L. Back and J. Solomos (eds) *Theories of race and racism: A reader*, London: Routledge, pp 1–32.

Bolles, A. (2001) 'Seeking the ancestors: Forging a black feminist tradition in anthropology', in I. McClaurin (ed) *Black feminist anthropology*, London: Rutgers University Press, pp 24–48.

Bowling, B. (1999) *Violent racism: Victimisation, policing and social context* (revised edn), Oxford: Oxford University Press.

Bowling, B., Graham, J. and Ross, A. (1994) 'Self-reported offending among young people in England and Wales', in J. Junger-Tas (ed) *Delinquent behaviour among young people in the western world*, Amsterdam: Kugler, pp 50–98.

Bowling, B. and Phillips, C. (2002) *Racism, crime and justice*, Harlow: Longman.

Bowling, B. and Phillips, C. (2003) 'Racist victimisation in England and Wales', in D. Hawkins (ed) *Violent crime: Assessing race and ethnic differences*, Cambridge: Cambridge University Press, 2003, pp 154–70.

Bridges, L. and Gilroy, P. (1982) 'Striking back', *Marxism Today*, pp 34–5.

Bryans, S. and Wilson, D. (1998) *The prison governor: Theory and practice*, Leyhill: Prison Service Journal.

Burnett, R. and Farrell, G. (1994) *Reported and unreported racial incidents in prisons*, Centre for Criminological Research, University of Oxford Occasional Paper 14, Oxford: Centre for Criminology.

Cain, M. (2000) 'Orientalism, occidentalism and the sociology of crime', *British Journal of Criminology*, vol 40, pp 239–60.

Chigwada-Bailey, R. (1997) *Black women's experiences of criminal justice: A discourse on disadvantage*, Winchester: Waterside Press.

Clancy, A., Hough, M., Aust, R. and Kershaw, C. (2001) *Crime, policing and justice: The experiences of ethnic minorities. Findings from the 2000 British Crime Survey*, Home Office Research and Statistics 223, London: Home Office.

Collins, P. (1998) *Fighting words*, Minneapolis: University of Minnesota Press.

CPS (Crown Prosecution Service) (2004a) *Addressing equality and diversity in the CPS: A stocktake report*, London: CPS, Equality and Diversity Unit.

CPS (2004b) *Equalities symposium, 1–2 July 2004*, London: CPS, Equality and Diversity Unit.

CRE (Commission for Racial Equality) (2003) *The murder of Zahid Mubarek*, London: CRE.

Dodd, V. (2006) 'The missed danger signals that led to a brutal murder', *The Guardian*, 30 June (www.guardian.co.uk/prisons/story/0,,1809443,00.html).

Edwards, R. and Ribben, J. (1998) 'Living on the edges: Public knowledge, private lives, personal experience', in J. Ribben and R. Edwards (eds) *Feminist dilemmas in qualitative research*, London: Sage, pp 1–24.

Fitzgerald, M. (1999) *Searches in London under Section 1 of the Police and Criminal Evidence Act*, London: Metropolitan Police.

Garland, J., Spalek, B. and Chakraborti, N. (2006) 'Hearing lost voices: Issues in researching hidden minority ethnic communities', *British Journal of Criminology*, vol 46, pp 423–37.

Gelsthorpe, L. (1993), 'Approaching the topic of racism: Transferable research strategies?', in D. Cook and B. Hudson (eds) *Racism and criminology*, London: Sage, pp 77–95.

Genders, E. and Player, E. (1989) *Race relations in prisons*, Oxford: Clarendon Press.

Gilroy, P. (1993) *The black Atlantic: Modernity and double consciousness*, London: Verso.

Graham, J. and Bowling, B. (1995) *Young people and crime*, Home Office Research Study 145, London: Home Office.

Hall, S., Critcher, C., Jefferson, T., Clarke, J. and Roberts, B. (1978) *Policing the crisis: Mugging, the state, and law and order*, London: Macmillan.

Harding, S. (1987) *Feminism and methodology*, Milton Keynes: Open University Press.

Harris, A. (1997) 'Race and essentialism in feminist legal theory', in A. Wing (ed) *Critical race feminism*, London: New York University Press, pp 11–18.

Heer, G. (2008, in press) '(In)visible barriers: The experience of Asian employees in the probation service', *Howard Journal of Criminal Justice*.

HM Government (2004) *Cutting crime, delivering justice, A strategic plan for criminal justice 2004–08*, Cm 6288, London: HMSO.

HMIC (HM Inspectorate of Constabulary) (2000) *Winning the race: Embracing diversity*, London: HMIC.

HMIP (HM Inspectorate of Probation) (2000) *Towards race equality*, London: HMIP.

HMIP (2004) *Towards race equality: Follow up inspection*, London: HMIP.

HMIP (2005) *Parallel worlds: A thematic review of race relations in prisons*, London: HMIP.

Holdaway, S. (1996) *The radicalisation of British policy*, Basingstoke: Macmillan.

Holdaway, S. (1997) 'Some recent approaches to the study of race in criminological research', *British Journal of Criminology*, vol 37, no 3, pp 383–400.

Home Office (2006) *Statistics on race and the criminal justice system 2005: A Home Office publication under Section 95 of the Criminal Justice Act 1991*, London: HMSO, (www.homeoffice.gov.uk/rds/pdfs06/s95race05.pdf).

Hood, R. (1992) *Race and sentencing*, Oxford: Clarendon Press.

hooks, b. (1990) *Yearning: Race, gender and cultural politics*, Boston: South End Press.

Kalunta-Crompton, A. (2004) 'Criminology and orientalism', in A. Kalunta-Crompton and B. Agozino (eds) *Pan-African issues in crime and justice*, Aldershot: Ashgate, pp 5–22.

Koffman, L. (1996) *Crime surveys and victims of crime*, Cardiff: University of Wales Press.

Lea, J. and Young, J. (1993) *What is to be done about law and order? Crisis in the nineties*, London: Pluto Press.

Macpherson, W. (1999) *The Stephen Lawrence inquiry*, London: HMSO.

Mawby, R. and Walklate, S. (1994) *Critical victimology*, London: Sage.

Maynard, M. (2002) 'Studying age, "race" and gender: translating a research proposal into a project', *International Journal of Social Research Methodology*, vol 5, no 1, pp 31–40.

McClaurin, I. (2001) 'Theorizing a black feminist self in anthropology: Toward an auto ethnographic approach', in I. McClaurin (ed) *Black feminist anthropology*, London: Rutgers University Press, pp 49–76.

Miles, R. (1982) *Racism and migrant labour*, London: George Allen and Unwin.

Modood, T. (1994) 'Political blackness and British Asians', *Sociology*, vol 28, no 4, pp 859–76.

NPD (National Probation Directorate) (2001) *A new choreography: An integrated strategy for the National Probation Service for England and Wales*, London: NPD.

NPD (2003) *The heart of the dance: A diversity strategy for the National Probation Service for England and Wales 2002–2006*, London: NPD.

Papadopoulos, I. and Lees, S. (2002) 'Developing culturally competent researchers', *Journal of Advanced Nursing*, vol 37, no 3, pp 258–64.

Penal Affairs Consortium (1996) *Race and criminal justice*, London: NACRO.

Phillips, C. and Bowling, B. (2002) 'Racism, ethnicity, crime, and criminal justice', in M. Maguire, R. Morgan and R. Reiner (eds) *The Oxford handbook of criminology* (3rd edn), Oxford: Oxford University Press, pp 579–620.

Phillips, C. and Bowling, B. (2003) 'Racism, ethnicity and criminology: developing minority perspectives', *British Journal of Criminology*, vol 43, pp 269–90.

Pitts, J. (1993) 'Thereotyping: Anti-racisms criminology and Black young people', in D. Cook and B. Hudson (eds) *Racism and criminology*, London: Sage, pp 96–117.

Poynting, S. and Mason, V. (2006) 'Tolerance, freedom, justice and peace? Britain, Australia and anti-Muslim racism since September 11th 2001', *Journal of Intercultural Studies*, vol 27, no 4, pp 365–92.

Puwar, N. (2000) 'The racialised somatic norm and the senior Civil Service', *Sociology*, vol 35, no 3, pp 351–70.

Quraishi, M. (2005) *Muslims and crime: A comparative study*, London: Ashgate.

Ramsay, M. and Percy, A. (1996) *Drug misuse declared: Results of the 1994 British Crime Survey*, Home Office Research Findings 33, London: Home Office Research and Statistics Directorate.

Ramsay, M. and Spiller, A. (1997) *Drug misuse declared in 1996: Latest results from the British Crime Survey*, Home Office Research Study 172, London: Home Office Research and Statistics Directorate.

Reiner, R. (1989) 'Race and criminal justice', *New Community*, vol 16, pp 5–21.

Report of the Zahid Mubarek Inquiry (2006) London: HMSO, vols 1 and 2.

Rhodes, P. (1994), 'Race-of-interviewer effects: A brief comment', *Sociology*, vol 28, no 2, pp 547–58.

Rowe, M. (2004) *Policing, race and racism*, Cullompton: Willan.

Russell, K. (1992), 'Development of a black criminology and the role of the black criminologist', *Justice Quarterly*, vol 9, no 4, pp 667–83.

Salisbury, H. and Upson, A. (2004) *Ethnicity, victimization and worry about crime: Findings from the 2001/02 and 2002/03 British Crime Surveys*, Home Office Research Findings 237, London: HMSO.

Shute, S., Hood, R. and Seemungal, F. (2005) *A fair hearing? Ethnic minorities in the criminal courts*, Cullompton: Willan.

Sim, J., Scraton, P. and Gordon, P. (1987) 'Introduction: Crime, the state and critical analysis', in P. Scraton (ed) *Law, order and the authoritarian state*, Milton Keynes: Open University Press, pp 1–70.

Sivanandan, A. (1981) 'From resistance to rebellion', *Race and Class*, vol 23, no 2, pp 111–52.

Spalek, B. (2005), 'Researching black Muslim women's lives: A critical reflection', *International Journal of Social Research Methodology*, vol 8, no 1, pp 1–15.

Spalek, B. (2006) *Crime victims: Theory, policy and practice*, Basingstoke: Palgrave Macmillan.

Walklate, S. (2003) 'Can there be a feminist victimology?', in P. Davies, P. Francis and V. Jupp (eds) *Victimisation: Theory, research and policy*, Hampshire: Palgrave Macmillan, pp 28–45.

Wiegman, R. (1999) 'Whiteness studies and the paradox of particularity', *Boundary 2*, vol 26, no 3, pp 115–50.

Wilmore, G. (1999) *Black religion and black radicalism* (3rd edn), New York: Orbis Books.

SEVEN

Faith identities, crime and criminal justice

Introduction

As illustrated in the previous two chapters, gender and 'race'/ethnic identities have, over the last three decades or so, attracted much research attention, lying at the forefront of criminological enquiry. This chapter will look at faith identities in relation to crime, victimisation and criminal justice, suggesting that religious identities are increasingly featuring in criminological discourse, as well as in criminal justice policy and practice. The significance of these developments must not be understated, as the inclusion of faith identities/communities in research, policy and practice not only heralds new areas of enquiry and new modes of engagement with communities, but, moreover, brings challenges to contemporary theorising and empirical analyses in relation to crime and victimisation in more forceful and radical ways than perhaps those challenges stemming from either ethnic or gender identities.

When engaging in work that places the notions of religiosity and/or spirituality at the centre of analysis, the secular underpinnings of criminology become apparent. Traditionally, experiences of crime and victimisation have been portrayed through the secular lens of 'race'/ethnicity rather than religious identity, thereby serving to marginalise, ignore or misrepresent experiences in relation to religion and/or spirituality. In this chapter it is argued that a focus upon faith identities can lead to the adoption of innovative research techniques and theoretical frameworks of enquiry. However, this work carries with it the potential to be delegitimised because of the predominance of secularism within contemporary western society, whereby an artificially constructed binary opposition of secular/sacred serves to place work that includes a focus on the sacred into the category of the deviant 'Other'.

This chapter will also focus upon faith communities in relation to a criminal justice context, whereby faith communities are being viewed as an important resource for tackling crime and incivility, and indeed for helping to undermine terrorism, through working in partnership with various statutory agencies. Faith communities are also being seen as an object of government intervention in themselves in order to reach wider goals in terms of fostering community cohesion and civil renewal. Following the terrorist attacks of 11 September 2001, and more recent attacks in Bali, Madrid and London, the issues of religious identification, religious freedom and citizenship have generated much discussion within social and political arenas, with Muslim communities in particular being scrutinised. Muslims are predominantly the targets of anti-terrorist legislation and counter-terrorism surveillance policing (see Poynting and Mason, 2006), while at the same time being viewed as an important resource for tackling terrorism. As a result, although faith communities in general are attracting much research and policy attention, Muslims in particular are the focus of government attention, with the notion of engagement with Muslim communities being the subject of considerable debate.

This chapter therefore will highlight some key areas for criminology and the criminal justice/community safety fields when taking into consideration faith identities. As a starting point, the key terms religion, religiosity and spirituality will be explored, as these notions rarely feature in, but are increasingly likely to be a focus of, criminological enquiry.

Religion, religiosity, spirituality: some key terms

Religion

Religion is, in many ways, easier to define and operationalise than spirituality. According to Lerner (2000: 5–6), 'religions are the various historical attempts to organise a set of doctrines, rituals and specific behaviours that are supposed to be the right way to live'. According to Gilbert (2005), religion constitutes a framework within which peole seek to understand and interpret, and can provide a world-view acted out in narrative, doctrine, symbols, rites, sacraments and gatherings. Moss (2005: 8) states that by religion we mean 'those major groupings within global societies which have particular names and identifiable sets of beliefs'. Furthermore, 'within these religious systems, there is a belief in the supernatural – a divine being or beings or spiritual forces which to some extent influence the behaviour of human beings' (Moss, 2005: 8). Importantly, while religions can embody spirituality, they may not do so; moreover, spirituality can emerge and exist outside religious frameworks and institutions (Lerner, 2000).

The major world religious traditions consist of Judaism, Christianity, Buddhism, Hinduism, Sikhism and Islam, although within these groupings there can be a large variety of sub-groupings. For example, Christianity includes Anglican, Catholic and Protestant groups as well as other sects. Islam is diverse, there being many different religious strands, including Sunni and Shi'a, and with there also being many different schools of Islamic thought. For example, within the Sunni tradition, there are a number of different movements, including Barelwis, Deobandis, Tablighi Jamat and Jama'at-I-Islami (Conway, 1997). Among Hindus and Sikhs there is also much diversity. For instance, within the Hindu faith there are caste, or jati, groupings that are of significance in how these communities are organised (Beckford et al, 2006). Over 2,000 new religious movements (NRMs) also exist, which include groups like the Children of God, Krishna Consciousness and Scientology (Moss, 2005).

Religiosity

Religiosity might be understood as the degree to which an individual expresses a sincere and earnest regard for religion, which might be understood as including attendance of religious services, giving donations to religious institutions and/or reading theological and/or sacred material. According to Johnson et al (2001: 25), religiosity might be defined as 'the extent to which an individual is committed to the religion he or she professes and its teachings, such that the individual's attitudes and behaviours reflect this commitment'. Religiosity has been examined through the use of surveys that measure factors such as the frequency with which an individual has attended a religious service in the past year, how much time has been spent on community-based religious activities, and how important religion is to an individual (Johnson et al, 2001: 39).

Spirituality

Spirituality is a more complex and fluid notion to define (Moss, 2005), and indeed Lerner (2000) argues that any attempts to define spirituality are inherently limited due to the richness and complexity of Spirit, which is beyond linguistic articulation and expression. Nonetheless, many attempts have been made to try to articulate the meaning of spirituality. For example, according to Haug (1998), spirituality consists of a personal, internalised set of beliefs and experiences that effect a person at a cognitive, affective, behavioural and developmental level. According to Morell (1996: 306), 'at the centre of most spiritual traditions (not specific religious ideologies) is a belief that human beings are united as expressions or emanations of a central energy or principle' and there is a recognition of the fundamental relatedness of humanity. In Moss's view (2005: 12), spirituality has both an inward-looking and outward-looking dimension, the former being a pathway through which individuals seek to find a sense of meaning and purpose in their lives, the latter fostering a sense of responsibility for others. For Lerner (2000: 5), spirituality is 'a lived experience, a set of practices and a consciousness that aligns us with a sense of the sanctity of All Being'.

Increasingly, social science researchers are focusing upon spirituality and religion in relation to issues such as mental health, nursing and social work, so that there is a thriving market of academic and practitioner-orientated books on these subjects (for example, Swinton, 2001; Hunt, 2002; Cottingham, 2005; Moss, 2005; Gilbert, 2007). Indeed, social workers, nurses, psychiatrists, psychologists and therapists are increasingly including a spiritual dimension to the techniques that they use. Haug (1998) argues that therapists' 'spiritual literacy' enables them to open space non-judgementally and respectfully for the discussion of religious or spiritual content that is important to clients. Within a criminal justice context, growing attention towards faith identities can be seen in the work of Beckford and Gilliat (1998), who examined policy and practice issues in relation to religion in prison; Clear et al (2000), whose research concentrated upon the importance of religion in a penal setting; Wardak (2000), who has focused upon Pakistani Muslim youth in Edinburgh in relation to social control and deviance; Spalek (2002a), whose book looks at Islam in relation to criminal justice; and Quraishi (2005), who has researched Muslims, crime and victimisation in Karachi, Pakistan and in Haslingden, Yorkshire. Prior to this, a substantial body of work has been developed looking at the links between religiosity and delinquency (Hirschi and Stark, 1969; Stark et al, 1982; Ellis, 1987; Cochran et al, 1994; Evans et al, 1995; Johnson et al, 2001). This work will be returned to later on in this chapter.

The research attention that religious and spiritual issues are generating suggests that despite the effects of the European Enlightenment and the emergence of the modern western liberal democratic state, religion and spirituality continue to constitute significant social and cultural phenomena, even though for many years social theorists have neglected this area of research through the mistaken view that modernisation leads to secularisation (Herbert, 2003). The next section will therefore examine the notion of secularism and the significance of religion and spirituality in contemporary western societies.

Secularism and contemporary western societies

Asad (2003: 25, in Caraballo-Resto, 2006: 2) has argued that 'the secular is neither singular in origin nor stable in its historical identity'. This means there are many different ways of understanding and conceptualising secularism. According to Caraballo-Resto (2006), secularism has been viewed as an integral part of modern western society, where religious considerations are excluded from civil affairs, and issues in relation to equality are viewed largely through the secular framework of multiculturalism. According to Berger (1999), secularisation might be viewed as being a widespread alienation from organised churches and religious institutions. For example, in Britain, ritual participation in religious services and attachment to religious institutions has declined considerably, so that in a survey carried out between 1999 and 2000, only 14.4% of British people said that they attended church once a week (Davie, 2002: 6).

The philosophical and historical underpinnings of secularism lie within the European Enlightenment, where scientific reasoning progressively replaced theological frameworks of understanding. At the same time, the influence of religious institutions on civil society declined with the emergence of modern institutions and professional bodies that came to be separated out from their religious roots (Beckford, 1996; Jürgensmeyer, 2003). As a result, religion did not keep its central position within social theory (Beckford, 1996), and sociologists have assumed that religion is a declining phenomenon and therefore requires little attention (Lyon, 1996).

More recently, however, a number of factors appear to have led to a heightened focus upon religious and spiritual matters within contemporary western societies, illustrating that although secularism has been considered to be a characteristic of western democratic societies, religions continue to occupy public as well as private space, with some religious institutions having more influence over policy and practice than others and, moreover, with faith and spirituality continuing to be used as cultural resources by individuals.

In many parts of the world, even those experiencing modernisation,[1] including Africa, Asia, European countries and the US, religion has been at the forefront of collective action, where religion has constituted a form of identity politics. For example, according to Wilmore (1999), Black communities in the US have been bound together through biblical stories and the event of worship. Indeed, Marx (in Horowitz, 2004: 129) has written that 'religious suffering is at one and the same time the expression of real suffering and protest against real suffering'. Moreover, the religious right in the US has gained significant influence and power (Lyon, 1996), with right-wing evangelism constituting a potent political force, profoundly influencing US elections and legislation on issues like abortion (Appleyard, 2006). Collectivised religious responses such as these might be viewed from a Durkheimian perspective, whereby religion is conceptualised as a form of collective memory or collective consciousness, based upon a community of past, present and future members, as well as tradition (Davie, 2002).

Within academia, particularly since the 1990s, researchers have been including a spiritual/religious dimension in their work. For example, according to King (1993: 215), although feminism might be viewed as being linked to the notion of secularism, the women's movement might also be seen as grounded in an act of faith for the possibility of a better society, so that the emergence of feminism 'points to new religious and spiritual developments which affirm the resacralisation of nature, the earth, the body, sexuality and the celebration of the bonds of community'. Beckford (1996) links Ulrich Beck's work in *Risk society: Towards a new modernity* (1992) to spirituality, arguing that there are religious or spiritual overtones to Beck's claim that the risks accompanying modernisation in contemporary western society are so severe that a new collective consciousness emerges, one which 'may even generate a solidarity of living things' (Beckford, 1996: 39). Social theorists have also turned a critical gaze towards contemporary western society, characteristic features of which include concerns about risk, anxiety and the construction of the self, whereby religion and/or spirituality may be viewed as constituting some of the material from which identities are built (Giddens, 1991; Beck, 1992; Beckford, 2003; Bauman, 2004).

Hervieu-Leger (1999, in Davie, 2002) argues that Western European societies are amnesic because religious institutional disciplines have declined and communities have fragmented, and so societies are less able to maintain memories bound by traditions that lie at the core of religious existence. However, personal beliefs persist, and so increasingly become 'personal, detached and heterogeneous', particularly so for young people (Davie, 2002: 8). Indeed, Beckford (1996) argues that, despite the effects of the Enlightenment, religion continues to be used as a cultural resource, and Giddens (1991) has stated that religion has undergone a resurgence in late modern society, as evidenced by the rising numbers of people joining new religious movements, or practising 'New Age' forms of spirituality (Lyon, 1996; Heelas and Woodhead, 2005; Heelas, 2006). Berger (1999) argues that secularisation on a societal level does not necessarily mean secularisation at the level of individual consciousness. According to Davie (2002: 162), the number of young people in Northern Europe who believe in life after death and in a 'god within' is growing. Luckmann (1996) has argued that although institutional forms of religion have declined in late modernity, new social forms of religion have emerged, at the core of which is the construction of meaning through the construction of the self. According to Lynch (2008), lifestyle television shows in Britain can be interpreted through Luckmann's (1996) framework, in that lifestyle media can be seen as illustrating a new form of religion, constituting an example of 'a secondary institution that supports the individual's project of trying to live a meaningful and fulfilled existence within the horizons of this life' (Lynch, 2008: in press).

It might be argued that late modern society, whilst providing a certain degree of material comfort, nevertheless contains mechanisms that have led to the marginalisation of moral questions, leaving people with little sense of a purpose in life (Giddens, 1991; Sacks, 2002). Indeed, Giddens (1991: 9) states that 'personal meaninglessness – the feeling that life has nothing worthwhile to offer – becomes a fundamental psychic problem in circumstances of late modernity'. Clinical psychologist Oliver James (1997) has claimed that late modernity signals the shift to a relatively toxic society, creating a higher proportion of people who are at risk from depression, aggression and compulsive disorders. He also argues that in post-Second World War western society, rates of depression, suicide, alcohol and illegal substance abuse have risen sharply. Interestingly, studies on religious conversion[2] suggest that personal problems that characterise life situations prior to religious conversion include those relating to the 'spiritual' (involving the meaninglessness of life, a lack of direction and poor self-image); the 'interpersonal' (including marital problems and parental problems); the 'material' (unemployment, school-related problems) and 'character' (including drugs, alcohol and uncontrollable temper) (Kose, 1996). Therefore, it seems plausible to suggest that in late modernity, although the influence of institutional religious settings may have decreased, the individual demand for religious and/or spiritual frameworks of understanding has increased, and is likely to continue rising.

At the same time, in a post-11 September 2001 context the concept and practical aspects of religion and spirituality are taking on greater political significance, with attention being placed particularly, although not exclusively, upon Muslim communities. The UK, alongside other European countries, is grappling with how to reconcile issues of citizenship and security with regard to minority Muslim populations, amid crises of identity and of ideology in dealing with and integrating non-European immigrant populations, especially Muslim groups. The threat of Islamist terrorism has therefore brought to crisis core tenets of the liberal democratic state relating to notions of citizenship and individual rights in multi-ethnic and multi-religious contemporary democratic societies, inevitably leading to an increased focus upon religious identities.

Faith communities in the UK

Indicating the increasing recognition of the social significance of religious identification, in the 2001 National Census the British government introduced a question about religion[3] (Francis, 2003). For England and Wales, data was collected in relation to the following categories: Christian, Buddhist, Hindu, Jewish, Muslim, Sikh or None. According to the census, 71.7% of the population in England say that their religion is Christianity. After Christianity, Islam is the most common faith recorded, with 3.1% of the population describing their religion as Muslim. Census information further reveals that in England, 1.1% of the population are Hindus and 0.7% are Sikhs (National Statistics Online, 2007). Additionally, 14.6% of the population of England indicated that they are of 'no religion' (Beckford et al, 2006).

It is important to note that religious identification is a more important aspect of self-identity for individuals belonging to minority ethnic groups than for white groups. For example, the 1994 National Survey of Ethnic Minorities revealed that 95% of Muslims, 89% of Hindus and 86% of Sikhs surveyed considered religion to be 'very' or 'fairly' important to the way that they lead their lives, in contrast to 46% of white members of the Church of England and 69% of white Roman Catholics (Modood et al, 1997: 301). According to findings from the 2001 Home Office Citizenship Survey, in contrast to the 17% of white respondents who said that religion was important to their self-identity, 44% of Black and 61% of Asian respondents said that religion was important. For Muslims, religion was ranked second only after family in terms of the importance to their self-identity (O'Beirne, 2004). O'Beirne (2004) has stressed that religious affiliation and ethnicity should be considered together rather than separately when carrying out research and when making policy decisions. Beckford et al (2006: 8) have argued that 'the religion dimension should not be completely collapsed into ethnicity and vice versa'. Furthermore, Francis (2003) maintains that religious affiliation, although being a poor predictor of religious practice, nonetheless should be viewed as constituting a key aspect of social identity as this may influence individuals' values and how they experience the world. Taking on board the latter point raised by Francis (2003), if faith identities are to feature significantly within criminological research agendas, they present important challenges for the subject discipline of criminology, as will be discussed next.

Criminology as a secular discipline

Criminology as a social scientific discipline arose very much out of Enlightenment philosophy and the belief that science can be used to study crime, as Morrison (1995: 5) cogently argues: 'Criminology claims the status of the rational and scientific attempt to study the phenomena of crime. It was born with the death of God. It was meant to aid in the journey, the construction of a secure modernity.' According to Garland, criminology is

> a specific genre of discourse and inquiry about crime – a genre which has developed in the modern period and which can be distinguished from other ways of talking and thinking about criminal conduct. Thus, for example, its claim to be an empirically grounded, scientific undertaking sets it apart from moral and legal discourses. (Garland, 2002: 17)

Earlier understandings of crime and criminals, stemming from medieval philosophical traditions, the theologies of the Church of Rome and the Protestant Reform tradition, featured concepts such as fate or demons, original sin, the devil or human depravity. While these concepts have not disappeared in contemporary society, it might be argued that they do not frame criminological enquiry. Certainly, the historical roots of modern criminology lie in Enlightenment writers such as Beccaria and Bentham, who, according to Garland (2002), wrote materialist, secular work. Although later criticised by members of the positivist school for being unscientific, these writers nonetheless saw themselves as working in a scientific way (Garland, 2002).

It might be argued that Enlightenment values underpinning criminology have helped to create an artificial separation between the secular and the 'spiritual/ sacred'. If the roots of criminology lie in secular, materialist analyses, then religious and spiritual matters are not likely to have featured significantly in criminological work. As previously indicated in this chapter, research suggests that faith identities are particularly important for minority ethnic individuals; however, within criminology, 'race'/ethnicity has been predominantly focused upon by researchers, leading to the marginalisation of faith identities. For example, in 1980, Mawby and Batta carried out one of the first studies of South Asians and crime. While informal control mechanisms in relation to community and family were highlighted as explaining low crime rates amongst South Asian communities, the role of Islam did not feature significantly in this piece of work, and yet many of the research participants here would have been Muslim because Pakistanis, Bangladeshis and Indians comprise almost 70% of UK Muslims, with 92% of Pakistanis and

Bangladeshis being Muslim (National Census, 2001). Another significant study that looked at crime and victimisation in relation to race and ethnicity is the Keighley Crime Survey, which was conducted by Webster in 1995, and included the experiences of Asian and White youths. In a journal article presenting the research findings, although Webster (1997) does refer to Islam, Muslim identities and Islamist youth groups, his work is skewed towards a discussion of young Asian masculine criminality rather than giving the role of Islam in these young men's lives and their understandings and experiences of crime a central focus. Thus, the article is headed 'The construction of British "Asian" criminality' and 'Asianness' appears to be the subject of considerable discussion rather than Islam or the construction of male Muslim identities. It is important to consider the wider context to criminological research, as this has substantially influenced the traditional focus upon 'race'/ethnic – rather than religious – identities as will now be examined.

Criminal justice and secular, race relations, approaches

When viewing the wider context to criminological research, Beckford's (1996) argument that religion was marginalised by social scientists as modern institutions such as education and welfare were split off from their religious roots can also be applied to the criminal justice sector. Historically, religious convictions have been a motivating factor for those individuals who have volunteered their services towards rehabilitating offenders and reducing crime. Thus, historical accounts of the influence of evangelical Protestantism on the penal system can be found (Beckford and Gilliat, 1998), and the historical roots of the probation service lie in the police court missionaries in England in the late 18th and early 19th centuries, many of whom had religious convictions. The 1907 Probation of Offenders Act put this work onto a statutory footing, which meant that courts could now appoint and pay probation officers, thereby absorbing the original court missionaries into these new services. The 1920s was the period when probation work moved away from religious, missionary ideals to become a professional-based service (Whitfield, 1998).

Added to the above, the principles of multiculturalism underpinning contemporary British society have meant that religion has been viewed largely as occupying private as opposed to public space. Equality and diversity issues have therefore traditionally been approached through the lens of 'race'/ethnicity rather than religious identity. Within the criminal justice context, agencies of the criminal justice system have approached diversity issues through a secular, race relations, framework, whereby 'race'/ethnic identities/groupings have been identified and used to guide service delivery and provision, so that religion/spirituality have traditionally been overlooked within contemporary criminal justice policy and practice. This can be seen most clearly in the monitoring procedures used by agencies of the criminal justice system to record the identities of suspects, offenders, victims and employees, whereby racial and/or ethnic (rather than faith) categories have traditionally been used, with only the prison service systematically recording offenders' religious identities. Thus, for example, statistics in relation to stop and searches conducted by police under counter-terrorism legislation use ethnic rather than religious categories. This means that although statistics may suggest an increase in the number of Asians stopped and searched, it is not possible to gauge the circumstances of young Muslims from these statistics (Garland et al, 2006). The British Crime Survey, which is a yearly household survey that seeks to document risks and experiences of criminal victimisation in England and Wales, includes minority ethnic booster samples. Since 2005/06 the faith identities of respondents are increasingly being monitored and so statistics in relation to the crimes that faith communities experience are likely to become available. The Home Office Citizenship Survey, which does include faith identities and looks at perceptions and experiences of prejudice and discrimination (though not experiences of criminal victimisation), reveals that Hindus, Muslims and Sikhs are substantially more likely to say that they feel very worried about being attacked due to their skin colour, ethnic origin or religion than Christians, those of other religions and those of no religion (Department for Communities and Local Government, 2006: 28).

The focus upon ethnicity, rather than religion, as an identity marker has meant that the significance of religious identity to the policies and practices of criminal justice agencies has traditionally been largely omitted. While direct and institutional racism by the police, the courts and the penal system has been extensively documented (Hood, 1992; Jefferson et al, 1992; Kalunta-Crompton, 1999; Bowling and Phillips, 2002; Shute et al, 2005), and policies have been implemented to tackle these issues, discrimination on the grounds of religion has rarely been addressed. The emphasis upon 'race'/ethnicity rather than religion has no doubt been partly due to the historical separation of religion from the welfare state. Nonetheless, mounting evidence of the significance of religious discrimination exists. For example, a Home Office report published in 2001, entitled *Religious discrimination in England and Wales*, found that while in theory it is difficult to disentangle discrimination based on religious grounds from discrimination based on ethnicity, in practice some of the persons who were questioned in this study did appear to be the targets of discrimination and violence as a result of their religious beliefs and practices (Weller et al, 2001). In a survey looking at the effects of the events of 11 September 2001 on discrimination and implicit racism in five religious and seven ethnic groups, religion was found to be more important than ethnicity in indicating which groups were most likely to experience racism and discrimination. Moreover, this research indicates the existence of modern and implicit religious discrimination. The phrase 'modern religious discrimination' indicates that prejudice against religious communities continues to exist in a 'post–civil rights era'. Implicit religious discrimination refers to daily life situations in which covert religious prejudice, such as being treated rudely or not being taken seriously, can be experienced. British 'Whites' also reported a rise in post-11 September discrimination, and of the white people in the study who said they faced religious discrimination, almost half were Muslim (Sheridan et al, 2003: 19).

In Britain, under the 2001 Anti-terrorism, Crime and Security Act, a religiously aggravated element to crime has been introduced, which involves imposing higher penalties upon offenders who are motivated by religious hatred. Following this piece of legislation, the Crown Prosecution Service (CPS) has been collecting information on the number of religiously aggravated prosecutions carried out in Britain. According to the CPS, for offences to be charged as specific religiously aggravated offences, prosecutors have to prove first that the offender committed one of the basic offences (including offences of assault, wounding, harassment, damage and public order offences such as causing people to fear violence or harassment) and then prosecutors have to prove that the offence was religiously aggravated in one of two ways: either that the accused person demonstrated hostility to the victim because the victim was thought to belong to a particular religious group, or that the accused person was motivated by hostility towards the victim for the same reasons (CPS, 2003: 5). There have been relatively few religiously aggravated prosecutions; nonetheless, the majority of victims involved here are Muslim. Thus, between 14 December 2001 and 31 March 2003, out of a total of 18 cases, 10 involved Muslim victims, two Sikh victims, two Hindu victims, one Jewish, one Jehovah's Witness, one Christian victim and one victim whose religion was not stated. (CPS, 2003: 36). Between 2005 and 2006, out of 43 cases of religiously aggravated crime, 18 incidents involved Muslims as victims, three involved Christians as victims, and one involved a Sikh victim, with 21 victims' religious identities being unknown or not stated (CPS, 2006: 45). Of course, the number of hate crimes that are prosecuted is tiny in comparison to the number of hate crimes that are actually committed, particularly as most victims do not report their experiences to the police (Victim Support, 2006). Community groups, often working in partnership with local police services, play an important role in monitoring and documenting instances of hate crime. For example, the Community Security Trust (CST), which represents the Jewish community on matters of anti-Semitism in the UK, recorded 455 anti-Semitic incidents in 2005, this being the second-highest annual total since the CST started recording incidents in 1984 (CST, 2006: 4). The Forum Against Islamophobia and Racism (FAIR), the Islamic Human Rights Commission (IHRC) and the Muslim Council of Britain are three community groups that monitor hate crimes committed against Muslim communities. According to the IHRC, there was a rise in the number of anti-Muslim attacks during the holy month of Ramadan (IHRC, 2006), including the case of a Muslim shopkeeper's car being firebombed. This serves to illustrate how the incidence of faith hate crimes can be influenced by particular national, international and cultural/religious events. Indeed, in the aftermath of the bombings in London on 7 July 2005, the Metropolitan Police

Service recorded a sharp increase in faith-related hate crimes, including verbal and physical assaults (European Monitoring Centre on Racism and Xenophobia, 2005).

If one approaches the study of crime, criminal justice and victimisation from a viewpoint that 'religion, spirituality, identity and lifestyle are interwoven so that a division into sacred and secular is neither practical nor appropriate' (Blain, 2004: 162), then the inclusion of religion and spirituality within criminological discourse is essential. Indeed, Francis (2003) has argued that it is important that we understand and recognise how religion affects individuals' lives and how it serves to shape social institutions. The following section, therefore, will discuss the ways in which researchers have engaged, and are continuing to engage, with religious/spiritual identities/communities when working on issues related to crime and victimisation.

Criminal justice researchers' and practitioners' engagement with religious/spiritual identities

One particular strand within criminological research that has focused upon religiosity is that in relation to youth offending, exploring the question of whether participation in religious activities, as well as having religious beliefs, has any effect on delinquency. The results that have been produced here are rather mixed, with some researchers rejecting the relevance of religiosity on delinquency (Hirschi and Stark, 1969; Ellis, 1987), whilst other researchers argue that the relationship between religiosity and delinquency varies according to different contexts and different types of offence (Stark et al, 1982). More recently, Johnson et al (2001: 37–8) have claimed that their study provides empirical evidence that the 'effects of religiosity are neither spurious nor completely indirect via secular (non religious) models of social control'. Rather, Johnson et al (2001) argue that religiosity can be linked to reduced delinquency, and this may be partly due to the finding that with increasing religious involvement an adolescent's disapproval of delinquent acts increases. Wardak (2000), in his study of Pakistani Muslim communities in Edinburgh, highlights that the mosque is the site at which numerous educational, social, religious and recreational activities take place. According to Wardak (2000), the more often that youths take part in their community's social, religious and cultural life, the less they deviate from its norms and therefore the less likely they are to commit crime. For Wardak (2000: 234), 'Islamic teachings constitute the basis of normative order in Edinburgh's Pilrig community'.

Within victimological work, researchers are increasingly acknowledging the role that religion and spirituality may play. Spalek (2002b), for instance, has highlighted how some Muslim women who experience victimisation may turn to prayer, meditation and their local imam as a way of helping them cope in the aftermath of crime. Critical black feminists have introduced the notion of 'spirit injury' as constituting an important aspect of the process of victimisation (Davis,

1997;Williams, 1997).According to Kennedy et al (1998), whilst some research has focused upon documenting the role that spirituality plays in individuals' reactions to stressful, non-criminal events, such as bereavement, virtually no studies have been carried out to examine spirituality in relation to individuals' responses to crime. In answer to this, Kennedy et al (1998: 322) looked at changes in spirituality for the female victims of sexual assault.They found that the majority of the female victims (60%) revealed an increased sense of the spiritual in the aftermath of the crimes that had been committed against them. Furthermore, those victims with increased spirituality appeared to cope better than those victims without increased spirituality. Indeed, according to Shorter-Gooden (2004), participation in a congregation or spiritual community may be part of a strategy that some African American women draw upon to help them cope with racism and sexism. Quraishi (2005) has placed Muslim identities at the centre of his comparative analysis of the crime and victimisation experiences of South Asians living in Haslingden in Yorkshire, and Karachi in Pakistan. According to Quraishi (2005: 116), there is a commonly shared sense of victimisation amongst the South Asian Muslims taking part in his study, this being linked to the concept of the ummah, which consists of the individual, community and global Muslim population, so that religious oppression and Islamophobia constitute important aspects to Muslims' perceptions as oppressed minorities.This work highlights the relevance of faith identities, and more specifically Muslim identities, to experiences of crime and victimisation. For example, Quraishi (2005: 62) highlights how some of the participants of the study, living in Haslingden, drew upon Shariah law when speaking about crime. Thus, some of his respondents considered zina (fornification and adultery) to be a crime: 'Zina is also one of the biggest crimes and the majority of our lads, if they get a chance, will commit zina.'

Religion may be used by individuals as a cultural resource in order to help them justify committing crime. For instance, in a study exploring domestic violence experienced by Black women, it was found that some men might invoke 'tradition' or 'religion' to justify their violent actions (Mama, 2000). It has also been claimed that within some Muslim youth subcultures, religion may be used to justify and/or absolve deviant or criminal acts. Justifications may include claims that the victims are not Muslim or that they belong to a different religious community, and individuals may pay some of the proceeds from crime to Islamic causes or centres as a way of absolving themselves from guilt (Pargeter, 2006). However, it is important to stress that this sort of work should not be used to demonise religions. It is perhaps useful here to draw upon the work of David Matza in relation to his book, *Delinquency and drift* (1964). According to Matza, the delinquent drifts between delinquent and conventional behaviour. Most young offenders recognise the legitimacy of the dominant social order, and so experience feelings of guilt from their behaviour. As a result, they will draw upon justifications in order to help neutralise their guilty or anxious feelings. Matza (1964) argues that young offenders may identify special groups to victimise, and there may also be a denial of responsibility, a denial of injury, a denial of the victim and so forth. Therefore, it may be the case that rather than motivating people to commit crime, religion may be used as a way of justifying deviant and/or illegal activities, to help reduce any feelings of discomfort or guilt that the offender may have, both consciously and subconsciously.

Clearly, religious identities and spirituality are increasingly featuring in criminological work. However, these bring forth new challenges for criminological enquiry, as traditionally work has largely consisted of secularised accounts – focusing upon ethnicity or the role of culture – that have overlooked or marginalised the religious and/or spiritual aspects of people's lives. The next section, therefore, briefly explores some of the key issues that criminological research will need to tackle if religiosity and spirituality are further focused upon. Indeed, that the production of criminological knowledge might incorporate new theoretical, methodological and epistemological positions is not something that requires justification if we take the view of Garland (2002: 24) that 'Criminology is a socially constructed and historically specific organisation of knowledge and investigative procedures. Our own ways are established conventions rather than unchallengeable truths.'

Incorporating religiosity and spirituality within criminological knowledge constructions: some key issues

To some extent, and as previously indicated in this chapter, the notions of religiosity and spirituality are already being incorporated into social science research frameworks. For example, researchers are using questionnaires that attempt to measure individuals' religiosity and spirituality, using statements like 'I read literature on my faith' or 'I try hard to carry my religion over into all other dealings in life' or 'My desire to understand events in spiritual terms has increased/decreased/stayed the same' (Kennedy et al, 1998: 324–7). Many social surveys that seek to explore and measure value systems also include questions about beliefs. For example, in the British Social Attitudes Survey, beliefs in god are explored (Francis, 2003; see Heelas, 2006 for further discussion of this). The social work curriculum is increasingly being discussed in terms of whether spirituality and religion can be incorporated into this (see SWAP, 2005).

However, there are deeper difficulties to consider here. Religion and spirituality potentially bring radical challenges to social scientific knowledge constructions, since with the emergence of the European Enlightenment, secular rationalism has valorised 'positivistic conceptions of science and the scientific endeavour', rendering 'some forms of knowledge legitimate and acceptable and other forms not' (Walklate: 2003: 35). Phenomena such as 'soul', 'spirit', 'god' or 'karma' are not directly open to empirical measurement or scientific experimentation (Humphrey, 2008), so that when exploring religiosity and spirituality it may be necessary to utilise approaches of investigation that lie outside conventional social scientific frameworks. For example, Lerner (2000) argues that concepts like 'spirit' or 'soul' may only be partially knowable through spiritual intuitions and insights. According to Humphrey (2008), it is important for researchers to cultivate an attunement to spirituality in their own lives if carrying out research in this area, and that researchers should not be afraid to inhabit other life-worlds that carry with them the risk of changing the researcher's own world sense-making schema.

The positions above, however, carry with them certain difficulties. Both Lerner (2000) and Humphrey (2008) acknowledge that phenomena such as 'spirit' or 'sacred' may be unnameable, with Lerner (2000: 32) stating that 'the deepest spiritual thinkers warn us that the realm of the Spirit is the realm of the ineffable'. This suggests that any knowledges that are produced around issues in relation to god or spirituality are likely to be partial and incomplete and indeed inaccurate. Nonetheless, it is important to stress here that so-called objective, scientific knowledge is also partial and open to many biases (for example see Cain, 1990, and her discussion of Bhaskarian realism). Another difficulty lies with the hegemonic positioning of secularism and scientific reasoning, so that knowledges derived from the realm of the 'sacred' stand to be automatically delegitimised, constituting the deviant 'Other' in the binary opposition consisting of secular/sacred. As a result, researchers are likely to struggle for their claims to be acknowledged and indeed run the risk of having their knowledges derogatorily dismissed.

Although it has been argued that good research requires active involvement with organisations and individuals in order to understand and portray their world-views and lifestyles (Gelsthorpe, 1993), a question that needs to be raised in the context of this chapter is, is there a safe space in contemporary western society within which to claim that active involvement with communities can include the researcher undertaking a spiritual journey that leads to more reflective research? Furthermore, might incorporating religious and/or spiritual notions into social science research methodologies delegitimise the work because of the hegemony of secularism, even though it might be argued that these are crucial when carrying out work in relation to religious and/or spiritual identities? Thus, for example, in a study carried out by Spalek and El-Hassan (2007), which involved interviewing individuals who had converted to Islam whilst inside British jails, the interviewer greeted and acknowledged the inmates as his Muslim brothers, drawing upon the Qur'an where believers are instructed to observe all Muslims as their brothers, to like for their brother what they would like for themselves, and this was an important aspect of the research study, so as to gain the trust of research participants. However, incorporating religious/theological notions into social science research methodologies is a contentious issue given that secular frameworks have dominated social research. It seems that a researcher who is seriously engaged in working with faith communities is placed within an uncomfortable position as, in gaining the trust of religious communities by taking on board notions of religiosity and/or spirituality, they are running the risk of their work being delegitimised and disrespected within broader social policy and research arenas, which have in modern times been underpinned by secular models.

When researching individuals for whom religion and/or spirituality is an important aspect of their everyday lives, standpoint epistemologies potentially offer a fruitful way forward. Whilst standpoint epistemologies are normally associated with feminism, shedding light upon dominant patriarchal structures in society (Gelsthorpe, 1990), they can be applied to other contexts. Thus, if the viewpoint is taken that a dominant structure operating in contemporary western societies, serving to oppress individuals in particular contexts, is secularism, then standpoint epistemologies offer the possibility of exploring secularism as a dominant social norm that can serve to delegitimise religious/spiritual experiences through documenting the voices of those people who experience, and in some cases struggle to overcome, this dominant norm. At the same time, standpoint epistemologies offer the potential to document situations where religious institutions and structures can oppress, by recording the voices of those individuals who have experienced oppression of this kind. Interestingly, theological frameworks of understanding, derived directly from religious/spiritual texts, may be used by individuals to challenge what they regard as being oppressive regimes that have more to do with cultural interpretations of religion than with religious/ theological frameworks of understanding.

It might further be argued that secularised sociological perspectives and frameworks of understanding are problematic if used to interpret the lives of individuals for whom religion/spirituality is a fundamental aspect of life. Although religious ideas and practices can be influenced by societal and cultural traditions, this does not mean that researchers should solely focus upon the transmission of such traditions, because in doing so they marginalise the centrality of religious beliefs and spiritual understandings. For example, for many followers of Islam, the Qur'an is the actual word of God that was recorded by Muhammad during the early part of the 7th century (Watson, 1994). For many followers of Islam, there is thus a legitimate, moral authority upon which the lives of men and women are based, so that referring solely to societal traditions and expectations undermines the authority of the Qur'an, and the importance of faith for many Muslims. There is thus a need for researchers to adopt a greater sensitivity. This is both time-consuming and demanding work. Trying to understand the role that religion plays in individuals' lives can be problematic, especially when the researcher may only have a rudimentary knowledge of the particular faith with which a research participant identifies. Indeed, this point raises the wider debate around how important it is for the researcher to belong to the same faith as their research participants, or, for that matter, whether it is important for the researcher to have any faith or belief in a higher being (Garland et al, 2006). At the same time, a researcher's own religious identity may directly or indirectly influence the research process, so that great reflexivity is to be encouraged here as well. For example, Yin (2005), when researching British lesbian, gay and bisexual Muslims and Christians, illustrates how the narratives that he collected from Christian gay males in relation to sexual non-monogamy challenged his own previously uncontested understandings of 'Christian' ethics in sexual relationships. Yin (2005: 4) argues that 'the line of demarcation some participants established between emotional fidelity and sexual fidelity was sociologically fascinating but personally disturbing' due to his religiously informed assumptions around fidelity.

Clearly, there are many unanswered epistemological and methodological questions here. With religion and spirituality constituting an increasingly significant aspect of social science research, work will, no doubt, in the future address some of these issues, and will probably generate many more. Another important aspect to the inclusion of faith identities within criminology and criminal justice is the issue of community engagement with faith communities, which will now be discussed, this being an important aspect of contemporary social and criminal justice policy.

Engagement with faith communities in a criminal justice/ community safety context

As already indicated in this chapter, faith communities, particularly those following a Christian tradition, have historically played a significant role in the criminal justice system in England and Wales, mirroring the involvement of faith communities in other social policy contexts, for example, in relation to childcare, poor relief and public health (Monsma and Soper, 1998). Although the social professions came to replace religious communities in the provision of services, so that the influence and work of faith communities gradually declined (Beckford, 1996; Beckford and Gilliat, 1998), over the last decade or so, policy makers have become increasingly interested in encouraging faith communities to work in partnership with statutory agencies for the provision of public services. Thus, for example, David Blunkett, then Home Secretary, in a speech headed 'One nation, many faiths', highlighted the following:

> Faith can be the building blocks and the glue of community. It plays a vital role in people's lives – even for those of us who are not overtly religious. All of us, our basic values, our sense of right and wrong, are shaped by our community and its religious heritage. Understanding the role faith plays in people's lives is vital to community cohesion and good race relations. Many faith groups reach out to the wider community, providing facilities, undertaking practical projects and harnessing their deep commitment and drive to improve everyone's lives. (Blunkett, 2003)

According to Home Office publications, the government sees faith communities as potentially valuable allies in tackling social exclusion, as they can provide access to some of the most marginalised groups in society (HM Government, 2004). As a result, faith communities are being encouraged to open up their services to other sections of the population, and to apply for statutory funding in the same way as other local welfare providers (Faith Communities Unit, 2004). Reflecting the importance with which faith communities are now viewed by policy makers, the Citizenship Survey, which is carried out by the Home Office every two years and asks a series of questions about people's trust in institutions, their perceptions of discrimination by public and private sector organisations and their participation within their local communities, includes questions about people's faith identities. Moreover, in 2004, *Working together: Co-operation between government and faith communities* was published, which aimed to enhance local authorities' dealings with faith communities (Faith Communities Unit, 2004).

The increased interest in faith communities can partly be linked to the promotion of a wider political agenda in relation to social cohesion, civil renewal and active citizenship, many aspects of which originated in the 1980s under Thatcherism. Within the notion of active citizenship, individuals are viewed as having certain responsibilities and so should be encouraged to offer their skills and knowledge to public service, thereby pushing back the contours of the State (Mawby and Walklate, 1994). At the same time, communities are increasingly being viewed by government as necessary partners in the delivery of policies and practices. In May 2006, the Department for Communities and Local Government (DCLG) was created, whose vision is 'of prosperous and cohesive communities, offering a safe, healthy and sustainable environment for all'. The role of the DCLG includes building the capacity of communities to shape and protect their own future, working together to offer more choice and quality in public services, and building cohesion and tackling extremism (DCLG website, www.communities.gov.uk).

According to Francis (2003), the government may be interested in two types of social capital with respect to faith communities, where social capital refers to 'the propensity of individuals to associate together on a regular basis, to trust one another, and to engage in community affairs' (Hall, 1999, in Francis, 2003: 55). Bonding social capital refers to the ways in which members of religious communities might provide services and support to members of their own communities. Bridging social capital, on the other hand, refers to the ways in which religious communities can provide support and services to members of the wider locale, through undertaking voluntary work, for example (Francis, 2003).

However, the renewed emphasis upon the role that faith communities can play in public service provision raises many questions. One issue is that although the importance of religion within faith-based organisations/initiatives will vary (Monsma and Soper, 1998), in some contexts religious beliefs can nonetheless have an impact upon service provision. For example, some religious organisations may refuse their services to people on the grounds of their sexual orientation. Faith groups may, in particular, refuse to engage with, and offer their services to, lesbian, gay, bisexual and transgender individuals as a result of their belief systems in relation to sexuality (Branigan, 2006). It may also be the case that certain faith communities are not consulted and are excluded by statutory and other voluntary organisations, as a result of biased, misplaced perceptions that organisations have of those communities.

As funding structures within local government and mainstream services have traditionally been organised around ethnicity rather than religious identity, local government agencies are more experienced and perhaps more comfortable in working with groups of a non-religious nature and so faith communities have often been excluded from participation and dialogue (McManus, 2002). For example, statutory guidance under the 1998 Crime and Disorder Act lays a duty on community safety partnerships to involve faith communities in their work. However, traditionally, faith communities have rarely been consulted by the lead agencies involved in crime and disorder reduction partnerships. In a survey conducted in 2002 by McManus, out of 200 crime and disorder reduction partnerships, only nine mentioned religious communities as part of their plans. There may be a biased, misplaced perception of faith communities, which might affect decision making at local and national level, leading to the exclusion of faith communities. At the same time, local authorities and other agencies involved in developing and implementing crime and disorder reduction partnerships may not know what religious organisations to contact, what individuals those organisations represent, and they may be suspicious of them (McManus, 2002). Nonetheless, it is likely that crime and disorder partnerships will increasingly include faith communities as a result of the rising importance with which faith communities are viewed by government.

It is also important to highlight here that it seems that the British government is particularly interested in learning about, and creating policies in relation to, non-Christian faith communities, as evidenced by the Office of the Deputy Prime Minister's publication in 2006, entitled *Review of the evidence base on faith communities* (Beckford et al, 2006). This sought to review the evidence base relating to the demographic, socio-economic and cultural characteristics of 'emerging' faith communities, specifically the Hindu, Muslim and Sikh populations, together with the likely future trends within them. This focus upon non-Christian faiths might be linked to broader concerns around issues of radicalisation, multiculturalism and integration, which have carried particular political currency in a post-11 September 2001 context and in the aftermath of the more recent terrorist attacks in London on 7 July 2005. Particularly with respect to Muslim communities, strategies that are being implemented to develop effective working partnerships between faith communities and agencies of the criminal justice system are being instigated not only to boost individuals' trust of, and engagement with, criminal justice as part of a wider governmental strategy to increase minority ethnic communities' confidence in the criminal justice system, to improve crime reporting and to more effectively respond to victims' needs, as detailed in numerous policy documents, but also are being developed as part of counter-terrorist policing strategies that seek to reduce the likelihood of another terrorist attack occurring within mainland Britain. For example, in the 2005–08 National Policing Plan (Home Office, 2005: 8) it is stated that the 'counter-terrorism strategy of Government is underpinned by strong intelligence processes within each force area and strong communities to build and increase trust and confidence within minority faith communities'. It might be argued that Muslims' responsibilities as active citizens have increasingly been framed by anti-terrorist measures that encourage internal community surveillance so that the responsible Muslim citizen is expected to inform the authorities about the activities, suspicious or perceived to be suspicious, of their fellow community members, and actively to help deal with any potential extremism. However, within government rhetoric in the UK regarding the involvement of Muslim communities in helping to combat extremism, an artificially constructed binary opposition of legitimate versus illegitimate Muslim can be clearly discerned. Those Muslims and community organisations that are viewed as being 'moderate' make up the legitimate side of the dichotomy and so can be drawn upon as allies in the prevention of terrorism. All other Muslim identities are deemed illegitimate; radicalism has been conflated with extremism, and so these Muslims are marginalised and excluded from policy-making processes, and thereby prevented from entering the borders of the legitimate domain. It appears that the British government is keen to stress a homogeneous Muslim community that is committed to tackling extremism, and radicalisation is not viewed as being a characteristic of this community. Conflating radicalisation with extremism is highly contentious, as radicalisation has a wide range of meanings, and so this approach carries the risk of alienating large numbers of British Muslims (see Spalek and Imtoual, 2008 for more discussion).

Conclusion

A focus upon faith identities in relation to crime and victimisation raises many important issues. At a theoretical level, a researcher engaged in work that features religious identity and/or spirituality is inevitably confronted by the secular underpinnings of modern criminology, whereby a binary opposition of secular/sacred is constructed, consigning the realm of the sacred to a deviant Other. As a result, faith identities have rarely featured in criminological analyses, and diversity has largely been viewed through a secular framework of understanding in relation to ethnicity. If taking the position that religious affiliation and spirituality may constitute important aspects of the self-identity of some individuals, then it seems that the artificial separation between the secular and the sacred is no longer tenable. When exploring experiences of crime and victimisation in relation to people's religious and/or spiritual identities researchers may have to develop new approaches, drawing upon intuition that might enable the realm of the 'sacred' to be explored, or through utilising standpoint epistemologies that draw upon the standpoints that research participants themselves take. This area is fraught with difficulties, however, as the dominance of secularism in contemporary western society means that research that is associated with religious or spiritual frameworks of investigation is likely to be delegitimised and not considered to constitute 'proper social science'. Nonetheless, the rising interest in religion and spirituality within social and political arenas means that innovative research strategies are likely to be developed.

This chapter has also shown that the British government is encouraging faith communities to work in partnership with statutory agencies so as to play a significant role in public service provision. This raises many questions, including how and in what ways the religious identities of members of faith-based organisations can impact upon, and influence, the services that they provide. At the same time, it may be the case that certain faith communities are excluded from partnership work as a result of biased perceptions that organisations have of those communities, particularly as funding structures within local government and mainstream services have traditionally been organised around ethnicity rather than religious identity. It is also important to highlight that the terrorist attacks in the US on 11 September 2001, and then subsequent attacks in Spain, Bali and London, have brought to crisis core tenets of the liberal democratic state relating to notions of citizenship and individual rights in multi-ethnic and multi-religious contemporary democratic societies. The post-11 September context raises many issues in relation to religious identification, religious freedom and citizenship, with Muslim minorities in particular being scrutinised, being the focus of anti-terrorist legislation and counter-terrorist surveillance policing. This context can detrimentally impact upon agencies' attempts to foster dialogue and engagement with Muslim communities. As a result, partnership work with Muslim organisations can be severely compromised. Future research is therefore likely to focus further upon exploring engagement issues with Muslim communities.

Notes

[1] According to Herbert (2003), modernisation involves industrialisation, urbanisation, communications development and scientific progress.

[2] Religious conversion can be defined as 'an experience of increased devotion within the same religious structure, a shift from no religious commitment to a devout religious life, or a change from one religion to another' (Kose, 1996, 1).

[3] The religious question was conceptualised in different ways in the 2001 Census for England and Wales and the 2001 Census in Scotland. In the former, all Christian denominations were placed together within one general 'Christian' category, while in the latter the denominations were differentiated (Francis, 2003: 45).

Chapter questions

What theoretical and methodological challenges does a focus upon faith identities bring to criminology?

How, and in what ways, are faith identities relevant when thinking about crime and victimisation?

What can faith communities bring to a criminal justice context?

Case study
Muslim converts in jails in England

Between April and June 2005, two men incarcerated in a Young Offenders Institution and six men incarcerated in an adult prison were interviewed at length in order to explore the process of conversion to Islam inside prison. The men were aged between 18 and 23, many had been in and out of prison on a number of occasions. Interestingly, out of the eight men that were interviewed, seven were Black Caribbean and one was white, so that the predominance of Black Caribbean converts in the sample appears to reflect the high rate of conversion amongst this ethnic group in prison. A semi-structured interview format was adopted. Importantly, a Black African male Muslim researcher played a crucial role in this piece of research, not only by conducting the interviews with the inmates but also in helping to formulate the interview questions and also in analysing the data. Many of the interviewees referred to key aspects of Islam, and used Arabic words, so the Muslim researcher's understanding of Islam was crucial to developing an understanding of the perspectives of this sample of Muslim converts. At the same time, the researcher could 'bond' with the participants as he was able to greet them as fellow Muslims and could immediately engage with them on issues relating to Islam. In particular, the researcher acknowledged the inmates as his Muslim brothers, since in the Qur'an believers are instructed to observe all Muslims as their brothers, to like for their brother what they would like for themselves. The interviewer himself also used to work as a prison imam and so was familiar with prison life and prison slang.

Source: Spalek and El-Hassan, 2007: 104

Question
The study above incorporates the faith identities of the researcher and researched into the research process. Can you think of any other research contexts in relation to criminal justice where the inclusion of faith identities in the methodological process might be important?

References

Appleyard, B. (2006) 'Is it time to take God out of the State?', *The Sunday Times*, 22 October, pp 14–15.

Asad, T. (2003) *Formations of the secular: Christianity, Islam, modernity*, Stanford, CA: Stanford University Press.

Bauman, Z. (2004) *Identity: Conversations with Benedetto Vecchi*, Cambridge: Polity Press.

Beck, U. (1992) *Risk society: Towards a new modernity*, London: Sage.

Beckford, J. (1996) 'Postmodernity, high modernity and new modernity: Three concepts in search of religion', in K. Flanagan and P. Jupp (eds) *Postmodernity, sociology and religion*, Basingstoke: Macmillan, pp 30–47.

Beckford, J. (2003) *Social theory and religion*, Cambridge: Cambridge University Press.

Beckford, J. and Gilliat, S. (1998) *Religion in prison: Equal rites in a multi-faith society*, Cambridge: Cambridge University Press.

Beckford, J., Gale, R., Owen, D., Peach, C. and Weller, P. (2006) *Review of the evidence base on faith communities*, London: Office of the Deputy Prime Minister.

Berger, P. (ed) (1999) *The desecularization of the world: Resurgent religion and world politics*, Grand Rapids, MI: William B. Eerdmans Publishing.

Blain, J. (2004) 'Paganism', in G. Taylor and S. Spencer (eds) *Social identities: Multidisciplinary approaches*, London: Routledge, pp 162–81.

Blunkett, D. (2003) 'One nation, many faiths: creating unity with diversity in multi-faith Britain', Speech given at University of York, 28 October (www.york. ac.uk/admin/presspr/pressreleases/newsoct2003.htm).

Bowling, B. and Phillips, C. (2002) *Racism, crime and justice*, Harlow: Longman.

Branigan, T. (2006) 'Lib Dems urge Kelly to drop equalities brief', *The Guardian*, 16 October, p 9.

Cain, M. (1990) 'Realist philosophy and standpoint epistemologies or feminist criminology as a successor science', in L. Gelsthorpe and A. Morris (eds) *Feminist perspectives in criminology*, Buckingham: Open University Press, pp 124-40.

Caraballo-Resto, J. (2006) 'The rhetoric of secularism among first generation Muslim migrants in Dundee', Paper presented at the ninth EASA Biennial Conference, Bristol University, September (www.nomadit.do.uk/easa/ easa06/).

Clear, T., Hardyman, P., Stout, B., Lucken, K. and Dammer, H. (2000) 'The value of religion in prison: An inmate perspective', *Journal of Contemporary Criminal Justice*, vol 16, no 1, pp 53–74.

Cochran, J., Wood, P. and Arneklev, B. (1994) 'Is the religiosity–delinquency relationship spurious? A test of arousal and social control theories', *Journal of Research in Crime and Delinquency*, vol 21, pp 57–86.

Conway, G. (1997) *Islamophobia: A challenge for us all*, London: Runnymede Trust.

Cottingham, J. (2005) *The spiritual dimension: Religion, philosophy and human value*, Cambridge: Cambridge University Press.

CPS (Crown Prosecution Service) (2003) *Racist incident annual monitoring report 2002–2003*, London: CPS.

CPS (2006) *Racist incident annual monitoring report 2005–2006*, London: CPS.

CST (Community Security Trust) (2006) 'Anti-Semitic incidents report 2005', at www.thecst.org.uk/docs/Incidents%5FReport%5F05.pdf (accessed 12 July 2007).

Davie, G. (2002) *Europe: The exceptional case*, London: Darton, Longman and Todd.

Davis, D. (1997) 'The harm that has no name: Street harassment, embodiment and African American women', in A. Wing (ed) *Critical race feminism: A reader*, New York: New York University Press, pp 192–202.

Department for Communities and Local Government (2006) *2005 Citizenship Survey race and faith topic report*, London: Department for Communities and Local Government.

Ellis, L. (1987) 'Religiosity and criminality from the perspective of arousal theory', *Journal of Research in Crime and Delinquency*, vol 24, pp 215–32.

European Monitoring Centre on Racism and Xenophobia (2005) *The impact of 7 July 2005 London bomb attacks on Muslim communities in the EU*, Vienna: EUMC.

Evans, T., Cullen, F., Dunaway, R. and Burton, V. (1995) 'Religion and crime re-examined: The impact of religion, secular controls and social ecology on adult criminality', *Criminology*, vol 33, no 2, pp 195–224.

Faith Communities Unit (2004) *Working together: Co-operation between government and faith communities*, London: Home Office Faith Communities Unit.

Francis, L. (2003) 'Religion and social capital: The flaw in the 2001 Census in England and Wales', in P. Avis (ed) *Public faith? The state of religious belief and practice in Britain*, London: SPCK Publishing, pp 45–64.

Garland, D. (2002) 'Of crimes and criminals: The development of criminology in Britain', in M. Maguire, R. Morgan and R. Reiner (eds) *The Oxford handbook of criminology* (3rd edn), Oxford: Oxford University Press, pp 17–68.

Garland, J., Spalek, B. and Chakraborti, N. (2006) 'Hearing lost voices: Issues in researching hidden minority ethnic communities', *British Journal of Criminology*, vol 46, pp 423–37.

Gelsthorpe, L. (1990) 'Feminist methodologies in criminology: a new approach or old wine in new bottles?' in L. Gelsthorpe and A. Morrison (eds) *Feminist perspectives in criminology*, Milton Keynes: Open University Press, pp 89–106.

Gelsthorpe, L. (1993) 'Approaching the topic of racism: Transferable research strategies?', in D. Cook and B. Hudson (eds) *Racism and criminology*, London: Sage, pp 77–95.

Giddens, A. (1991) *Modernity and self identity*, Cambridge: Polity Press.

Gilbert, P. (2005) 'Spirituality and religion in the social work curriculum: Everybody's business', unpublished paper presented at the 'Spirituality, Religion and the Social Work Curriculum: The Neglected Dimension?' conference, at Staffordshire University, organised by the Centre for Health and Spirituality, Staffordshire University and SWAP, the Higher Education Academy, 28 April.

Gilbert, P. (2007) 'The spiritual foundation: awareness and context for people's lives in Britain today', in M.E. Coyte, P. Gilbert and V. Nicholls (eds) *Spirituality and values in mental health: Jewels for the journey*, London: Jessica Kingsley, pp 14–67.

Hall, P. (1999) 'Social capital in Britain', *British Journal of Political Science*, vol 29, pp 417–61.

Haug, I. (1998) 'Including a spiritual dimension in family therapy: Ethical considerations', *Contemporary Family Therapy*, vol 20, no 2, pp 181–94.

Heelas, P. (2006) 'Challenging secularization theory: The growth of New Age spiritualities of life', *Hedgehog Review. Critical Reflections on Contemporary Culture*, vol 8, nos 1 and 2, pp 46–58.

Heelas, P. and Woodhead, L. (2005) *The spiritual revolution: Why religion is giving way to spirituality*, Oxford: Blackwell.

Herbert, D. (2003) *Religion and civil society*, Aldershot: Ashgate.

Hervieu-Leger, D. (1999) *Le pelerin et le convert: la religion en mouvement*, Paris: Flammarion.

Hirschi, T. and Stark, R. (1969) 'Hellfire and delinquency', *Social Problems*, vol 17, pp 202–13.

HM Government (2004) 'Confident communities in a secure Britain. The Home Office strategic plan 2004–08', Cm 6287, London: HMSO.

Home Office (2005) *National Policing Plan 2005–2008*, London: HMSO.

Hood, R. (1992) 'Discrimination in the courts?', in R. Hood (ed) *Race and sentencing*, Oxford: Clarendon Press, pp 179–92.

Horowitz, D. (2004) *Unholy alliance*, Washington, DC: Regnery Publishing.

Humphrey, C. (2008: in press) 'Turning the world upside down', in B. Spalek and A. Imtoual (eds) *Spirituality and social science research*, Bristol: The Policy Press.

Hunt, S.J. (2002) *Religion in western society*, Basingstoke: Palgrave.

IHRC (Islamic Human Rights Commission) (2006) 'Islamophobia rampant in Ramadan in UK', press release, 5 October, (www.ihrc.org.uk/show.php?id=2147).

James, O. (1997) *Britain on the couch*, London: Century.

Jefferson, T., Walker, M. and Seneviratne, M. (1992) 'Ethnic minorities, crime and criminal justice: A study in a provincial city', in D. Downes (ed) *Unravelling criminal justice*, London: Macmillan, pp 138–64.

Johnson, B., Jang, S., Larson, D. and De Li, S. (2001) 'Does adolescent religious commitment matter? A re-examination of the effects of religiosity on delinquency', *Journal of Research in Crime and Delinquency*, vol 38, no 1, pp 22–43.

Jürgensmeyer, M. (2003) *Terror in the mind of God*, London: University of California Press.

Kalunta-Crompton, A. (1999) *Race and drug trials*, Aldershot: Avebury.

Kennedy, J., Davis, R. and Taylor, B. (1998) 'Changes in spirituality and well-being among victims of sexual assault', *Journal of the Scientific Study of Religion*, vol 37, no 2, pp 322–8.

King, U. (1993) *Women and spirituality* (2nd edn), London: Macmillan.

Kose, A. (1996) *Conversion to Islam: A study of native British converts*, London: Kegan Paul International.

Lerner, M. (2000) *Spirit matters*, Charlottesville, VA: Hampton Roads.

Luckmann, T. (1996) 'The privatization of religion and morality', in P. Heelas, S. Lash and P. Morris (eds) *Detraditionalization: Critical reflections on authority and identity*, Oxford: Blackwell, pp 72–86.

Lynch, G. (2008: in press) 'The dreams of the autonomous and reflexive self: Exploring the religious significance of contemporary lifestyle media', in B. Spalek and A. Imtoual (eds) *Spirituality and social science research*, Bristol: The Policy Press.

Lyon, D. (1996) 'Religion and the post-modern: Old problems, new prospects', in K. Flanagan and P. Jupp (eds) *Postmodernity, sociology and religion*, Basingstoke: Macmillan, pp 14–29.

McManus, J. (2002) 'Faith communities and community safety', in J. Howarth (ed) *Report of the fourth interfaith meeting held by the Churches' Criminal Justice Forum*, London: Churches' Criminal Justice Forum.

Mama, A. (2000) 'Woman abuse in London's black communities', in K. Owusu (ed) *Black British culture and society*, London: Routledge, pp 89–110.

Matza, D. (1964) *Delinquency and drift*, New York: Wiley.

Mawby, R. and Batta, L. (1980) *Asians and crime: The Bradford experience*, Middlesex: Scope Communications.

Mawby, R. and Walklate, S. (1994) *Critical victimology*, London: Sage.

Modood, T., Berthoud, R., Lakey, J., Nazroo, J., Smith, P., Virdee, S. and Beishon, S. (1997) *Ethnic minorities in Britain: Diversity and disadvantage*, London: Policy Studies Institute.

Monsma, S. and Soper, C. (eds) (1998) *Equal treatment of religion in a pluralistic society*, Grand Rapids, MI: William B. Eerdmans Publishing.

Morell, C. (1996) 'Radicalising recovery: Addiction, spirituality and politics', *Social Work*, vol 41, no 3, pp 306–12.

Morrison, W. (1995) *Theoretical criminology: From modernity to post-modernism*, London: Cavendish Publishing.

Moss, B. (2005) *Religion and spirituality*, Lyme Regis: Russell Publishing House.

National Census (2001) *Religion in Britain*, London: Office for National Statistics.

National Statistics Online (2007) 'Religious populations' (www.statistics.gov. uk/cci/nugget.asp?id=954).

O'Beirne, M. (2004) *Religion in England and Wales: Findings from the 2001 Home Office Citizenship Survey*, London: Home Office.

Pargeter, A. (2006) 'North African immigrants in Europe and political violence', *Studies in Conflict and Terrorism*, vol 29, no 8, pp 731–47.

Poynting, S. and Mason, V. (2006) 'Tolerance, freedom, justice and peace? Britain, Australia and anti-Muslim racism since September 11th 2001', *Journal of Intercultural Studies*, vol 27, no 4, pp 365–92.

Quraishi, M. (2005) *Muslims and crime: A comparative study*, London: Ashgate.

Sacks, J. (2002) *The dignity of difference*, London: Continuum.

Sheridan, L., Gillett, R., Blaauw, E. and Winkel, F. (2003) *Effects of the events of September 11th on discrimination and implicit racism in five religious and seven ethnic groups*, Leicester: University of Leicester School of Psychology.

Shorter-Gooden, K. (2004) 'Multiple resistance strategies: How African American women cope with racism and sexism', *Journal of Black Psychology*, vol 30, no 3, pp 406–25.

Shute, S., Hood, R. and Seemungal, F. (2005) *A fair hearing? Ethnic minorities in the criminal courts*, Cullompton: Willan.

Spalek, B. (ed) (2002a) *Islam, crime and criminal justice*, Cullompton: Willan.

Spalek, B. (2002b) 'Muslim women's safety talk and their experiences of victimisation: A study exploring specificity and difference', in B. Spalek (ed) *Islam, crime and criminal justice*, Cullompton: Willan, pp 50–71.

Spalek, B. and El-Hassan, S. (2007) 'Muslim converts in prison', *Howard Journal of Criminal Justice*, vol 46, no 2, pp 99–114.

Spalek, B. and Imtoual, A. (2008: in press) '"Hard" approaches to community engagement in the UK and Australia: Muslim communities and counter-terror responses', *Journal of Muslim Minority Affairs*, vol 27, no 2.

Stark, R., Kent, L. and Doyle, D. (1982) 'Religion and delinquency: The ecology of a lost relationship', *Journal of Research in Crime and Delinquency*, vol 19, pp 4–24.

SWAP (Social Policy and Social Work) (2005), 'Spirituality and religion in the social work curriculum: a neglected dimension?' (www.swap.ac.uk/docs/workshops/multifaith.doc).

Swinton, J. (2001) *Spirituality and mental health care: Rediscovering a 'forgotten' dimension*, London: Jessica Kingsley.

Victim Support (2006) *Crime and prejudice: The support needs of victims of hate crime. A research report*, London: Victim Support National Office.

Walklate, S. (2003) 'Can there be a feminist victimology?', in P. Davies, P. Francis and V. Jupp (eds) *Victimisation: Theory, research and policy*, Hampshire: Palgrave Macmillan, pp 28–45.

Wardak, A. (2000) *Social control and deviance*, Aldershot: Ashgate.

Watson, H. (1994) 'Women and the veil: Personal responses to global processes', in A. Ahmed and H. Donnan (eds) *Islam, globalisation and postmodernity*, London: Routledge, pp 141–59.

Webster, C. (1995) *Youth crime, victimisation and racial harassment*, Community Studies 7 (revised edn), Ilkley: Centre for Research in Applied Community Studies, Bradford and Ilkley Community College.

Webster, C. (1997) 'The construction of British "Asian" Criminality', *International Journal of the Sociology of Law*, vol 25, pp 65–86.

Weller, P., Feldman, A. and Purdam, K. (2001) *Religious discrimination in England and Wales*, Home Office Research Study 220, London: HMSO.

Whitfield, D. (1998) *Introduction to the probation service* (2nd edn), Winchester: Waterside Press.

Williams, P., (1997) 'Spirit-murdering the messenger: The discourse of finger pointing as the law's response to racism', in A. Wing (ed) *Critical race feminism: A reader*, New York: New York University Press, pp 229–36.

Wilmore, G. (1999) *Black religion and black radicalism* (3rd edn), New York: Orbis Books.

Yin, A. (2005) 'Religion and the politics of spirituality/sexuality: Reflections on researching British lesbian, gay and bisexual Christians and Muslims', *Fieldwork in Religion*, vol 1, no 3, pp 271–89.

EIGHT

Lesbian, gay, bisexual and transgender communities: crime, victimisation and criminal justice

Introduction

The experiences of lesbian, gay, bisexual and transgender (LGBT) communities in relation to crime, criminal justice and victimisation have traditionally been marginalised by policy makers and researchers, reflecting the bias towards heterosexuality that dominates western society, whereby same-sex desire has often been viewed through the lens of deviance. Nonetheless, LGBT communities have attracted some research and policy concern, particularly in relation to their experiences of hate crime and domestic violence, this work illustrating that hate crime and domestic violence are significant issues for LGBT minority groups and that, moreover, while there are similarities between the experiences of LGBT communities and heterosexuals, there are nonetheless significant differences that need to be taken into account.

This chapter looks at LGBT minorities in relation to crime, victimisation and criminal justice. It is argued that when considering LGBT minority experiences, it is important to consider the oppositional binary heterosexual–homosexual that is said to underpin western society, which casts same-sex desire into the category of the Other, the delegitimised. Not only have LGBT groups had to struggle against scientific medical constructions of sexuality that represent any kind of sexual orientation that lies outside of heterosexuality as pathological, abnormal and unnatural, but LGBT minorities have also had to challenge the institutions of heterosexuality, marriage and family, for example, for oppressing them. Within a criminal justice context, LGBT communities have criticised agencies of the criminal justice system for assuming that all peoples are heterosexual, and for acting in discriminatory ways towards those that are not. At the same time, LGBT minorities are increasingly arguing that agencies of the criminal justice system need to recognise differences between lesbian, gay, bisexual and transgender communities, and should respond with greater specificity and sensitivity to their needs.

This chapter also briefly considers some of the methodological issues and implications for knowledge production that the inclusion of LGBT identities poses for criminologists. It is argued that if heteronormativity underpins agencies like the police, offender management or Crown Prosecution Services, then LGBT minority groups may experience prejudice and disadvantage as employees, offenders, suspects and/or victims. However, obtaining quantitative evidence of prejudice or discrimination within a criminal justice context is highly problematic as sexual orientation tends not to be monitored by agencies, and individuals may be unwilling to disclose their sexual orientation. Utilising qualitative approaches can also be problematic. For example, gaining access to LGBT minorities for the purposes of research can be extremely difficult. Other research issues include how the usage of terms such as lesbian, gay, bisexual or transgender may serve to obscure the distinct experiences of specific groups. Hidden within these labels is a wide range of hidden peoples with hidden experiences who may have received little research attention. Moreover, the impact of a researcher's sexual orientation and sexuality upon criminological data collection and analysis has rarely been discussed and yet reflexivity over the research process requires that a researcher engage in self-reflexivity, examining how their own identities might play a role in the research that they carry out. It is important to stress that in contrast to gender and 'race'/ethnic identities, LGBT minorities have generated little research attention in relation to crime and victimisation; as a result, this chapter is rather exploratory.

Lesbian, gay, bisexual and transgender minorities and identity constructions

The 1960s heralded the development of the lesbian and gay liberation social movements, aimed at protesting against, and dismantling forms of, oppression and discrimination arising out of a dominant regime of power in western society in relation to heterosexuality. As Cruikshank (1992: 10) observes, 'because it [homophobia] is widespread, deeply rooted, and apparently ineradicable, gay and lesbian liberation must be a radical force to counteract it'. Lesbians and gay men have historically been criminalised, harassed and subjected to violence as a result of homophobia. For example, after Christianity became the predominant religion in the Roman Empire, homosexuality was punishable by death. The armed services in many countries have historically punished and/or dismissed any personnel found to be engaged in homosexual acts, and homosexuality has often been penalised through sodomy laws. A key moment in the gay and lesbian liberation movements appears to be the Stonewall rebellion in the US, relating to an incident that occurred in a Greenwich Village bar on 27 June 1969. When police raided this bar, lesbians and gay patrons responded by throwing beer cans and bottles at police, which resulted in a riot that lasted two nights, involving a crowd of 2,000 people fighting with 400 police officers (Cruikshank: 1992: 69).

The gay and lesbian liberation movements have constituted a critique of mainstream discourses that view homosexuality as perverse, and have reacted against institutions of heterosexuality that oppress those forms of sexual orientation that lie outside heterosexism (Seidman, 1997). The lesbian and gay liberation movements have involved building social identities with respect to homosexuality, with emphasis being placed upon the analytical centrality of sexuality so as to promote the interests of lesbians, bisexuals and gay men (Abelove et al, 1993). Often, lesbian, bisexual, gay and transgender existence has been omitted from scholarly work across a wide range of different fields, including feminism (with the focus here being upon gender rather than sexuality), and so the lesbian and gay liberation movements have included a focus upon documenting the experiences of LGBT minorities (Rich, 1993). Thus, for Abelove et al (1993), lesbian and gay studies involve placing sex and sexuality at the centre of analysis, expressing and advancing the interests of lesbians, bisexuals and gay men, and contributing to the lesbian and gay movements.

It is important to note that although lesbian and gay identity has been the focus around which resistance has been organised, by the early 1980s the fragmentation of a group collective identity can be witnessed, with critics arguing that collective identity has reflected a white middle-class position, thereby serving to exclude and marginalise other standpoints within lesbian and gay communities, such as those linked to ethnicity, age or 'race' (Seidman, 1997; Merck et al, 1998). Critics include queer theorists, who argue that identity is multiple. Queer theory involves a concern to dismantle the heterosexuality–homosexuality binary opposition. Inherent within this project is an objection to homosexuality as a category from which to formulate resistance strategies, as this simply reproduces the heterosexuality–homosexuality binary that pervades society (Seidman, 1997). As a result, queer theory consists of a concern to 'disrupt the binary construction, to "embrace the indeterminacy of the gay category" (Stein and Plummer, 1994: 181), for the category is implicated in our oppression at the same time that it is used by our liberation movements' (Whisman, 1996: 36).

Lesbian, gay, bisexual and transgender minorities and hate crime

As alluded to in the paragraphs above, LGBT minorities have been subjected to criminalisation, oppression and victimisation. It is unsurprising, therefore, that community organisations representing LGBT groups have been documenting the extent and level of homophobic hate crimes that are committed against LGBT minorities. A large number of surveys carried out with LGBT minority groups illustrate that hate crimes experienced by LGBT groups are significant, and that, moreover, most crimes are not reported to the authorities, distrust of the police being a significant factor here. According to a study of violence against lesbians and gay men in Britain carried out by the pressure group Stonewall in 1995, entitled *Queer bashing* (Mason and Palmer, 1996), one in three gay men and one in four lesbians had experienced at least one violent attack during the period 1990–95. Because of the fear of becoming the victim of homophobic violence,

65% of respondents always or sometimes avoided telling people they were gay, and 59% of respondents always or sometimes tried to avoid looking obviously gay. According to a report published by the National Advisory Group on Policing Lesbian and Gay Communities, *Breaking the chain of hate* (see Stonewall, 2007), 65.9% of the lesbian, gay and bisexual people taking part in the study here had been the victim of at least one homophobic hate crime. 29.4% were victims of verbal abuse, 13.2% experienced threats and intimidation, and 22.7% experienced violent assaults (in Tatchell, 2002: 59). According to Mason (2002: 39), surveys carried out in the US, Canada, Great Britain, Australia and New Zealand suggest that 70–80% of lesbians and gay men report experiencing verbal abuse in public on the basis of their sexuality; 30–40% report threats of violence; 20% of gay men report physical violence, and 10–12% of lesbians report physical violence. Incidents include being chased, sexually assaulted, pelted with objects, spat upon, and having property vandalised (Mason, 2002). Although random attacks by strangers appear to be common, Mason (2002) argues that lesbians may experience a significant level of abuse at home or at work, involving ongoing campaigns of abuse perhaps perpetrated by a person known to the victims. This may also be the case in relation to the experiences that gay men have of abuse, although due to the limited amount of research that has been conducted in this area it is not possible to make any such claims. Mason (2002) interviewed 75 lesbians and found that almost every woman had experienced a verbally, physically or sexually abusive reaction to her sexuality at least once in her life. Words commonly used to insult lesbians include 'dirty' and 'butch'. Mason (2002) argues that in order to understand violence committed against lesbians it is important to look at the regime of heterosexuality, as well as patriarchy, as the binary heterosexuality–homosexuality can serve to produce and perpetuate prejudices that underpin violence against lesbians.

Hate crimes against LGBT minorities affect all individuals, not only those who have directly experienced violence, as violence against LGBT groups serves to influence how individuals negotiate their personal safety, a predominant aspect of which is likely to include hiding their sexuality, thereby performing secretive homosexualities, confined largely to those private spaces deemed as being 'safe'. Felsenthal (2004) argues that, due to the transphobic violence and abuse experienced by transgender people, individuals may limit their use of public space, remaining behind closed doors. Weatherford and Weatherford (1999) reveal that some black men and women who engage in same-sex sexual behaviour might remain invisible within the black Churches that they belong to out of a fear of possible expulsion. Indeed, some individuals may pretend to be heterosexual due to the fear of possible violence (Mason, 2002). According to Stanko and Curry (1997), the self-surveillance that lesbians and gay men engage in may include passing off as heterosexuals as a way of managing the risk of violence. As Mason (2002: 94) argues: 'In avoiding or flouting danger, in negotiating safety, in hiding or flaunting sexuality, lesbians and gay men are involved in the complex daily management of a plethora of choices around the relation between homosexuality and visibility.' Hate crimes committed against LGBT minorities might thus serve as a warning to individuals to remain hidden behind closed doors, confining them within the boundaries of the 'closet', keeping individuals on the margins of mainstream society (McGhee, 2003).

Hate crimes are not the only component driving LGBT minorities underground, as historically these minorities have been subject to criminalisation and therefore have been policed and charged with criminal offences as a result of engaging in homosexual acts. Nonetheless, over the last two decades or so the police and prosecution authorities have striven to engage with LGBT communities, and homosexuality has largely been decriminalised. However, distrust of the police amongst LGBT communities remains significant, so that only a small proportion of crimes committed against LGBT groups is reported; even serious crimes such as rape or blackmail often remain unreported. Indeed the Association of Chief Police Officers (2001, cited in McGhee, 2003: 359) has acknowledged that many LGBT individuals believe that homophobia is widespread within the police service and many believe that information about an individual's sexuality passed on to the authorities will be revealed to their families, neighbours or employers. Other reasons for the under-reporting of hate crimes include a belief that an incident will not be taken seriously by the authorities, and a belief that an incident is not serious enough to report (McGhee, 2003: 359).

When writing about hate crimes perpetrated as a result of homophobia, it is important to note that hate crime legislation may not necessarily incorporate crimes committed on the basis of sexual orientation because not all minority groups feature in hate crime legislation. For instance, in the US, the 1990 Hate Crime Statistics Act (HCSA) requires the Attorney General to collect data 'about crimes that manifest evidence of prejudice based on race, religion, sexual orientation, or ethnicity, including where appropriate the crimes of murder, non-negligent manslaughter, forcible rape, aggravated assault, simple assault, intimidation, arson and destruction, damage or vandalism of property', suggesting that hate crimes carried out against LGBT communities are taken into account by law enforcement authorities. However, there are state differences in the number of groups protected so that while some states will include hate crimes on the basis of sexual orientation, others will not. In 2003, for example, while 46 American states had hate crime laws, only 29 had provision for hate crimes related to sexual orientation or disability (McVeigh et al, 2003: 844). In England and Wales, unlike for crimes committed through racial or religious prejudice, there is no specific offence of aggravation for homophobic crimes. However, under the 2003 Criminal Justice Act, judges are required to state in court any extra elements of a sentence that they are giving for an offence aggravated by hostility in relation to sexual orientation. Section 146 of the 2003 Criminal Justice Act came into effect on 4 April 2005. This section requires a court to treat hostility based on sexual orientation (or presumed) as an aggravating feature for sentence.

Prosecutors can now remind the court that they must treat homophobia as an aggravating feature, rather than requesting that they do so (CPS, 2005a). Statistics released by the Crown Prosecution Service (CPS) for 2004–05 reveal that out of 317 cases identified as having a homophobic element, 190 resulted in a guilty plea and a further 34 resulted in conviction after trial, the conviction rate being 71%. Principal offences were offences against the person, followed by public order offences (CPS, 2005a).

Diversity within and between LGBT minorities

It is important to note that there are significant differences between and within LGBT communities, these differences having implications not only for research but also for policy and practice-related issues. For instance, Mason (2002) suggests that minority ethnic lesbian and gay men report higher levels of homophobia-related violence than their white counterparts, suggesting that ethnicity intersects with sexuality, thereby serving to influence the extent of violence committed against minority ethnic LGBT individuals. This would suggest that strategies aimed at minimising the extent, and the impacts, of violence upon LGBT individuals should be aimed particularly at those individuals of minority ethnic status. Moran and Sharpe (2004) highlight the diversity of experiences contained within the umbrella term 'transgender', which emerged in the 1990s to capture the multiplicity of gender experiences that lie between the medically constructed categories of transvestite and transsexual. Transgender categories include the cross-dresser, drag queen, drag king, transgender male, transgender female, intersexed, stone butch and nellie queen.

Moran and Sharpe (2004) argue that there may be significant differences between transgender males and transgender females when experiencing violence and that law enforcement and victim services need to take these differences into account. Thus, transgender women may approach their personal safety as a man might and so they may be placing themselves at higher risk of victimisation. Police may then view transgender women as being engaged in overtly risky behaviour, and therefore may judge them as being illegitimate victims, thereby responding inappropriately to their experiences. Transgender men may have a significant fear of rape, which is not likely to be taken seriously by law enforcement agencies. Transgender men may also be less likely to report crimes to the police than transgender women. This may be because the perceptions that transgender men have of violence are likely to be informed by their previous experiences as women. Moreover, victim services that help women who have experienced gender violence are not likely to cater to the needs of cross-dressers or transgender women (Moran and Sharpe, 2004).

Older people within LGBT minority groups are also likely to have specific issues that agencies of the criminal justice system, as well as victim services, need to take into account. Older lesbians, gay men, bisexuals and transgender individuals are less likely to access services and to report crimes because they have lived a large part of their lives in less liberal times and therefore encounter unique problems as they age, particularly as mainstream service providers regularly assume that all older people are heterosexual (Age Concern, 2002). LGBT individuals with a religious identity also raise a number of issues. For example, service providers may not raise LGBT issues with Muslims, assuming that LGBT minorities cannot also be Muslim and that Muslims cannot also hold LGBT identities. Moreover, while there may be specific services for faith minorities and specific services for LGBT minorities, these compartmentalised approaches overlook the specific needs and experiences of individuals who hold both faith and LGBT identities (see, for example, Safra Project, 2003). Thus, diversity among and between LGBT minorities deserves more research and policy attention.

Community consultation

Agencies of the criminal justice system have recently worked towards establishing ongoing contact and consultation with LGBT communities. For example, the Crown Prosecution Service has held meetings with representatives of LGBT communities in order to inform communities about its vision for the future, also to listen to key concerns and to engage in dialogue and establish effective links (CPS, 2005b). Police services have also striven to develop good relations with LGBT communities, particularly in relation to homophobic attacks. For example, some police forces have held conferences on responding to homophobic attacks, some have developed consultation mechanisms led by gay and lesbian communities, some have tried to develop anonymous reporting of homophobic attacks via third parties, and some police services have community contact officers with a specific responsibility to liaise with gay and lesbian groups (Jones and Newburn, 2001).

Community consultation raises a number of issues. It appears that although considerable advances have been made with respect to consultation with gay men, lesbians' needs have tended to be overlooked because of a lack of political organisation and power. At the same time, even where good relationships have been fostered between the police and gay and lesbian groups, these only pertain to those individuals who have 'come out', with those individuals whose sexualities remain hidden not being part of consultation processes. There is also a whole population of men that might be characterised as being socially invisible since these individuals may engage in homosexual or bisexual behaviour but may not lead openly gay lives. Indeed, many of these men may keep their sexuality secret, perhaps due to being married, or because they may not view themselves as being gay. This population is viewed as being at high risk from homophobic violence and yet is particularly unlikely to report any offences to the police. This population therefore poses particular difficulties for any community engagement undertaken by agencies of the criminal justice system. There may also be radical gay or lesbian groups whose opposition to the police makes it impossible for them to engage with police services (Jones and Newburn, 2001).

Police culture

When writing about policing in relation to homophobic violence, it is perhaps important to write something about police culture and the difficulties that this poses for gay and lesbian officers. According to Miller et al (2003), policing is a gendered and sexualised institution, and police culture might be viewed as embracing aggressive masculinity, including traits such as toughness or physical strength. Questioning a police officer's sexuality can be a tactic frequently used by officers to devalue the actions of those officers who do not conform to popular macho models. Those police officers who remain in 'the closet', and therefore who hide their sexual orientation, are under pressure to engage in banter about heterosexual conquests so as to avoid being scrutinised by their colleagues. Some research seems to suggest that homosexuals are the social group most disliked by police (see Miller et al, 2003: 360). Police officers who are gay or lesbian may face barriers in terms of career progression, or may experience hostility from co-workers or supervisors.

Over the last two decades, gay and lesbian police associations have been formed, thereby challenging the dominance of heterosexuality within policing. In the UK, the Gay Police Association (GPA) exists to work towards equal opportunities for gay police service employees, to offer advice and support to gay police service employees and to promote better relations between the police service and the gay community. The association is also involved in policy development, victim care and family and community liaison in relation to homophobic hate crime. The GPA has taken part in an initiative to introduce the monitoring of sexual orientation for all police officers and police staff in all police services across the UK, which will be voluntary and rely on self-classification. The monitoring of sexual orientation is viewed as constituting an important initiative to help promote equality for gay staff in the police service (GPA, 2006).

Lesbian and gay minorities and domestic violence

The issue of domestic violence within lesbian and gay partnerships has attracted some research attention. It is important to stress that the prevalence of domestic violence within lesbian and gay partnerships is difficult to uncover because lesbian and gay minorities often conceal their sexual orientation and so drawing a large, random sample of this population is extremely problematic (Renzetti, 1998). At the same time, it may be the case that individuals hide the issue of domestic violence from researchers and public authorities because they do not wish to propagate negative imagery of gay relationships within a homophobic society (Merrill, 1998). In a survey of 100 self-identified battered lesbians, Renzetti (1998: 119) found that physical forms of violence commonly cited included being pushed and shoved, being hit with open hands or fists, being scratched or hit in the face and having things thrown at them. Psychological or emotional abuse was also experienced, which might include being demeaned in front of family, friends or strangers and having property damaged or destroyed. Being outed, whereby the abuser threatens to reveal or actually does reveal their partner's sexual orientation against their wishes, is a further significant dimension to domestic violence within lesbian partnerships, and indeed in Renzetti's (1998: 119) study 21% of participants had said their partners had threatened to out them. This can have significant effects upon victims, who may be shunned by their family and friends or may experience job loss. This illustrates how the dynamics of domestic violence between lesbian partners can include dimensions that heterosexual partnerships do not have; in this way, there is a danger in relying upon models of domestic violence that have been developed from heterosexual partnerships. Indeed, domestic violence has traditionally been viewed as the product of aggressive masculinity; however, when looking at the issue of domestic violence within lesbian partnerships it seems that abusers are not consistently more masculine than the victims and that some victims are larger and less 'feminine' than their abusers. However, the myth that perpetrators of domestic violence are more masculine than their victims may mean that it is more difficult for lesbian victims to get help. At the same time, services helping the victims of domestic violence may only cater to the needs of heterosexual victims. Renzetti (1998: 123–4) found that of 566 service providers, only 9.3% offered services specifically designed for battered lesbians and that of the 527 organisations that used volunteers, 56.2% indicated that volunteers received homophobia training but just 40.6% said that their volunteers receive training specifically on lesbian battering. It is therefore unsurprising that many battered lesbians do not seek help from domestic violence hotlines and shelters, as they perceive these services to be for heterosexual women. Moreover, lesbian victims of domestic violence report being insulted or dismissed by police officers (Renzetti, 1998).

Violence within gay partnerships is also a largely hidden problem. Domestic violence is mainly viewed as a male–female phenomenon, and so abuse within gay and bisexual partnerships remains under-investigated and under-explored. Moreover, victim services are often constructed on the basis that victims are female and perpetrators are male, and so victims of domestic violence within gay and bisexual partnerships do not gain the kind of help that they need. Indeed, battered gay and bisexual men who call for police assistance have often been mistaken for perpetrators (Merrill, 1998). Gay and bisexual men experiencing domestic violence have reported forms of physical, emotional, sexual and financial abuse similar to heterosexual and lesbian victims. It has often been assumed that batterers are larger than their victims; however, this is not true in the case of gay and bisexual partnerships. Moreover, gay and bisexual men who experience domestic violence may not recognise it as violence because many may have become conditioned to accepting abuse as a result of commonly experiencing homophobia. At the same time, victims are unlikely to seek out help because programmes helping victims of domestic violence tend to be directed at women and not men, and victims may not disclose being battered to their families from fear of their families reacting homophobically towards them (Merrill, 1998).

Models attempting to explain violence in intimate relationships that are based on heterosexual relationships may not be appropriate for explaining violence that takes place within gay or lesbian partnerships. For instance, feminist models that view intimate violence as the product of sexism and patriarchy may not be applicable in explaining domestic violence in male-to-male or female-to-female relationships (Merrill, 1998). Renzetti (1998) argues that internalised homophobia may be a reason why partner abuse occurs within homosexual relationships, as some lesbians and gays may accept mainstream society's negative evaluations of them and incorporate these into their self-concepts. Merrill (1998) suggests that gay batterers have character traits similar to those of heterosexual male batterers: they are emotionally dependent on their partners, feel emotionally out of control when in love and fear abandonment. A study of Muslim lesbian, bisexual and transgender women highlights how not conforming to the gender and sexual norms of the wider community can result in women experiencing domestic violence. Being lesbian, bisexual or transgender in a Muslim community can bring shame and dishonour to a family, and so some families or family members will resort to domestic violence to control or hide transgressions of sexual or gender norms. Indeed, some lesbian, bisexual or transgender victims of domestic violence may feel that they deserve this because of their feelings of guilt or shame stemming from their sexual orientation being viewed as sinful or morally wrong. Victims may not report their abuse to the police as the police may be viewed by victims as being racist or homophobic, or victims may think that in going to the police they are being disloyal to their families or wider community (Safra Project, 2003).

Batterer programmes often operate according to a heterosexual model, whereby offenders are assumed to be male, thereby posing difficulties for lesbian batterers. Lesbian batterers may be put into treatment programmes provided for heterosexual male batterers, which is problematic as these programmes tend to view domestic violence as being connected to masculinity, sexism and those patriarchal social norms that institute violence against women (Renzetti, 1998). In relation to integrating gay male batterers within group therapy, this is likely to be problematic as many of the men making up a group are likely to be homophobic (Merrill, 1998).

Summary

The discussions above clearly illustrate how the dominant social norm of heterosexuality has served not only to make the experiences of LGBT minority groups invisible, but can also be implicated in the hate crimes that LGBT minorities experience as well as perhaps playing a role in domestic violence within same-sex partnerships. It seems that too often policy makers and service providers have assumed that all people are heterosexual, thereby leading to a lack of initiatives aimed specifically at LGBT communities. At the same time, there has been insufficient attention paid to differences between and within LGBT groups, as heterogeneity in relation to age, faith, 'race'/ethnicity and so forth also has important policy and practice implications.

The next section examines the inclusion of LGBT identities within criminological research and some of the methodological challenges that these pose. It might be argued that heterosexuality is an invisible norm that underpins criminological knowledge production and criminal justice practices, thereby leading to the marginalisation of LGBT experiences. In the same way that the preceding three chapters have shown that gender, 'race'/ethnic and faith identities pose significant challenges for criminological research, the section below will discuss the implications of LGBT identities for criminological work.

Researching LGBT communities: criminological knowledge production

A theme underpinning this book is that of reflexivity increasingly being a characteristic feature within criminological research, whereby dominant knowledge constructions and research approaches are being challenged through an inclusion of, and focus upon, social difference, with a concomitant acknowledgement of the fluidity and fragility of any knowledge claims as associated with postmodern processes within late modernity. As demonstrated in Chapters Five and Six of this book, a focus upon gender and 'race'/ethnic identities has had a pronounced effect in terms of questioning assumptions within criminology, leading to the development of alternative epistemological and methodological positions. Moreover, as highlighted in Chapter Seven, faith identities are now also posing challenges for approaches to the production of criminological knowledge. Therefore, it is perhaps pertinent to explore LGBT identities and some of the issues that arise here in relation to criminological research, as the following paragraphs will elucidate.

When looking at LGBT minorities in relation to criminology and a criminal justice context, a number of issues come to light. It is important to highlight heteronormativity as a dominant, yet largely invisible, social norm that underpins all social institutions, a norm that has been institutionally elaborated in criminological practices and knowledges. If heteronormativity underpins agencies like the police, offender management or Crown Prosecution Services, then LGBT minority groups may experience prejudice and disadvantage as employees, offenders, suspects and/or victims. For example, employees might face promotional barriers and/or verbal abuse and harassment as a result of their sexual orientation and, moreover, may be involved in an intricate management of their sexuality that may involve their remaining in 'the closet'. However, getting hold of quantitative, statistical evidence of prejudice or discrimination of LGBT offenders, suspects, victims or criminal justice employees is extremely problematic as sexual orientation is rarely monitored by agencies. In contrast to the vast amount of data available in relation to 'race'/ethnicity and gender, very little information can be gleaned regarding sexual orientation in relation to the criminal justice system. Therefore, there is very little statistical information available to back up any claims made by LGBT minority groups regarding any prejudice that they may experience within the criminal justice context. Nonetheless, new legislation may lead to sexual orientation being increasingly monitored by agencies of the criminal justice system. The introduction of the 2003 Employment Equality (Sexual Orientation) Regulations, which outlaw discrimination on the grounds of sexual orientation in employment and vocational training, and the introduction of the 2006 Equality Act, which extends the protection afforded on the basis of sexual orientation from employment to the provision of goods, facilities and services in education and in the execution of public functions, are likely to have an impact upon monitoring procedures, so that more data in relation to discrimination and the experiences of LGBT minorities in relation to criminal justice will be made available.

Producing qualitative data regarding LGBT minorities' experiences is equally problematic. It is likely to be extremely difficult to find a sample of LGBT employees of the criminal justice system because of the ways in which people may hide their sexual orientation, and many potential participants may be dissuaded from taking part in any study as a result of a fear of their sexuality being made public. Similarly, it is difficult to get a sample of LGBT offenders and/or suspects to interview and explore any homophobic experiences that they might have in a criminal justice context, or to explore the ways in which individuals manage their sexual orientation so as to reduce their risks of being victims of homophobic attacks by, say, other offenders. LGBT victims are also very unlikely to inform the authorities or victim support organisations of their plight, and so this creates difficulties for any researcher trying to gain access to a sample of victims to interview. A report by Victim Support (2006), setting out the results of a study about the victims of hate crime, highlights the difficulties of gaining access to individuals who have experienced homophobic or other types of violence motivated by hatred. The study commissioned by Victim Support used community researchers to contact potential research participants as it was viewed that community researchers would have more success in getting individuals from minority communities to take part in interviews since they would have a particular affinity with the particular communities being studied. This point relates to a wider question about whether LGBT researchers are best placed to understand the lived experiences of LGBT communities. Similar to debates within research relating to 'race'/ethnicity and researcher insider/outsider status, it might be argued that heterosexuals can legitimately study such issues, but that this requires active involvement with LGBT organisations and individuals in order to understand and portray their world-views and lifestyles. On the other hand, it might also be argued that, as 'insiders', LGBT researchers are better placed to do this work since they have greater awareness and understanding of LGBT issues and so can provide accounts of experiences and perceptions that are more genuine and legitimate.

Within social scientific research, some reflexive methodological accounts of the work carried out by LGBT individuals can be found. Here, self-reflexivity features a discussion of the researcher's sexuality and its role in, and impact upon, the research process. For example, according to Goodman (1996), lesbian and gay anthropologists think about the implications that the disclosure of their sexual orientation will have upon research participants. La Pastina (2006), in discussing the implications of an ethnographer's sexuality when carrying out fieldwork, argues that his memories of growing up 'in the closet' in Brazil informed some of his research choices. La Pastina (2006) was fearful of disclosing his sexual orientation to the research participants due to fears of being made an outcast. This caused him considerable anxiety and depression, as the fieldwork became an extension of the repressive environments that La Pastina had experienced when he was younger. While La Pastina's (2006) research account focuses largely upon the role that a researcher's sexual orientation can play in the research choices that are made and in data collection, other researchers have written about the role that erotics, attraction and possibly sex might have in fieldwork. Thus, Kong et al (2002) have argued that researchers engaged in interpretative accounts should discuss their attraction to the people that they interview and the role that this plays in the research.

This discussion illustrates how a researcher's sexual orientation and sexuality might impact upon data collection and analysis. This might therefore be a significant contribution that LGBT minorities can potentially make to challenging dominant criminological knowledge constructions that have generally failed to consider LGBT identities and sexuality more generally. If Seidman's (1997) claim is legitimate, that the human sciences are underpinned by a political unconscious that suppresses epistemological and social difference, then the inclusion of LGBT identities poses challenges to the epistemological basis and methodological processes within criminology, especially when considering that the sexual orientation of researchers and researched has generally been omitted.

Another issue raised by the documentation of LGBT minority groups' experiences is that focusing upon the lives of LGBT communities may be perpetuating the heterosexual–homosexual binary that underpins western society and thereby serves to reinforce, rather than to dismantle, heteronormativity. This argument has been made by queer theorists, who emerged in the 1980s when the idea of gay and lesbian identity as a way of building community and organising resistance was challenged for reflecting a middle-class white perspective, and who drew extensively upon the work of Michel Foucault, psychoanalytic theory and feminist studies (Seidman, 1997; Filax, 2006). Queer theory constitutes a method of enquiry and political action. According to Seidman (1997: 93), 'queer theory articulates an objection to a homosexual theory and politics organised on the ground of the homosexual subject: this project reproduces the hetero–homosexual binary'. It is argued that heteronormativity pervades all social institutions and so to 'queer' is to 'notice, call into question and refuse heterosexuality as the natural foundation of social institutions' (Filax, 2006: 140), particularly when the social dominance of heterosexuality involves the demonising of its Other: the homosexual. Queer theorists have argued that LGBT identities should not be completely abandoned, but rather should be viewed as being permanently open and contestable, so that decisions about the identity categories that a researcher uses might be linked to wider political, pragmatic and conceptual aims (Seidman, 1997). Another strategy to avoid reinforcing heteronormativity might be to deconstruct, make visible and particularise this social norm through a focus upon, and study of, heterosexuality.

A further issue to raise here is in relation to the usage of terms such as lesbian, gay, bisexual or transgender. These terms may serve to obscure the distinct experiences of specific groups. Within these labels are a wide range of hidden peoples with hidden experiences, and who may have received little research attention. As illustrated previously in this chapter, the category 'transgender' can include a range of people, each having specific identities and experiences that policy makers and service providers need to take into account (Moran and Sharpe, 2004). Similarly, Stein's edited collection (1993) highlights the multiplicity of lesbian identities, and Hiestand and Levitt (2005) write about the construction and development of butch lesbian identities. Focusing upon the specific lives of specific groups of individuals whose identities might be linked to the more general categories in relation to lesbian, gay, bisexual and transgender might help to dispel any prejudices or assumptions about LGBT minorities.

Conclusion

LGBT minority groups as offenders, suspects, victims or employees of the criminal justice system have largely been marginalised from research and policy arenas. Moreover, LGBT minorities have historically been subjected to criminalisation, oppression and victimisation. Nonetheless, the brief outlines here illustrate how hate crime and domestic violence are significant issues for LGBT minorities. Hate crimes committed against LGBT communities are extensive and, moreover, LGBT individuals may hide their sexual orientation so as to reduce their risk of violence. Individuals rarely report crimes to the authorities as a result of heteronormative structures pervading mainstream society. At the same time, victim and offender initiatives tend to be directed at heterosexuals and so the needs of LGBT minorities are rarely addressed. Research also suggests that diversity within

LGBT communities is significant, so that sexual orientation can intersect with other social differences in relation to 'race'/ethnicity, faith, gender and so forth. At the same time, differences between LGBT communities can also be significant. As a result, in this chapter it has been argued that policy and practice must engage more with difference and specificity of experience.

This chapter also illustrates that the inclusion of LGBT identities in criminological research raises many methodological questions. For example, can heterosexual researchers carry out research with LGBT minorities? What impact might the sexual orientation of the researcher and the researched have upon the research process? How can researchers carry out work with LGBT minorities without reinforcing the heterosexual–homosexual binary that underpins western society? There are many questions here and it is likely that some of these issues will be discussed further as more work is carried out. Another area that requires further focus is disability and age in relation to crime, victimisation and the criminal justice system, and these are the focus of the next chapter.

Chapter questions

How, and in what ways, are differences between lesbian, gay, bisexual and transgender communities significant in a criminal justice context?

What implications do LGBT identities raise for criminological research?

How might the norm of heteronormativity have a negative impact upon LGBT communities, particularly in relation to crime and victimisation?

Case study
Hate crimes against LGBT minorities

There has been a 3.3% increase in homophobic crimes recorded between April and September 2005 compared with the same period the previous year. Latest data available shows the proportion of victims of homophobic crime who are female increasing from 18.6% to 27.6%, with a 52.9% or 72 victim increase in the actual number of female victims recorded. The proportion of victims who are BME has also increased, rising from 13.7% to 27.9%. The current sanction detection rate for homophobic crime is 15.5%, a similar rate recorded for the period last year. The MPS have recently provided the MPA with data on transgender crime. The number of transgender crimes recorded between April and September 2005 is 46, compared to 34 recorded in the same period in 2004.

Source: MPA, 2007

Question
To what extent are hate crimes committed against LGBT communities the result of individual action or the result of homophobia in wider society?

References

Abelove, H., Barale, M. and Halperin, D. (1993) 'Introduction', in H. Abelove, M. Barale and D. Halperin (eds) *The lesbian and gay studies reader*, London: Routledge, pp xv–xviii.

Age Concern (2002) *Survey of fear of street crime amongst older people*, London: Age Concern, Policy Unit.

CPS (Crown Prosecution Service) (2005a) 'CPS publishes first full set of homophobic crimes', press release, 25 July (www.cps.gov.uk/news/west_yorkshire/news_events/press_releases/homophobic_crime_figures_released/index.html).

CPS (2005b) *Business Strategy 2005-08* (Draft V1.3, 10 January 2005), London: Equality and Diversity Unit, CPS.

Cruikshank, M. (1992) *The gay and lesbian liberation movement*, London: Routledge.

Felsenthal, K. (2004) 'Socio-spatial experiences of transgender individuals', in Jean Lau Chin (ed) *The psychology of prejudice and discrimination: Bias based on gender and sexual orientation, volume 3*, London: Praeger, pp 201–25.

Filax, G. (2006) 'Politicising action research through queer theory', *Educational Action Research*, vol 14, no 1, pp 139–45.

GPA (Gay Police Association) (2006) 'Sexual orientation monitoring' (www.gay.police.uk/monitoring.html).

Goodman, L. (1996) Rites of passage', in E. Lewin and W. Leaps (eds) *Out in the field: Reflections of lesbian and gay anthropologists*, Urbana: University of Illinois Press, pp 49–57.

Hiestand, K. and Levitt, H. (2005) 'Butch identity development: The formation of an authentic gender', *Feminism and Psychology*, vol 15, no 1, pp 61–85.

Jones, T. and Newburn, T. (2001) *Widening access: Improving police relations with hard to reach groups*, Police Research Series Paper 138, London: Home Office Research, Development and Statistics Directorate.

Kong, T., Mahoney, D. and Plummer, K. (2002) 'Queering the interview', in J. Gulbrium and J. Holstein (eds) *Handbook of interview research*, Thousand Oaks, CA: Sage, pp 239–58.

La Pastina, A. (2006) 'The implications of an ethnographer's sexuality', *Qualitative Inquiry*, vol 12, no 4, pp 724–35.

McGhee, D. (2003) 'Joined-up government, community safety and lesbian, gay, bisexual and transgender active citizens', *Critical Social Policy*, vol 23, no 3, pp 345–74.

McVeigh, R., Welch, M. and Bjarnason, T. (2003) 'Hate crime reporting as a successful social movement outcome', *American Sociological Review*, vol 68 (December), pp 843–67.

Mason, G. (2002) *The spectacle of violence: Homophobia, gender and knowledge*, London: Routledge.

Mason, A. and Palmer, A. (1996) *A national survey of hate crimes against lesbians and gay men*, London: Stonewall.

Merck, M., Segal, N. and Wright, E. (1998) 'Introduction', in M. Merck, N. Segal and E. Wright (eds) *Coming out of feminism?*, Oxford: Blackwell, pp 1–10.

Merrill, G. (1998) 'Understanding domestic violence among gay and bisexual men', in R. Bergen (ed) *Issues in intimate violence*, London: Sage, pp 129–41.

MPA (Metropolitan Police Authority) (2007) 'Equal opportunities and diversity management information report', 1 December (www.mpa.gov.uk/committees/eodb/2005/051201/12.htm).

Miller, S., Forest, K. and Jurik, N. (2003) 'Diversity in blue: Lesbian and gay police officers in a masculine occupation', *Men and Masculinities*, vol 5, no 4, pp 355–85.

Moran, L. and Sharpe, A. (2004) 'Violence, identity and policing: The case of violence against transgender people', *Criminal Justice*, vol 4, no 4, pp 395–417.

Renzetti, C. (1998) 'Violence and abuse in lesbian relationships: Theoretical and empirical issues', in R. Bergen (ed) *Issues in intimate violence*, London: Sage, pp 117–28.

Rich, A. (1993) 'Compulsory hetereosexuality and lesbian existence', in H. Abelove, M. Barale and D. Halperin (eds) *The lesbian and gay studies reader*, London: Routledge, pp 227–54.

Safra Project (2003) *Identifying the difficulties experienced by Muslim lesbian, transgender and bisexual women in accessing social and legal services, Initial findings*, London: Safra Project.

Seidman, S. (1997) *Difference troubles: Queering social theory and sexual politics*, Cambridge: Cambridge University Press.

Stanko, E. and Curry, P. (1997) 'Homophobic violence and the self at risk: Interrogating the boundaries', *Social and Legal Studies*, vol 6, no 4, pp 513–32.

Stein, A. (ed) (1993) *Sisters, sexperts, queers beyond the lesbian nation*, Harmondsworth: Penguin.

Stein, A. and Plummer, K. (1994) 'I can't even think straight: Queer theory and the missing sexual revolution in sociology', *Sociological Theory*, vol 12, no 2, pp 178–87.

Stonewall (2007) 'Breaking the chains of hate summary' (www.stonewall.org.uk/information_bank/violent__hate_crime/resources/192.asp).

Tatchell, P. (2002) 'Some people are more equal than others', in P. Iganski (ed) *The hate debate*, London: Profile Books Ltd, pp 54-70.

Victim Support (2006) *Crime and prejudice: The support needs of victims of hate crime: A research report*, London: Victim Support National Office.

Weatherford, R. and Weatherford, C. (1999) *Somebody's knocking at your door.: AIDS and the African-American Church*, New York: Haworth Pastoral Press.

Whisman, V. (1996) *Queer by choice*, London: Routledge.

NINE

Ageing, disability, criminology and criminal justice

Introduction

Two further minority groupings that have traditionally been marginalised by criminologists are those consisting of older people, and people with disabilities. In criminology, there is a tendency to focus upon the experiences of young people, particularly as offenders, although some research in relation to the fear of crime and victimisation has included a consideration of older people. On the other hand, disabled people who experience crime have been labelled 'invisible victims' because crimes committed against these individuals are often hidden and not reported to agencies of the criminal justice system. Disability in relation to crime is a developing research area, particularly in relation to the experiences of mentally disordered offenders, where mental disorder might be viewed as a disability of mind.

This chapter presents key research and policy issues in relation to older people and people with disabilities, as offenders and victims of crime. Elder abuse is highlighted as a key issue, but it is stressed that older people can also be victims of a wide range of offences, including burglary, physical assault and corporate crime. Older people can also commit crime, and the proportion of older prisoners in jails in England and Wales has been rising over the last decade or so. Hate crimes are a significant issue for people with disabilities, leaving individuals feeling scared, embarrassed, humiliated and stressed. Increasingly, policy makers and agencies of the criminal justice system are considering the needs of people with disabilities, with special measures being implemented to help disabled victims and witnesses cope better with the criminal justice process. At the same time, mental disorder is widespread amongst the prison population, with the issue of the needs of people who suffer from mental illness who come into contact with the criminal justice system constituting increasing policy concern.

This chapter also explores some of the issues that the inclusion of identities in relation to ageing and disability pose for criminological knowledge construction. It is argued that research with older people and people with disabilities puts focus upon the body, the body as ageing or the body as 'impaired'. At the same time, wider social and cultural processes, such as consumerism, individualism and valued norms in relation to being young and healthy, and how these influence experiences of ageing and/or disability are also of concern. It is also argued that the voices of older people and people with disabilities are often marginalised, and so researchers should include these individuals as active participants in the research process, providing space for voices to articulate experiences of oppression in relation to dominant norms that serve to stigmatise older and disabled people.

Ageing and older people

Critical perspectives on ageing

Over the last three decades, critical perspectives have emerged, challenging traditional, largely medical-based, theories of ageing. Critical perspectives incorporate a reflexive stance, whereby dominant ideas are critiqued and placed within their broader social, cultural and historical context (Achenbaum, 1997). Critical perspectives go beyond the 'mere appearance' of everyday life, and in relation to ageing, direct attention is turned towards the body as a site of regulation and control in conditions of late modernity, including an exploration of the wider social structures that have an impact upon, and influence, experiences of ageing. It has been argued that ageing has been seen as a problem since the creation of the welfare state, whereby older people have increasingly come to be viewed as constituting a burden for the younger population through their apparent dependency (Phillipson, 1998). Moreover, different institutional settings give different narratives on ageing identities, which may pose significant challenges for older people (Estes et al, 2003).

When focusing upon identities in relation to ageing, it is important to highlight that older people hold a number of identities, for example in relation to their gender, 'race'/ethnicity or faith, and these will all influence their everyday experiences. Indeed, Blakemore (1997) argues that ethnic and cultural factors significantly influence not only the ageing process but also professionals' perceptions of older people's needs. It may be the case that Asian Sikh or Muslim family members tend to care for their older relatives; also, older people from minority ethnic groups might have language difficulties or may have special religious and dietary needs (George, 1997). Blakemore (1997) notes that in the UK, although policy makers have focused predominantly upon 'racial' identities within older people, other minorities also have specific needs, for example older Irish, Jewish or Polish people. While acknowledging differences between older people is important, researchers adopting a critical position nonetheless suggest that a common identity in relation to ageing should be maintained as this contains the possibility of collective action against inequalities and prejudices that are experienced on the basis of being older (Estes et al, 2003).

A critical perspective also involves highlighting that an oppositional binary of young/old underpins western society, with the category of 'old' constituting the devalued, the Other, thereby perceived as being inferior and so excluded and prevented from entering the borders of the 'young'. Wahidin and Cain (2006: 4) use the category of the 'unyoung' to define those individuals 'deemed beyond the pale of the human because of their perceived frailties, dependence, failure to be contributing members of society'. However, this categorisation might be criticised on the basis that it fails to empower older people, as it is unable to propose a collective identity that lies beyond the 'young', and serves to perpetuate the binary opposition of young/old through valuing 'young' as the norm through which to view older people. Furthermore, there is considerable debate over the definition of 'old' or 'older'. Some researchers have used the age categories of 65–75 and 75+, others have categorised individuals over 50 as constituting older people, whilst more have used 60+ or 70 (Phillips, 2006; Wahidin and Cain, 2006).

A critical perspective further involves drawing attention to the erosion of traditional social structures associated with conditions of modernity, so that the body is viewed as the site through which governmental power operates, and so individual subjects are constructed according to the objectives of governing authorities (Foucault, 1977; Turner, 1995). In a consumerist society, the body provides access to, and enables the expression of, a broad range of consumer identities. However, an ageing body might be viewed as one that is increasingly rigid, thereby preventing the expression of a number of identities (Featherstone and Hepworth, 1995). As Estes et al (2003: 37) argue, 'the progressive betrayals of the body accumulate and force themselves onto identity's agenda. There may be younger selves trapped in ageing bodies'. This position, in seeing ageing as a cage that surrounds a younger self, appears to be a rather negative and disempowering view of the ageing process. As a result, some attempts have been made to stress the fluidity of identities. Nonetheless, these attempts have been criticised as themselves constituting mechanisms through which new forms of restriction emerge, since attempts to construct 'agelessness' themselves consist of a series of demands upon the body (Estes et al, 2003). It is important to note, however, that in denying the expression of consumer identities, ageing bodies might be viewed as directly challenging consumerism, since it might be argued that technologies that construct individuals as consumers are unable to work through the bodies of older people. This is not necessarily to argue that older people are free to claim a number of identities, merely to suggest that ageing bodies and the restrictions that these impose upon the expression of various identities can directly challenge consumer society, regardless of whether older individuals themselves have any choice over these restrictions. As a result, ageing bodies and the restrictions that these impose upon individuals might be viewed as a form of collective empowerment, posing challenges for a society that is underpinned by ideals related to consumerism and individualism.

The paragraph above suggests that when exploring issues around ageing, the body should constitute a core aspect of research. This represents a significant departure from mainstream social scientific knowledge production, where the body has often been marginalised, as western thought separates the mind from the body (Estes et al, 2003). Moreover, a focus upon the body includes a consideration of emotionality, as emotions are expressed through bodies. But the body here is not to be viewed in isolation from wider cultural, social and political structures, as these influence how people feel within particular situations, and so emotions should not be viewed as wholly biologically and psychologically driven (Hochschild, 1998).

These analyses highlight some issues raised by critical perspectives on ageing, which, it might be argued, are relevant to other fields of study where a focus upon older people is pursued. The next section therefore considers criminology and some of the research issues raised here by a consideration of, and focus upon, older people.

Ageing and criminological research

When specifically focusing upon research in the criminological arena in relation to ageing, a number of issues appear to be particularly relevant. The first issue relates to the body as a key feature of research, as highlighted in the above section. Therefore, it might be argued that criminological research exploring older people's experiences of crime and/or the criminal justice system necessitates a focus upon bodies. Research by Phillips (2006), Wahidin (2002), the Chief Inspectorate of Prisons (2004) and Crawley and Sparks (2006) about older prisoners does indeed refer to bodily issues. For instance, Phillips (2006) highlights that physical decline and vulnerability are a cause of anxiety amongst older prisoners, as physical strength is highly valued within a penal setting. Many older prisoners report illness and/or disability. For example, older women prisoners experience gynaecological problems and osteoporosis (Wahidin, 2002), many older prisoners also have problems with incontinence, personal hygiene, mobility, and also have a preoccupation with a fear of dying (Chief Inspectorate of Prisons, 2004; Crawley and Sparks, 2006).

But bodies are not the only focus of concern when researching older people. Another important factor to consider is the ways in which older people's voices have been marginalised, or indeed silenced, within criminology. For example, feminist work focusing on women as offenders has tended to focus upon younger rather than older women's experiences of criminal justice, leading to Wahidin and Cain's (2006) argument that feminist analyses should include a focus upon the experiences and identities of older women. At the same time, within penal and other institutions, the voices of older people are often silenced, replaced by the voices of professionals working in those environments, as a result of power inequalities and institutions' operational needs (Wahidin and Cain, 2006). In this way, the voices of older people should take central position within research, as these voices can be used to highlight ageist structures and processes that serve to disempower and victimise older people. Links here can be made with feminist research, which has used women's voices to shed light on patriarchy and women's experiences of violence. Furthermore, research models that view research subjects as participants in the research process should be actively encouraged, whereby older people are encouraged to take an active role in the research design, process and outcomes. Barnes (1995) provides an excellent example of the ways in which older people can be active participants in the research process, and how older people's voices and experiences can take a central position. A further pertinent issue to raise here is in relation to who should conduct research about older people, whether older researchers are best placed to understand the lived experiences of older individuals as victims or offenders, or whether younger people as 'outsiders' can legitimately study older people's experiences. It might be argued that in order to prevent older people's experiences from being marginalised within criminology, both younger and older researchers should be encouraged to carry out work here. Indeed, Wahidin and Cain (2006) have argued that any political movement by older people needs the involvement and support of younger people.

Turning now specifically to older people as offenders and/or victims, the next sections will highlight the main research studies in these areas; analyses around older people's fear of crime will also be presented, as the fear of crime has generated substantial research and policy attention.

Older people and crime

According to Wahidin and Cain (2006), although age constitutes a key variable in the study of criminality, the tendency has been for researchers to focus upon young offenders. Nonetheless, over the last decade or so, researchers and policy makers have increasingly turned their attention towards older people as the perpetrators of crime. This is due to a number of factors, including that there is an increasingly ageing population in the UK, and that there are rising numbers of lifers in English and Welsh prisons (Phillips, 1996; 2006).

Prison statistics show that over the last two decades the proportion of older prisoners in England and Wales has been rising. According to Phillips (2006: 56), the proportion of older prisoners between 1990 and 2000 more than doubled, constituting 1% of prisoners in 1990 and rising to 2.3% by 2000. Many older prisoners have been convicted of sex crimes or violent offences, most being men; however, the proportion of older female prisoners has also risen significantly since 1992 (Phillips, 2006: 56). Older prisoners present particular issues for the prison service. Researchers have found that depression, illness or disability are significant issues for older prisoners, and indeed, older prisoners' health appears to be worse than that of older people living in the community. The prison authorities have been criticised for not being sensitive to, or considering, older prisoners' social and health needs (Chief Inspectorate of Prisons, 2004).

There is also significant diversity within the population of older prisoners. Some prisoners may, for example, be career criminals whose experiences may be very different from lifers who have aged in prison (Phillips, 2006). According to a study by Crawley and Sparks (2006), which involved interviewing male prisoners aged between 65 and 84, older men in prison often have painful preoccupations, including the fear of dying and the loss of contact with their families. Older female prisoners may also have different needs to older male prisoners. According to a study by Wahidin (2002) of older women prisoners, women's health issues are different from men's as older women may have gynaecological problems or osteoporosis. Interestingly, while feminists have looked at women's experiences of criminal justice, they have focused almost exclusively upon younger women, leading Powell and Wahidin (2006) to argue that a feminist analysis in gerontology is required, which engages with the experiences and identities of older women.

Older people as victims of crime

Turning to the issue of older people as the victims of crime, elder abuse is a key research and policy area, and so there is an expanding literature on this issue (see Slater and Eastman, 1999; Fitzgerald, 2006; Gorgen, 2006). The available evidence on elder abuse provides only an approximate figure in relation to the number of people who experience it, as there are many difficulties involved in obtaining accurate data. Elder abuse takes place at home or in institutional settings, and so tends to be hidden away from public gaze. Most incidents are not reported to the authorities as victims may be fearful of criminalising the offender, whom they may rely on and therefore may be worried that reporting this might lead to them being taken out of their homes and being institutionalised. At the same time, victims may be ashamed that the offender is their own child. The very notion of 'elder abuse' is also open to criticism as this can serve to decriminalise individuals' experiences of victimisation, so that elder abuse is not viewed as 'real crime' by the authorities and therefore not responded to by the police but by social workers (Brogden and Nijhar, 2000).

Sources of data on elder abuse are available through reports of abuse received by adult protection services, or through probability samples taken from populations; also, the work carried out by groups campaigning for equal rights for older people, like Help the Aged and Age Concern, now includes a focus upon elder abuse. Action on Elder Abuse (AEA), a national organisation aiming to prevent the abuse of older people, was established in 1993. A helpline was set up in 1997, offering a free and confidential service. According to the AEA, elder abuse is 'a single or repeated act or lack of appropriate action occurring within any relationship where there is an expectation of trust which causes harm or distress to an older person'. This may involve physical, psychological, financial, sexual abuse and/or neglect. An analysis of the calls received by the AEA telephone helpline reveals that between 1997 and 1999 most calls were about abuse in people's own homes, although a quarter referred to abuse in hospitals, nursing and residential homes; two-fifths of the calls reported psychological abuse, one-fifth physical and one-fifth financial abuse; over a quarter of calls identified workers as the abuser (Jenkins et al, 2005). According to Fitzgerald (2006), the prevalence of elder abuse in the UK is difficult to estimate because there has been only one study on the community prevalence of elder abuse and no research into abuse within institutions catering to the welfare and social needs of older people. According to a survey carried out by the Office of Population Census and Surveys in 1992, which included 593 individuals aged over 60, 5% of this sample of 593 reported having been orally abused, 2% reported experiencing physical abuse, and 2% reported experiencing financial abuse (in Fitzgerald, 2006: 96). However, these figures are likely to be an under-estimate of the true extent of elder abuse, as those individuals who were in institutions or too ill or disabled did not take part in this survey. Researchers suggest that older women are more likely to experience elder abuse and domestic violence than older men (Pain, 1995; Fitzgerald, 2006). The higher incidence of elder abuse among women may be due to women living longer than men and therefore women being more likely to be living in institutional settings. At the same time, it may be the case that women are more likely than men to indicate that they have experienced abuse (Fitzgerald, 2006).

A House of Commons Select Committee report on elder abuse in 2004 has stressed that while the profile of child abuse has been raised significantly in the last few years, elder abuse remains largely hidden. This report suggests that as many as 500,000 older people might be being abused at any one time in England. However, much of this abuse is not reported because many older people are either unable or too frightened or embarrassed to go to the authorities. The report also highlights the lack of training of professionals in recognising, reporting and treating elder abuse (Health Committee, 2004). Increasingly, it is being suggested that elder abuse should be viewed as a specific crime area, and that the Crown Prosecution Service (CPS) should be working with organisations like AEA to understand how and where it occurs, how to prevent it and what action needs to be taken when it does occur (CPS, 2004). As such, the issue of elder abuse is likely to feature more and more as an aspect of the work of agencies of the criminal justice system.

Older people can also be the victims of a wide range of other crimes, including burglary or physical assault. Indeed, older people can be the victims of corporate crime, this being a particularly under-researched area (Brogden and Nijahar, 2006; Powell and Wahidin, 2006). A study of victimisation by corporate crimes by Spalek (1999) illustrates how older people can experience substantial psychological, emotional, physical, behavioural and financial impacts, similar to victims who experience 'street crimes' such as physical and sexual assault. Spalek (1999) interviewed older people whose company pension schemes were decimated by the actions of Robert Maxwell, a business magnate. Upon the death of Robert Maxwell on 5 November 1991, it became apparent that hundreds of millions of pounds were missing from the pension funds of companies belonging to Maxwell's business empire, and that the lives of approximately 30,000 Maxwell pensioners across the UK were affected (Bower, 1994). Data from interviews with a sample of Maxwell pensioners reveal that these individuals experienced the fraud committed against them as older people, as working-class retired printers, caught up in the risk society associated with conditions of late modernity where pension schemes are unstable and insecure (Spalek, 1999, 2001).

Older people and the fear of crime

Crime survey data suggest that older people display higher levels of fear of crime than younger people, even though younger people appear to be more likely to be victims of crime. This echoes crime data in relation to women and their fear of crime, which implies that, while men are more likely to experience street crime against them than women, women nonetheless report significantly more fear. Such anomalies have been termed the 'fear of crime paradox' (Clemente and Kleiman, 1976; Cook and Cook, 1976; Lee, 1982; Ortega and Myles, 1987). Moreover, older people (as well as women) have been deemed as having irrational levels of fear, where a rational level of fear is viewed as being that which corresponds to the likelihood of victimisation from street crime according to the socio-demographic space that an individual occupies. An irrational level of fear, on the other hand, is one that does not correspond to the likelihood of victimisation (Hough and Mayhew, 1983).

A number of reasons have been suggested for the high levels of fear of crime that older people seem to display. Researchers have suggested that older people (defined as those over the age of 60) are more socially and physically vulnerable to the effects of crime than are other groups of individuals, and this is why they portray 'irrational' levels of fear (Goldsmith and Tomas, 1974; Conklin, 1975; Harris, 1978; Skogan and Maxfield, 1981). It is thought that older people are more sensitive to risk than are younger people, so that although their level of risk from victimisation might be lower, they nonetheless show high levels of fear (Warr, 1984). Also, the mass media tend to sensationalise crimes against older people more than crimes against younger persons, which might have an effect upon levels of fear (Yin, 1982). Finally, the way in which fear is measured has also been questioned, since different types of measurement reveal different levels of fear. The general conclusion to be reached here is that when fear towards specific types of crime is measured rather than fear of walking alone at night, older people do not portray higher levels of fear than younger people. This is perhaps because fear of walking alone conjures up images that frighten older people, images that have little to do with specific instances of crime but might have more to do with being old in today's society (Garofalo and Laub, 1978; Yin, 1982).

More radical accounts argue that the gender component among the older population has been ignored, and yet there is a consistent finding that older women report higher fear levels than older men. Since there are more older women than there are older men, it follows that gender constitutes one reason why older people in general show higher levels of fear than younger people do. Secondly, many surveys operate upon the assumption that crime is something that occurs outside the household, so that the full extent of the victimisation experiences of older people are not revealed. Private violence in nursing homes, individuals' own homes and so forth, surely plays a factor in fear, so that perhaps the high fear level of older people accurately reflects their extent of victimisation when private violence is accounted for. Perhaps it might be suggested that older people's high levels of fear really relate to anxieties that accompany ageing. Thirdly, there tends to be an assumption in surveys such as the British Crime Survey that only those abusive events that have occurred relatively recently have an impact upon fear levels. Yet this surely needs to be questioned, since fear of crime might be viewed as a cumulative process, taking place over a long period of time and therefore relates not only to recent experiences but also to distant ones as well (Pain, 1995). Indeed, Wahidin and Cain (2006) argue that most older people have witnessed their own parents getting older, and so understand the vulnerability of older people at the hands of their carers, which is likely to be a source of anxiety for them.

Summary

Older people as offenders and victims of crime are research areas that are developing. Older people raise a number of issues for policy makers, researchers and practitioners, as they may have specific needs as a result of ageing processes. For example, older people as prisoners raise key health issues for the prison service, and older people's high levels of fear of crime raise concerns for policy makers as well as criminal justice and community safety practitioners. Older people also raise some interesting methodological issues, including a focus upon bodies and emotions, as well as the use of standpoint epistemologies as a way of utilising older people's voices so as to shed light on ageist structures and processes operating in western society. The next section focuses upon another minority grouping, a grouping that traditionally has been marginalised by researchers and policy makers: comprised of people with disabilities.

Disabled people

Disabilities and critical social research

Critical perspectives in relation to disability have also emerged, challenging the social exclusion of disabled people from mainstream society because of perceived impairment. Medical approaches to disability have been criticised for individualising disability, and for viewing people with disabilities as passive, powerless and incapable (Liggett, 1988). Cultural representations of impairment have been explored, and researchers have argued that these representations are disabling and constitute a form of oppression for people with disabilities (Riddell and Watson, 2003). A disability movement emerged during the 1970s and 1980s, so that a politics of disability has developed, with disability constituting a collective identity around which a social movement has taken shape, for the redress of social inequalities and tackling discrimination experienced by disabled people. At the same time, the stigmatisation, and negative portrayal, of disability as illness or constituting impairment, has been rejected, with positive disabled identities being actively pursued and promoted, involving their private and public affirmation, and including a demand for acceptance and integration within society (Oliver and Barnes, 1998). Alongside other minority groupings, the fragmentation and fluidity of identities have, more recently, been stressed, as identities in relation to 'race'/ethnicity, gender and so forth influence the ways in which disability is experienced (Riddell and Watson, 2003). For instance, gender has been highlighted as a key component to take into consideration when exploring the nature and experience of disability; Fine and Asch's (1988) work suggests that patriarchal structures enable disabled men to oppose the stigma and oppression associated with disability, so that they can aspire to adopt traditional male roles. Disabled women, on the other hand, do not have the same resources available to them to challenge their oppression.

Definitions of disability have constituted a site at which there have been struggles between policy makers and disabled people. People with disabilities have criticised and rejected definitions used by state officials, because these definitions have predominantly been used to aid policy making (Oliver and Barnes, 1998). Disability might therefore be viewed as a social construct, and definitions the result of power struggles between officials and groups representing disabled people's interests. Disability might therefore be thought of as intrinsically linked to the use of language, so that the true nature of disability is flexible and open to discussion (Liggett, 1988). Some critical studies in relation to disability have included a focus upon the body. It has been suggested, for example, that contemporary western society has become increasingly concerned with the body, with the focus upon creating and maintaining a healthy self through the utilisation of appropriate diets and exercise. The devalued Other in this instance constitutes the unhealthy, and so disabled people can experience stigmatisation, especially in contexts where individual responsibility for keeping healthy is stressed (Crawford, 1994).

Disabled people as victims of crime

Disabled people who experience crime have been labelled 'invisible victims' because crimes committed against these individuals are often hidden and not reported to agencies of the criminal justice system. At the same time, little research has been generated regarding the incidence of crimes against people with disabilities, and crimes that may take place in institutional care are not included in the British Crime Survey (Williams, 1995). Sanders et al (1997) carried out a study exploring the issues facing victims with learning disabilities, where they argued that offences against learning-disabled people are more likely to be difficult to investigate and prove than are other offences. These authors also highlight how learning disability is a blanket term covering many conditions, with varied manifestations. Therefore, individuals should be responded to as individuals, and their specific needs assessed by agencies of the criminal justice system. This research also highlights how people with learning disabilities as victims/witnesses raise a number of important issues. For example, while some individuals may have difficulties with recalling events to police officers or prosecutors; this is not necessarily the case as some people have very good memories, for instance some autistic individuals may have extremely good recall of incidents. Some learning-disabled witnesses may have language difficulties, and so they may have difficulty in putting their memories into words; also, some witnesses may have difficulty in understanding what they are being asked. Sanders et al (1997) further highlight that repeated questioning, often used both in the investigation and prosecution of cases, may adversely affect people with learning difficulties as this may serve to emphasise their relative powerlessness compared to other people. Furthermore, as police response to relatively minor offences may be dismissive, with there being little appreciation of the severe impact of minor crime upon individuals with learning difficulties, interviews should always be carried out with police officers who have received appropriate training.

A number of surveys have been carried out with disabled respondents, and these show that hate crimes are a significant issue for people with disabilities. For example, in a survey carried out in Scotland by the Disability Rights Commission (2004), 22% of disabled respondents had experienced harassment in public because of their impairment. Out of 158 completed questionnaires, it was found that approximately half the disabled people who responded experienced hate crime because of their disability. It was also found that 31% of disabled people surveyed who were the victims of hate crime experienced the attacks at least once a month. In a survey carried out by Mencap, it was found that nearly nine out of ten respondents with a learning disability had experienced bullying in the previous year, with two-thirds of respondents revealing that they are bullied on a regular basis (Mencap, 2000).

Hate crimes against people with disabilities is a rising area of policy concern, especially as the implementation of the 2003 Criminal Justice Act provides an increased sentence for offences involving or motivated by hostility based on disability or their presumed disability. Therefore, when an offender has pleaded guilty or been found guilty and the court is deciding on the sentence to be imposed, it must treat evidence of hostility based on disability as something that makes the offence more serious. The court must also state that fact openly so that everyone knows that the offence is being treated more seriously because of this evidence of hostility based on disability (CPS, 2007). Hate crimes leave people feeling scared, embarrassed, humiliated and stressed. Moreover, individuals are likely to avoid specific places and change their usual routines, and many may also move home as a result of being victimised. Crimes that are motivated by a hatred of disability can have an impact upon the broader population of disabled people, since individuals may be afraid to leave institutional care settings to live in wider society if they are aware of acquaintances who have been victimised in the community, and who may not have had their complaints taken seriously by the authorities responsible for investigating and prosecuting cases (Williams, 1995).

Other developments, in relation to equality legislation, taking place in the 1990s suggest that agencies of the criminal justice system will increasingly consider the needs of people with disabilities. For example, the 2005 Disability Discrimination Act places a duty on all public sector authorities to promote disability equality, which means that all public sector bodies will have a duty to promote the equalisation of opportunities for disabled people through preparing and publishing disability equality schemes (Directgov, 2007). Agencies of the criminal justice system will therefore be committed to preparing and publishing a disability equality scheme, which should demonstrate how these organisations will promote disability equality for staff and for the public that they serve, and this includes a focus upon arrangements for consulting on proposed policies and to monitor any adverse impact of policies on the promotion of disability equality. Through the No Witness No Justice programme, the CPS established witness care units across all of its 42 areas. In the Home Office report (HM Government, 2004), 'Cutting crime, delivering justice', it is argued that these units are essential to achieving a criminal justice system in which the public have confidence, whereby victims and witnesses are treated with respect and understanding, and where more offences are brought to justice. For the CPS, witness care units are seen as an important way of increasing victim and witness satisfaction with their treatment by the criminal justice system and as a way of reducing ineffective trials as a result of witness issues. Also, they are viewed as a way of making further progress on equality and diversity issues. Thus, community engagement has been an important component to establishing witness care units, and some units have been developed to acknowledge the needs of a more diverse range of victims (CPS, 2004). Following the implementation of an innovative project based in Liverpool, specifically helping vulnerable witnesses with learning disabilities, the CPS has reviewed whether there is scope for implementing this across all 42 areas, especially in light of the introduction of a disability equality scheme in 2006, so that disability issues will be mainstreamed into work that the CPS undertakes (CPS, 2004).

Disabilities and offending

Statistics suggest that mental disorder is widespread among the prison population in England and Wales, where mental disorder might be viewed as 'mental illness, arrested or incomplete development of mind, psychopathic disorder and any other disorder or disability of mind' (Mind, 2003: 3). The Social Exclusion

Unit (Singleton et al, 2002) has estimated that 72% of sentenced male prisoners suffer from two or more mental health disorders, with many prisoners having a personality disorder, a psychosis, neurosis or a substance misuse problem (Singleton et al, 1998). Indeed, prison life can cause or exacerbate mental health issues as a result of prison overcrowding, a lack of privacy and the prevalence of violence. It is also important to note that suicide in prison is a significant issue, with one study showing that between 1999 and 2000 there were 172 suicides among prisoners (Shaw et al, 2003). Indeed, in 1999 the Chief Inspectorate of Prisons carried out a thematic review of suicide in prisons.

Policy makers have acknowledged that offenders with mental health issues are of significant concern, and so efforts are being made to meet the needs of these offenders when they come into contact with the criminal justice system, whether this is at the point of arrest, while incarcerated or upon release into the community (Department of Health, 2005). Court diversion or criminal justice mental health liaison schemes are aimed at preventing people with mental health issues from going to prison, and medical assessments can be used to make any appropriate arrangements for individuals' support and treatment. However, diversion schemes have often not received the level of funding that they require and so some areas in the UK have limited schemes or no schemes available at all.

Traditionally, the mental health care available in prisons does not often compare favourably with standards outside penal settings, and so it might be argued that prisons cause unnecessary suffering to individuals with mental health issues (Cavadino, 1999). As a result, policy makers have set up initiatives aimed at improving prison mental health care. For example, wing-based services, day care, in-patient services and transfer to NHS facilities have been promoted, as well as improved training of prison staff and NHS teams working in prisons. In April 2006 the NHS took over responsibility of prison health care from the prison authorities (Sainsbury Centre for Mental Health, 2006).

More recently, people with learning disabilities or learning difficulties have attracted some policy attention. The Prison Reform Trust is undertaking a piece of research exploring the experiences of people with learning difficulties and learning disabilities who come into contact with the criminal justice system throughout the UK, entitled 'No One Knows'. This study will look at the issue of people with learning difficulties and learning disabilities from initial arrest and police custody through to court appearance and sentencing, including a focus upon the available opportunities for diversion into health and social care settings, community and custodial sentences, rehabilitation and resettlement. Prisoners' experiences will also be a focus of concern, and how best these individuals' particular needs can be responded to. The Prison Reform Trust highlights how there is a lack of opportunity for screening and diagnostics in some prisons and how this can disproportionately affect people who are the most disadvantaged (Prison Reform Trust, 2007).

Summary

Clearly, disability in relation to crime, victimisation and a criminal justice context raises many important issues. Heightened awareness amongst policy makers and criminal justice agencies of issues such as the difficulties experienced by people with learning disabilities when interacting with the criminal justice system as victims/and or witnesses, the high proportion of prisoners exhibiting personality and other mental disorders, and the detrimental impacts of hate crime committed against people with disabilities is leading to the development of initiatives aimed at supporting people with disabilities and is leading to more research in these areas. The increasing focus upon, and inclusion of, individuals with disabilities in criminological research is likely to raise a number of important methodological concerns, including the ways in which people with disabilities can become active participants in research, and the importance of giving their voices a central position in order to help critique broader social and cultural processes that serve to oppress them.

Conclusion

This chapter has focused upon two minority groupings that have traditionally generated very little research and policy attention within a criminological context: older people and people with disabilities. This chapter highlights key issues that these minority groups raise, as victims and offenders, not only for the policy arena, but also in relation to research processes. It seems that agencies of the criminal justice system need to take into consideration the needs of older people and people with disabilities, including an acknowledgement that while there may be issues common to individuals within these broad collective groupings, there are nonetheless specific needs that arise as a result of considerable diversity within these groupings in terms of 'race'/ethnicity, gender, religion and so on. A focus upon both minority groupings further highlights how ageing and disabilities are experienced through bodies, which constitute a site through which technologies of governmental power are at play, so that wider social and cultural processes can have an impact upon and influence experiences of ageing and disability. Researchers engaged in work with older and disabled people therefore need to give central attention to bodies and allow for the voices of these individuals to articulate their experiences. This is a developing research field within criminology, and as such is likely to generate interesting research strategies and research data.

Chapter questions

Why have disabled people who experience crime been labelled as invisible victims?

What theoretical and methodological challenges does researching people with disabilities and older people bring to criminology?

What insights into ageing do critical perspectives bring?

Case study
Older people in prison

No one seems to know the whole of Harry's story, but this is what they do know. He was born in Kilmarnock, worked on the railways, became an alcoholic after his parents died. They know he lived rough and that in 1991 he was sentenced to life for starting a series of fires. He is 71.

It was never easy to get through to Harry at the best of times, and a couple of years ago it began to get even harder. Depending on who you ask, he was suffering from either Alzheimer's or a form of alcohol-induced dementia. Everyone agrees that he frequently did not know where he was, that he began falling over regularly and became incontinent. Once he borrowed a lighter to light a cigarette and accidentally set his hair on fire. They put him in a cell with a CCTV camera because they were so worried he would do himself an injury. Recently, when he could no longer walk without help, he was moved to a nearby prison hospital. Doctors there said he should be released, but to where? 'It's difficult to find nursing homes that are prepared to take people like that,' says Stuart McLean, who retired as governor of Portsmouth's Kingston Prison last week. 'The last thing they want is to have someone who may be disruptive.'

Harry's case highlights one of the thorniest questions facing our penal system: when, if ever, is someone too old or infirm to be kept behind bars? It is a delicate balancing act between compassion and risk, and right now the scales are tipped heavily against compassion.

Source: Katz, 2001

Question
What issues do older prisoners pose for the prison service?

References

Achenbaum, W. (1997) 'Critical gerontology', in A. Jamieson, S. Harper and C. Victor (eds) *Critical approaches to ageing and later life*, Buckingham: Open University Press, pp 16–26.
Barnes, M. (1995) 'Partnerships in research', in G. Wilson (ed) *Community care: Asking the users*, London: Chapman, pp 228–41.

Blakemore, K. (1997) 'From minorities to majorities: Perspectives on culture, ethnicity and ageing in British gerontology', in A. Jamieson, S. Harper and C. Victor (eds) *Critical approaches to ageing and later life*, Buckingham: Open University Press, pp 27–38.

Bower, T. (1994) *Maxwell the outsider*, London: Mandarin Paperbacks.

Brogden, M. and Nijhar, P. (2000) *Crime, abuse and the elderly*, Cullompton: Willan.

Cavadino, P. (1999) 'Diverting mentally disordered offenders from custody', in D. Webb and R. Morris (eds) *Mentally disordered offenders, managing people nobody owns*, London: Routledge, pp 40-76.

Chief Inspectorate of Prisons (2004) *No problems, old and quiet: Older prisoners in England and Wales*, London: HMSO.

Clemente, F. and Kleiman, M. (1976) 'Fear of crime amongst the aged', *Gerontologist* vol 16, pp 207–10.

Conklin, J. (1975) *The impact of crime*, New York: Macmillan.

Cook, F. and Cook, T. (1976) 'Evaluating the rhetoric of crisis: a case study of criminal victimisation of the elderly', *Social Science Review*, vol 50, pp 632–46.

CPS (Crown Prosecution Service) (2004) *Addressing equality and diversity in the CPS: A stocktake report*, London: Equality and Diversity Unit, CPS.

CPS (2007) 'Policy statement on disability hate crime'(www.cps.gov.uk/ publications/prosecution/disability.html).

Crawford, R. (1994) 'The boundaries of the self and the unhealthy other: Reflections on health, culture and AIDS', *Social Science and Medicine*, vol 38, no 9, pp 1347–65.

Crawley, E. and Sparks, R. (2006) 'Is there life after imprisonment?', *Criminology and Criminal Justice*, vol 6, no 1, pp 63–82.

Department of Health (2005) 'Offender mental health care pathway (www.dh.gov. uk/en/Publicationsandstatistics/Publications/PublicationsPolicyAndGuidance/ DH_4102231).

Directgov (2007) 'The Disability Discrimination Act' (www.direct.gov.uk/en/ DisabledPeople/RightsAndObligations/DisabilityRights/DG_4001068).

Disability Rights Commission (2004) 'Research reveals impact of hate crime on disabled Scots' (www.drc-gb.org/about.us/drc_scotland/news/research_reveals_ impact_of_hat.aspx).

Estes, C., Biggs, S. and Phillipson, C. (2003) *Social theory, social policy and ageing*, Maidenhead: Open University Press.

Featherstone, M. and Hepworth, M. (1995) 'Images of positive ageing', in M. Featherstone and H. Wernick (eds) *Images of ageing*, London: Routledge, pp 42–70.

Fine, M. and Asch, A. (eds) (1988) *Women with disabilities: Essays in psychology, culture and politics*, Philadelphia: Temple University Press.

Fitzgerald, G. (2006) 'The realities of elder abuse', in A. Wahidin and M. Cain (eds) *Ageing, crime and society*, Cullompton: Willan, pp 90–106.

Foucault, M. (1977) *Discipline and punish: The birth of the prison*, London: Allen Lane.

Garofalo, J. and Laub, J. (1978) 'The fear of crime: Broadening our perspective', *Victimology*, vol 3, pp 242–53.

George, J. (1997) 'Racial aspects of elder abuse', in M. Eastman (ed) *Old age abuse* (2nd edn), London: Chapman and Hall, pp 163–72.

Goldsmith, J. and Tomas, E. (1974) 'Crimes against the elderly: A continuing national crisis', *Ageing*, (July) pp 10–13.

Gorgan, T. (2006) 'As if I just didn't exist – elder abuse and neglect in nursing homes', in A. Wahidin and M. Cain (eds) *Ageing, crime and society*, Cullompton: Willan, pp 71–89.

Harris, C. (1978) *Fact book on aging: A profile on America's older population*, Washington, DC: National Council on Aging.

Health Committee (2004) 'Elder abuse', (www.parliament.uk/parliamentary_committees/health_committee/hc190404_14.cfm).

HM Government (2004) 'Cutting crime, delivering justice, A strategic plan for criminal justice 2004–08', Cm 6288, London: HMSO.

Hochschild, A. (1998) 'The sociology of emotion as a way of seeing', in S. Williams and G. Bendelow (eds) *Emotions in social life*, London: Routledge, pp 3–15.

Hough, M. and Mayhew, P. (1983) *The British Crime Survey*, Home Office Research Study 76, London: HMSO.

Jenkins, G., Asif, Z. and Bennett, G. (2000) 'Listening is not enough', *The Journal of Adult Protection*, vol 2, no 1, pp 60–87.

Katz, I. (2001) 'Grey area', *The Guardian*, 30 January (www.guardian.co.uk/prisons/story/0,,467180,00.html).

Lee, G. (1982) 'Residential location and fear of crime among the elderly', *Rural Sociology*, vol 47, no 4, pp 655–69.

Liggett H. (1988) 'Stars are not born: An interpretive approach to the politics of disability', *Disability, Handicap and Society*, vol 3, no 3, pp 263–76.

Mencap (2000) *Living in fear: The need to combat bullying of people with learning difficulties*, London: Mencap.

Mind (National Association for Mental Health) (2003) *The Mental Health Act 1983: An outline guide*, London: Mind.

Oliver, M. and Barnes, C. (1998) *Disabled people and social policy*, Essex: Addison Wesley Longman.

Ortega, M. and Myles, J. (1987) 'Race and gender effects on fear of crime: an interactive model with age', *Criminology*, vol 25, no 1, pp 133–52.

Pain, R. (1995) 'Elderly women and fear of violent crime: The least likely victims?', *British Journal of Criminology*, vol 35, pp 584–98.

Phillips, J. (1996) 'Crime and older offenders', *Practice*, vol 8, no 1, pp 43–55.

Phillips, J. (2006) 'Crime and older people: The research agenda', in A. Wahidin and M. Cain (eds) *Ageing, crime and society*, Cullompton: Willan, pp 53–70.

Phillipson, C. (1998) *Reconstructing old age: New agenda in social theory and practice*, London: Sage.

Powell, J. and Wahidin, A. (2006) 'Rethinking criminology: The case of "ageing studies"', in A. Wahidin and M. Cain (eds) *Ageing, crime and society*, Cullompton: Willan, pp 17–34.

Prison Reform Trust (2007) 'No one knows: learning disability and learning difficulties in prison', at http://www.prisonreformtrust.org.uk/subsection.asp?id=525

Riddell, S. and Watson, N. (2003) 'Disability, culture and identity: Introduction', in S. Riddell and N. Watson (eds) *Disability, culture and identity*, London: Pearson, pp 1–18.

Sainsbury Centre for Mental Health (2006) *London's prison mental health services: A review*, London: Sainsbury Centre for Mental Health.

Sanders, A., Creaton, J., Bird, S. and Weber, L. (1997) *Victims with learning disabilities*, Occasional Paper 17, Oxford: Centre for Criminological Research, University of Oxford.

Shaw, J., Appleby, L. and Baker, D. (2003) *Safer prisons: A national study of prison suicides 1999–2000*, National Confidential Inquiry into Suicides and Homicides by People with Mental Illness, London: Department of Health.

Singleton, N., Meltzer, H., Gatward, R., Coid, J. and Deasy, D. (1998) *Psychiatric morbidity among prisoners: Summary report*, London: Office of National Statistics.

Skogan, W. and Maxfield, M. (1981) *Coping with crime*, Beverly Hills, CA: Sage.

Slater, P. and Eastman, M. (1999) *Elder abuse: Critical issues in policy and practice*, London: Age Concern.

Spalek, B. (1999) 'Exploring victimisation: A study looking at the impact of the Maxwell scandal upon the Maxwell pensioners', *International Review of Victimology*, vol 6, pp 213–30.

Spalek, B. (2001) 'Policing the UK financial system: the creation of the new FSA and its approach to regulation', *International Journal of the Sociology of Law*, vol 29, no 1, pp 75–87.

Turner, B. (1995) 'Ageing and identity: Some reflections on the somatisation of self', in M. Featherstone and H. Wernick (eds) *Images of ageing*, London: Routledge.

Wahidin (2002) 'Reconfiguring older bodies in the prison time machine', *Journal of Aging and Identity*, vol 7, no 3, pp 177–93.

Wahidin, A. and Cain, M. (2006) 'Ageing, crime and society: An invitation to criminology', in A. Wahidin and M. Cain (eds) *Ageing, crime and society*, Cullompton: Willan, pp 1–16.

Warr, M. (1984) 'Fear of victimisation: Why are women and the elderly more afraid?', *Social Science Quarterly*, vol 65, no 3, pp 681–702.

Williams, C. (1995) *Invisible victims: Crime and abuse against people with learning difficulties*, London: Jessica Kingsley.

Yin, P. (1982) 'Fear of crime as a problem for the elderly', *Social Problems*, vol 30, no 2, pp 240–5.

Conclusion

Communities, identities and criminology

The subject of social identity in contemporary western societies is an area that has received considerable research interest. While traditionally class, gender and 'race'/ethnic identities have generated substantial social scientific research attention, other group collectivities are now receiving greater focus, specifically those relating to sexual orientation, religion, disability and age. At the same time, work on identities includes a focus upon the construction of self in late modernity since it is argued that increasing individualisation means that human identity is a task under continual construction. *Communities, identities and crime* illustrates how the construction of social identities might best be conceptualised as consisting of the interplay, tensions and contradictions between modernity's 'imperative of order', including the expression of collective identities and interests, and the fragmentation, individualisation, and fluidity of identities associated with conditions of late modernity. Both processes are at play, and serve to produce, perpetuate, deconstruct and influence the nature of, identity formations within particular contexts.

This book further highlights the fact that equality and diversity issues feature significantly in the policies and practices of all criminal justice agencies. The concern shown towards gender, 'race'/ethnicity, faith, sexual orientation, disability and age reflects wider social processes occurring in contemporary western societies, whereby questions of identity are increasingly important. The phrase 'equality and specificity within diversity' might be used to capture contemporary developments within the criminal justice system. Traditionally, there has been a hierarchy between different groupings in terms of the levels of protection and research afforded them, with 'race'/ethnicity and gender generating most attention. However, recent trends suggest that this hierarchy is levelling out, so that minority groupings in relation to faith, sexuality, disability and age are attracting more research and policy attention. At the same time, there is a growing awareness that the distinct voices and experiences of certain specific groups of individuals are obscured within such broad-based approaches, and so increasingly, more nuanced approaches are being adopted, whereby the needs of specific communities are being taken into account.

Communities, identities and crime also considers the relevance of social identities to researching the social world. It appears that, despite the temporal and sliding nature of identities, it might be argued that identities nonetheless constitute the sites at which the social world is experienced and the sites through which power relations are at play. However, postmodern perspectives that stress the fluidity and situated nature of identities, while highlighting the transient and multitudinous nature of subject positions, fail to engage in critical discursive practice. As a result, this book has stressed that a potentially useful epistemological position to take is that of perspectival realism. This acknowledges the fluidity and multitude of subject positions, and takes the position that, at any given moment, the social world can be viewed rationally in more than one perspective. At the same time, however, this approach also stresses and seeks to challenge those wider norms that perpetuate inequalities.

Communities, identities and crime further highlights the significance of the notion of community in criminal justice policy and practice. Underpinned by the principle of 'active citizenship', communities are viewed as an important resource for tackling crime and incivility. The inclusion of communities in criminal justice constitutes a form of institutional reflection, which involves criminal justice institutions opening themselves up to the communities that they serve, with the lay public engaging with, as well as critiquing, rival forms of expertise. However, the notion of 'community' is itself contentious and open to many different interpretations, particularly within the context of late modernity, where modern and postmodern processes combine and interact to create multiple forms of belonging. Nonetheless, within government discourse the notion of community tends to be treated rather simplistically, the term 'community' constituting a catch-all phrase used by government as a way of simplifying, merging and combining complex social identities and groupings for the purposes of policy development and implementation. Furthermore, although the term 'community' gives the outward impression of neutrality, the ways in which the term is used and operationalised by government suggest that it is loaded with assumptions about the kinds of social identities that are included, as well as fostered, for the purposes of community participation, engagement and scrutiny of performance. Moreover, the notion of community participation can also be critiqued, since it seems that managerial imperatives and strategic decisions on what can and cannot be done often influence the scope of community participation.

The discussions featured in *Communities, identities and crime* also link in to broader discussions about the narrow confines of the subject discipline criminology. The subject of social identities serves to widen the lens of analysis from a rather narrow, criminal justice, focus to a wider exploration of social injustice, including a focus upon social harm. Minority groupings in relation to gender, 'race'/ethnicity, faith, sexual orientation, disability and age, and their experiences of the social world, raise wider questions about justice and equality, about how the harms that people can experience may not necessarily be viewed or be labelled as crime, and therefore how social justice might be achieved outside a criminal justice framework. This book also uses the subject of social identities to challenge the narrow confines of criminological knowledge production, whereby criminology might be viewed as being complicit in the suppression of social difference, not only through largely focusing on those harms defined criminal by regimes of power, but also through insufficiently exploring social difference and insufficiently engaging with the voices of those who occupy the margins, thereby leading to the homogenisation of knowledge production. *Communities, identities and crime* therefore raises questions about how a focus upon minority groupings in relation to gender, 'race'/ethnicity, faith, sexual orientation, disability and age raises epistemological questions for criminology.

This book is therefore a political project, a reaction against increasingly scientised conceptions of criminology. A focus upon identities necessarily involves looking at subjectivities, both those of the researcher and of the researched. Exploring the complex nature of subjectivity includes taking into account human emotion. A greater focus upon emotions can help develop a psychosocial criminology. Moreover, a focus upon emotion can help develop a criminology that is less dispassionate and more compassionate. Researchers should be encouraged to focus upon the emotions that they experience while they carry out their research, and should be more open to the emotions that their research subjects are experiencing. Moreover, looking at the multitudinous nature of subjectivity for both the researcher and the researched can help develop a research position that goes beyond a simplistic oppressor–oppressed dichotomy, acknowledging that all peoples are involved in reproducing silent, invisible norms that can lead to discrimination and suffering. For a researcher, examining the role that their own subjectivity plays in reproducing dominant, repressive norms can constitute part of an ethical position that places great value upon researcher reflexivity. Certainly, the subject of social identities in relation to crime, criminal justice and victimisation has much potential for criminology.

Index

Page references for notes are followed by *n*